Praise for *Powering Up*

For those wanting to take their primary classroom practi̶c̶e̶ ̶·̶·̶·̶·̶ ̶·̶·̶·̶t̶s̶ and bolts of teaching, *Powering Up Children* provides a great starting point – offering a wealth of ideas on how to build character in young children and develop them as learners who are motivated, confident, and curious.

It is a book full of exciting possibilities for those teachers and leaders looking to move beyond the recent focus on passing statutory tests and towards a way of teaching that gives children so much more.

Aidan Severs, Deputy Head Teacher, Dixons Allerton Academy Primary

Rich in both practical and theoretical value, *Powering Up Children* is a captivating contribution to the field of pedagogical literature. The book can function as both an educator's rubric and a perfect guide for professional introspection, as Guy Claxton and Becky Carlzon present a generous array of classroom strategies and scientific references that invite teachers to carefully craft a paradigm shift in their own practice.

All of the tools and techniques have been designed to excite the very core of the modern learner, and teachers will easily imagine their use throughout their pupils' educational journey.

A must-read for anyone with the true calling of a teacher and a curious mind.

Ana María Fernández, educator and creator of the VESS Educational Model

How to equip children for a complicated and fast-changing world is now a global question, and this book offers a giant stride in the right direction. It provides educators with both a clear philosophy and a valuable theoretical framework, combined with vivid, exciting, and highly practical methods for "powering up" their learners.

Powering Up Children should transform the thinking of all primary school teachers and policy makers, both in my native Japan and indeed across the whole world.

Asato Yoshinaga, Associate Professor, Kokugakuin University

In this refreshing book, Guy Claxton and Becky Carlzon demonstrate that knowledge-rich learning works best when children are given the opportunity to interrogate their understanding and harness their learning power. Guy and Becky then go on to offer a clear analysis of how this opportunity can be brought to life in the primary school classroom through the Learning Power Approach. You are left with the feeling that if all schools could adopt this approach, young people really could change the world for the better.

Debra Kidd, teacher and author

Who doesn't want children to have active, imaginative, and discerning minds? In *Powering Up Children*, Guy Claxton and Becky Carlzon share strategies and approaches to help achieve just that. It demonstrates the importance of the Learning Power Approach in preparing children for the tests they need to pass and for the world they will inhabit both now and in the future.

Informed by cutting-edge research and real-world practice, *Powering Up Children* is a brilliantly thought-out book of ideas to power up the hard-working teacher.

Hywel Roberts, teacher, writer and humourist

If you're looking for a book packed with ideas on how to become an even better teacher, this is it. In *Powering Up Children* Guy and Becky demystify the culture of a great learning environment and offer educators a complete mindset shift for creating more agile teaching and learning.

Just like your savings account, the Learning Power Approach requires investment – but the pay-off is enormous. Get stuck in! The worst thing that can happen is that you get it right the first time and miss out on an opportunity to build your own learning muscles!

Jaz Ampaw-Farr, 'Resilience Ninja' at Why First Ltd

Powering Up Children could not have come at a better time, as the current educational landscape is buzzing with a renewed interest in developing learner agency. And while there is an abundance of resources written on the subjects of building independence, amplifying student voice, and helping them own their own learning, few provide the kind of clear and practical advice so readily shared in this wonderful book.

My hope is that all teachers of primary school aged children will take the opportunity to read this book and put into practice its many valuable suggestions. Whether linked to reconsidering the choreography of one lesson, rethinking the way you use language, or redesigning the learning environment, there is a starting point to build on for everyone.

I am excited by the prospect of sharing *Powering Up Children* with teachers around the world and am so grateful for its contribution to the field – it is just the guidebook to accompany any teacher as they venture out on a journey of change.

Kath Murdoch, education consultant

Powering Up Children is a must for all primary school educators, and is certain to be peppered with sticky notes and highlighter in no time as you read, reread, and share it with every teacher you know.

As a passionate educator of little learners my aim is always for our pupils to be amazingly capable little people who grow up to be amazingly capable bigger people, so I cannot recommend this book highly enough – as it paves the way to achieve that goal.

Kellie Morgan, Director of Early Learning and Junior Years, Melbourne Girls Grammar

Powering Up Children is impressive, practical, and wise – and it's not often you can put those three things together. It picks up Guy Claxton's latest thinking about "learning power" and, with the help of expert practitioner Becky Carlzon, embeds it firmly in the primary school classroom (and it applies just as well to early childhood too). Guy and Becky include a host of practical methods to help children develop their learning muscles, and I especially valued their ideas on how to encourage children to think of themselves as learners by speaking "learnish".

Margaret Carr, Professor of Education, University of Waikato, and co-author
of *Learning Stories: Constructing Learner Identities in Early Education*

In *Powering Up Children* Claxton and Carlzon have produced that most unusual of publications: a book that will appeal to anyone interested in children's learning at all levels of expertise and experience. It is especially remarkable in that it simultaneously provides page upon page of practical, easy-to-implement advice for teachers while also reflecting a deep understanding of the nature of education and the forces that are shaping the future of the profession.

All teachers, as well as school leaders and educational innovators, will find enormous value in this book. Its provocations will spark new ideas, challenge some existing thinking, and provide clarity about new ways forward.

Martin Westwell, Chief Executive, South Australian Certificate of Education Board

Powering Up Children is so enjoyable – I love the way Guy and Becky bring the Learning Power Approach to life so vividly in the primary school classroom. Containing lots and lots of strategies you can put straight into action, this book is a one-way journey to transforming the way you look at teaching for ever. Enjoy the trip!

Melina Furman, PhD, Associate Professor, School of Education,
Universidad de San Andrés

With all the talk of 21st century skills and the need to prepare children for the challenges and opportunities ahead, *Powering Up Children* not only sets out the design principles of the Learning Power Approach but also shows teachers how – through subtle adjustments in their practice – skills such as collaboration and craftsmanship can be developed in learners.

A perfect and timely read for classroom teachers and school leaders alike.

Rae Snape, Head Teacher, The Spinney Primary School, National Leader of Education, The Kite Teaching School Alliance

Powering Up Children provides a perfect marriage of Guy Claxton's very accessible refreshing of the research behind the Learning Power Approach and Becky Carlzon's practical, detailed, and imaginative lesson descriptions, which bring the design principles to life beautifully.

Any teacher reading this book will feel inspired and empowered to get going with the Learning Power Approach straight away, because it all seems so doable.

Shirley Clarke, formative assessment expert

This exceptionally detailed and practical book draws into sharper focus the sheer lunacy of rejecting those lessons that actually interest children. It really is time to knock that nonsense on the head and get on with a more humane approach to educating young children for life – and *Powering Up Children* tells us how.

As someone with experience as a primary school governor, I could see this book being particularly useful as a jargon-free guide that not only enables you to detect what makes really good teaching and why, but also helps you make specific observations – rather than relying on intuitive hunches – of what your school is doing right. It would also be really helpful for parents who are curious about the current debates in education and would like to know what an enlightened education looks like on paper.

Madeleine Holt, co-founder of Rescue Our Schools and More Than a Score

Building on the foundations of *The Learning Power Approach*, *Powering Up Children* challenges us to reflect and to go beyond: to customise and improve our practice so that we help children develop as learners – not just to get top grades, but also to build character in readiness for the tests of life.

Tom Wallace, Specialist Leader of Education in Formative Assessment, Ignite TSA, and co-founder of Balance Assessment

POWERING UP CHILDREN

CHILDREN

The Learning Power Approach to Primary Teaching

POWERING UP CHILDREN

The Learning Power Approach to Primary Teaching

Guy Claxton and **Becky Carlzon**

Foreword by Ron Berger

Crown House Publishing Limited

www.crownhouse.co.uk

First published by

Crown House Publishing
Crown Buildings, Bancyfelin, Carmarthen, Wales, SA33 5ND, UK
www.crownhouse.co.uk

and

Crown House Publishing Company LLC
PO Box 2223, Williston, VT 05495, USA
www.crownhousepublishing.com

First published 2019. Reprinted 2019 (twice).

Note from the publisher: The authors have provided video and web content throughout the book that is available to you through QR (quick response) codes. To read a QR code, you must have a smartphone or tablet with a camera. We recommend that you download a QR code reader app that is made specifically for your phone or tablet brand.

British Library Cataloguing-in-Publication Data

A catalogue entry for this book is available from the British Library.

Print ISBN: 978-178583337-3
Mobi ISBN: 978-178583381-6
ePub ISBN: 978-178583382-3
ePDF ISBN: 978-178583383-0

LCCN 2018961111

Printed and bound in the UK by
TJ International, Padstow, Cornwall

For Dr Teo, who gave Becky her life back.

Foreword by Ron Berger

All educators and families agree on this, and research consistently affirms it: the character of children has a profound effect on their academic and life success. Students who are respectful, responsible, courageous, and compassionate do better in school and life. Students who show determination and resilience in their learning, who have high standards for craftsmanship in what they do, are better equipped for everything that comes their way.

Remarkably, many schools feel that they cannot focus on these skills and habits during the school day because there is just not enough time. They see time in school as a trade-off: we can focus on academic learning to prepare for exams – the measure of our accountability – or we can focus on cultivating student character. Given limited time, character must be put aside. The irony is that these things are not separate. Focusing on character at the same time as academics builds students who are stronger at both. They work together: the dispositions that make students good and effective human beings also make them successful learners. We don't need to choose.

In *Powering Up Children: The Learning Power Approach to Primary Teaching*, Guy Claxton and Becky Carlzon bring together a vision, models, and resources to help primary teachers build classrooms where "learning dispositions" are explicitly cultivated in concert with academic skills and content. This book provides a framework for a "learning-powered classroom" and fleshes out that framework with concrete strategies and models that primary teachers can put to use right away. In every chapter I found myself nodding in affirmation: this is how a classroom should be.

All teachers understand that the biggest determinant to student success lives in each student themself: how committed and determined they are to succeed; how much confidence and clarity they have in order to improve; what strategies they have in order to move forward. We often mistakenly attribute a student's strengths in this realm to innate qualities or family background – a student is either motivated or not – it is an individual issue. In truth, we adjust to the cultures we enter. If a school or classroom community expects more of students, challenges them and supports them more deeply, believes in their capacity and refuses to let them drift, students behave entirely differently. They step up. We can create classroom cultures, school cultures, of high standards and success for all students.

Powering Up Children describes what a classroom culture of high standards for academics and learning dispositions can look like, and uses models and stories to make that clear. It provides instructional strategies and templates that teachers can use, and, just as importantly, coaches teachers to move beyond a teacher-centric classroom to one in which students take significant responsibility for their own learning. It supports teachers to gradually release responsibility to students to set goals, critique their own and each other's work, and to reflect on their challenges and growth.

Students are capable of much greater things than we imagine. *Powering Up Children* is an excellent guide to building schools and classrooms that empower teachers to challenge and support children more deeply, to believe in them more authentically, and to bring out their best as scholars, citizens, and human beings.

Ron Berger, Chief Academic Officer, EL Education

Acknowledgements

We would like to say thank you to the many people from whom we have learned so much, and who have generously given their time, their experience, and their materials. Without them this book would be much slimmer and poorer. Our intellectual friends and mentors include: Ron Berger, Margaret Carr, Art Costa, Angela Duckworth, Carol Dweck, Michael Fullan, Bena Kallick, James Mannion, Kath Murdoch, Dame Alison Peacock, David Perkins, Ron Ritchhart, Sir Ken Robinson, Chris Watkins, and David Yeager. Previous collaborators we are indebted to include: Maryl Chambers, Leanne Day, Jenny Elmer, Janet Hanson, Bill Lucas, Ellen Spencer, and Steve Watson.

The primary teachers and head teachers who have showed us the way include: Julie Barlow, Birgitta Car, Andrea Curtis, Reagan Delaney, Robyn Fergusson, Amrita Hassan, Rakhsana Hussain, Peter Hyman, David Kehler, Karen McClintock, Kellie Morgan, Bojana Obradovic, Lorraine Sands, Nicole Stynes, Adam Swain, Luke Swain, Julian Swindale, Emma O'Regan, Katriona Rae, Judith Reid, Sarah Saddington, Victoria Scale-Constantinou, Mariyam Seedat, Rebecca Senior, Heath Venus, Anna Weinert, and Michelle Worthington. We would like to acknowledge the help we have received from teachers at the following schools: Bangkok Patana International School, Bangkok; Blaise Primary School, Bristol; Bushfield Primary School, Wolverton; Carlogie Primary School, Angus; Christian College Geelong, Geelong; Corngreaves Academy, Cradley Heath; Flinders Christian College, Victoria; Melbourne Girls' Grammar, Melbourne; Nayland Primary School, Suffolk; Prospect Primary School, Adelaide; The Regent's International School, Bangkok; Sefton Park School, Bristol; and St John Fisher Catholic Primary School, Liverpool. Special thanks go to: Andy Moor, Nicola Suddaby, and colleagues at St Bernard's RC Primary School; Robert Cleary, Gemma Goldenberg, and their colleagues at Sandringham Primary School; Diane Pumphrey, Katrina Williamson, and the teachers at West Thornton Academy; Bryan Harrison and colleagues at Miriam Lord; Lisa Cook and the team at Challenging Learning; Tom Wallace and the team at Balance; and Hannah Coles, Alice Stott, and the team at Voice 21, as well as Nicky Clements, Michelle Forrest, Michelle Green, James Mannion, and Anton de Vries.

Finally we would like to thank the good folk at Crown House, especially David Bowman, Tom Fitton, Tabitha Palmer, Louise Penny, Beverley Randell, Bethan Rees, and Rosalie Williams. Louise's sharp eyes, in particular, have helped our book to be much clearer in both structure and language. You couldn't wish for a better bunch.

Contents

Introduction

This book on the Learning Power Approach (LPA) is for primary, or elementary, school teachers.[1] But it is not for all of them. It is only for those who are really serious about teaching in a way that builds character alongside delivering the traditional curriculum. It is for teachers who are hungry for ideas and information about how to do that, and ready to change their way of being in the classroom to achieve that end. Let us explain.

School is about more than examination results. Everyone knows that. Everyone agrees. No school proudly claims on its website, "Send your children to us and we will squeeze the best grades we can out of them, by hook or by crook. And that is all we care about." If pressed, every school protests that "we are not just an exam factory, you know". There is always some acknowledgement that forming powerful habits of mind in children matters too: that we all want them to grow in confidence, kindness, resilience, or "mental agility". "Fulfilling their potential" doesn't just mean "getting top marks". We want good results,

> We want good results, but we want *results plus*: grades *plus* a character that is ready for the challenges and opportunities of the mid to late 21st century.

but we want *results plus*: grades *plus* a character that is ready for the challenges and opportunities of the mid to late 21st century, as best we can predict what those will be. We can't imagine a school that wants *results minus*: children with good grades but who are timid, dependent, unimaginative, and unadventurous.

---

1   Throughout the book, we will tend to use our native UK terminology of primary schooling, years, and key stages – except when referring to case studies from other educational systems. The UK system runs from "Reception" (which children enter at age 4, roughly) through Years 1 (5–6-year-olds), 2, 3, 4, 5, and 6 (10–11-year-olds). Often these are divided into two "Key Stages": Key Stage 1 comprises Years 1 and 2; Key Stage 2 comprises Years 3 to 6. In the USA school years are called "grades", and they tend to be one year "behind" the English years, so fifth grade corresponds roughly to Year 6.

The key question is: what does that *plus* amount to? What exactly do we want our kids to be *like* when they leave our class, or move up to their high school? And how exactly is our school – and especially our teaching – going to look different if we take this plus as seriously as we could? How are we going to teach maths differently if we want our children to be growing an adventurous and creative spirit at the same time? How are our displays of children's work going to look different if we want them to develop a sense of craftsmanship – a genuine pride in having produced the best work of which they are capable? We all want our children to become more resilient – to be inclined and equipped to grapple intelligently with things they find hard. So how are our forms of assessment going to tell us whether we are succeeding: whether our Year 4s are indeed more resilient than they were in Year 3?

Lots of teachers and school leaders espouse these values. Some of them have thought through – in detail – exactly what it will take, and set in motion – with the requisite degree of precision – the necessary changes. But many are still hesitant, awaiting clearer guidance and support from departments of education or academic "thought leaders". Or they have got a firm hold on part of the challenge, but not yet figured out the whole if it. They work on resilience, but not imagination; on collaboration, but not concentration; on self-esteem, but not critical thinking; or, conversely, on higher order thinking skills, but not empathy.

> The LPA shows in systematic detail how to go beyond the soundbites and the posters to create classrooms that really do grow robust, inquisitive, imaginative, and collaborative learners – lesson by lesson, week by week, year on year.

It is this detailed and comprehensive help that the LPA provides. It is for teachers and schools that really want to take the plus seriously, and have begun to realise the implications of doing so. They know that "team games" are not enough to grow collaboration; that becoming a good collaborator is as much to do with the way in which we teach English as it is to do with sports day. They know that a few fine words on the home page of the school website, or in a policy document on teaching and learning, are not enough. They have quickly realised that some glossy posters downloaded from Pinterest about growth mindset and the power of *yet* are not enough. You have to "live it, not laminate it", as the Twittersphere pithily puts it!

For example, Sam Sherratt, who teaches the Primary Years Program of the International Baccalaureate (IB) in Ho Chi Minh City, wrote in his blog back in 2013, "All too often, in IB schools, the Learner Profile [a list of desirable attributes] exists in the form of displays and catchphrases, but doesn't exist as a way of life, as a code of conduct or as an expectation for all stakeholders. We are not going to let that happen at ISHCMC [his school]!"[2] The LPA shows in systematic detail how to go beyond the soundbites and the posters to create classrooms that really do grow robust, inquisitive, imaginative, and collaborative learners — lesson by lesson, week by week, year on year.

So this book is crammed full of practical illustrations, advice, and hints and tips. It is designed for busy primary teachers who want to get started on the LPA journey, and for others who have already made good progress but may feel a bit stuck for fresh ideas or are wondering about the next step to take. And there is always a next step. As our understanding of the LPA has deepened, the horizon of possibility keeps receding in front of us. The further you go in training children to take control of their own learning, the deeper the possibilities that are opened up.

Depending on where you are on your journey, some of our suggestions will be very familiar to you, and some might seem rather pie in the sky. The spot we try to hit, as much as possible, is the area in between "I do it already. Tell me something new", and "in your dreams, mate": the spot where you sense a new possibility for tweaking your existing style and it feels plausible and doable with the real live children you teach. That's what we want you to be on the lookout for. So if something seems familiar, we invite you to think about how you could stretch what you already do just a little more. And if a suggestion seems far-fetched it may nevertheless spark a train of thought that leads to a more fruitful idea.

> The further you go in training children to take control of their own learning, the deeper the possibilities that are opened up.

---

2   Sam Sherratt, "Parent Workshops: The IB Learner Profile", *Making PYP Happen Here* [blog] (7 October 2013). Available at: https://makingpyphappenhere.wordpress.com/2013/10/07/36/.

In a talk he gave a while ago that Guy attended, David Perkins suggested that each of us is either more of a "do-think-do" person – someone who likes to dive in, give things a go, then reflect and try again – or a "think-do-think" person – someone who prefers to gather all the information, then gives things a go and thinks again.[3] Whichever you think you might be, we hope that you can use the ideas outlined in this book as a guide to improving your LPA practice. Feel free to dive into whichever chapter is most appealing to you, although we do suggest reading the whole book from cover to cover at some point!

The LPA is not a set of rigid "recipes for success"; it is a set of tools, ideas, and examples that we hope you will critique and customise to suit your own situation. All we ask is that you hold fast to the spirit and the values while you are developing your own version. Sometimes we have seen people introduce – without meaning to – the "lethal mutation" that kills the spirit. For example, if you slip into seeing the LPA mainly as a way to rack up those conventional test scores, you have missed something really essential. Rather, we develop habits of mind like resilience and resourcefulness mainly *because* they are valuable outcomes of education in their own right – and then we keep an eye on making sure that the results go up too.

> We are aiming to develop strong mental habits in our children that will stand them in good stead for a lifetime, and that takes time and consistency.

The LPA is very far from being a quick fix or the latest fad. It is actually quite demanding because it requires us to re-examine our natural style of teaching, and to make small but real experiments with our own habits in the classroom. As Sir Ken Robinson has said, "If you want to shift culture, it's two things: its habits and its habitats – the habits of mind, and the physical environment in which people operate."[4] The LPA requires some honest self-awareness and reflection, and that can be quite effortful and sometimes even uncomfortable. We told you the LPA wasn't for everyone!

---

3   Guy has asked David if he has a published reference for this idea, but he can't find it!

4   Cited in Ron Ritchhart, *Creating Cultures of Thinking: The 8 Forces We Must Master to Truly Transform Our Schools* (San Francisco, CA: Jossey-Bass, 2015), pp. 230–231.

But our experience tells us that nothing less will do. Just adding some shiny new techniques on top of business as usual – what we call the "tinsel approach" – does not work in the long term because the same underlying messages of the medium persist. We are aiming to develop strong mental habits in our children that will stand them in good stead for a lifetime, and that takes time and consistency. Habits take months, even years, to develop and change. Children's development depends on the day-to-day cultures we create for them to inhabit, not on something special we remember to pay attention to every so often. And to create those cultures, we teachers have to be conscious, resilient, and imaginative learners too.

The beauty of the LPA, though, is that it relies on a series of adjustments that are worked into your natural style one by one, gradually and cumulatively. You are not being asked to transform yourself from a leopard into a tiger overnight. It is evolution, not revolution. The LPA is a direction of travel, supported by signposts and resources to guide you along the way, and everyone can go at their own pace. The good news is that, on the journey, teaching the LPA way becomes highly satisfying and rewarding. A roomful of enthusiastic, resourceful learners, who are keen to sort things out for themselves, is a sight to behold – and a joy to teach. Instead of doing a lot of informing, explaining, and interrogating, your role develops a subtler side to it in which you spend more time nudging and challenging the children to "go deeper".

> The LPA is a direction of travel, supported by signposts and resources to guide you along the way, and everyone can go at their own pace.

In every context in which Becky has taught, this is exactly what she has found – small tweaks to her practice have often made the biggest difference. For example, just by positively and consistently weaving in the language of the LPA, as we will show in Chapter 5, children have quickly locked on to "what learning is about" and realised how they can explore and express their own learning. An illustration of this occurred when a new child started in Becky's class in the middle of the academic year. By the end of his first day he was talking about how he was going to challenge himself, who he had been collaborating effectively with, and what he had learned from his mistakes that day. Children are usually very quick to pick up cues from adults and their peers.

Children can also surprise us. For example, when reflecting on their learning process, the 5- and 6-year-olds in Becky's class have been known to make comments such as:

"I'd prefer to collaborate today because I need to share ideas with a friend."

"I noticed everyone was really absorbed in their learning today because the classroom was so quiet."

Because this book is designed to be really practical, there isn't much in the way of background or rationale about the LPA in it. We only say a little about where the approach comes from, what the scientific underpinnings are, and what the evidence for its effectiveness is. You will find all of that, if you are not familiar with it already, in the first book in this series, *The Learning Power Approach: Teaching Learners to Teach Themselves* (published by Crown House in the UK and Corwin in the US). The only thing worth noting here is that the LPA is not another "brand" competing for your attention in the crowded education marketplace. It is our attempt to discern the general principles behind a number of initiatives that have been developing, often independently of one another, over the last twenty years or so. It is a new school of thought about the kind of teaching that effectively stimulates the growth of agile, tenacious, and inventive minds – as well as getting the grades. You will find examples and ideas from a wide range of sources, and from different countries, as well as from our own research and practice.

The book you are reading now is actually the second in a series of four books, of which *The Learning Power Approach* is the first, providing the background to the approach. This volume will be followed by two other, equally practical, books: one for high school teachers, and another for school leaders. But we wanted to focus the first of these books on younger children because those vital qualities of mind – the general-purpose "learning muscles", as we call them – are being shaped most powerfully, for good or ill, in the early years. Set children on the right trajectory in their primary school and they will have a precious asset for life – even if, as sometimes happens, they go on to find themselves in a high school that is not yet as ready to welcome their independence and maturity as it could be.

Will the LPA work in your school? We are sure it will. We have seen it work well in early years settings in disadvantaged areas of New Zealand; in remote rural primary schools in the forests of Poland; in international schools in Bangkok and Buenos Aires; and in big urban primary schools across the UK, as well as in private preparatory schools in the Home Counties and in special schools in London and Birmingham. The examples, tools, and techniques with which this book is crammed have been tried and tested in a wide range of settings.

But you will probably still have to experiment with them in the specific conditions of your classroom and often make adjustments to get them to work. Every school and every class is different; there's no getting around that. One size rarely fits all. The key is to be ready to adapt the ideas to each context and to be open to problem-solving and to sharing your LPA journey with your learners. For example, when Becky moved from teaching in a Reception class in Bristol, England, to teaching business English in Argentina, it took a few months

> ... those vital qualities of mind – the general-purpose "learning muscles", as we call them – are being shaped most powerfully, for good or ill, in the early years.

before she could really make headway with developing her students as learners as well as fluent English speakers. But by patient trial and error she found methods that worked to get them to take more responsibility for their learning.

She invented marking schemes which built curiosity around mistake-making and also developed a willingness to be more playful with the English language. She found ways to tap into her students' imaginations and make her lessons more attractive to them. One of her business classes invented new smoothies and sent videos of their creations to the renowned smoothie brand Innocent in the UK to see what they thought. To their delight, Innocent replied with their own video! In the process, Becky's students learned about phrasal verbs, improved their pronunciation, and developed their instruction writing – as well as building accuracy with language, reflection skills, and the ability to collaborate with colleagues. While learning how to teach in this new context, Becky was constantly asking herself questions like:

"How can I build my students as strong, collaborative, and reflective learners?"

"Is there a different way I could approach this to build persistence and learning from mistakes?"

"How can I make learning English more meaningful to my students?"

"How can I hand more responsibility over to my students?"

"How can I encourage my students to push and challenge themselves and not take the easy option?"

By experimenting with different possible answers to these questions, Becky was able to apply and develop the LPA in a new and unfamiliar context.

A learning-power classroom has many varied sides to it. Teachers lay the furniture out in a different way. They choose different things to display on the walls. They involve the children more than usual in designing their own learning. They use a specific vocabulary when they are talking to the children, and encourage specific kinds of talk between the children. They create particular kinds of activities and challenges. They comment on children's work and write reports differently. Over time, we have distilled a clear set of design principles that teachers can follow if they want to make their classroom a highly effectively incubator of powerful learning.

The central chapters in this book are structured around thematic clusters of these design principles, and generally follow a common format:

1. First we explain why the design principles we are focusing on are important; including what's in it for you – the teacher – and what's in it for the children.

2. Next, we offer a menu of practical low-risk tweaks to classroom practice that enable you to engage with the design principles and experience some quick wins.

3. Then we give you some ideas about how to embed the principles more deeply in the ongoing life of your classroom, including some rich lesson examples from across the primary age range, and from different school subjects.

4. Finally, we address some of the common bumps and issues that may crop up along the way, and offer some advice on how to creatively adapt and modify the LPA until it begins to bear fruit.

And with that, let's now dive into Chapter 1 and see what the LPA is all about.

Chapter 1

An Overview of the Learning Power Approach

This chapter provides a brief sketch of the LPA: what it is, where it comes from, why it matters, how it differs from other approaches, and what it asks of teachers. These questions are dealt with in more detail in the first book in the series, *The Learning Power Approach*, which we hope you will refer back to as your appreciation of the LPA grows and deepens.

What Is the LPA?

In essence, the LPA is a newly emerging school of thought about teaching and learning. It is about how to teach in a particular way if you value certain outcomes for the children in your classes. If you want your children to be quiet and well-behaved, to remember what you have told them, and to get good marks – if those are the behaviours and attitudes that matter to you most – then there is a kind of teaching that will steer children in that direction (although, kids being kids, not all of them will comply!). But that is not the LPA. The LPA is a way of teaching for teachers who value politeness and success, but who value other outcomes even more. They want to see children do as well as they can on the tests, to learn to read and write and do their maths, but – more than that – they also want them to grow in their independence, resourcefulness, creativity, curiosity, and capacity for thinking about and exploring important matters deeply – for themselves.

Traditional teaching doesn't reliably produce this second set of outcomes. On the contrary, some children learn how to get good marks in a way that makes them more, not less, reliant on the teacher. They can become more interested in getting right answers than in really thinking and wondering about the things they are exploring.

They grow more conservative and cautious in their approach to learning, rather than more adventurous and resilient.

So whether you like the LPA or not will depend on your values. If you don't think independence, resilience, and curiosity are important characteristics for the next generation, then you can stick to more conventional teaching methods. Nobody can force you to change your style. But if you think, as we do, that such dispositions are vital if our children are to flourish in a turbulent and fast-changing world, then the LPA will be more likely to appeal.

> The LPA is a way of teaching for teachers who ... want to see children do as well as they can on the tests, to learn to read and write and do their maths, but – more than that – they also want them to grow in their independence, resourcefulness, creativity, curiosity, and capacity for thinking about and exploring important matters deeply – for themselves.

Put more formally, the goal of the LPA is this:

> To develop all students as confident and capable learners – ready, willing, and able to choose, design, research, pursue, troubleshoot, and evaluate learning for themselves, alone and with others, in school and out, for grades and for life.

All of the words in this statement matter.

Develop reminds us that cultivating these character traits takes time. We can't just throw children in at the deep end and expect them to be powerful learners straight away. We have to constantly provide them with manageable opportunities to stretch and strengthen their confidence and ability to work things out for themselves.

All says that this is vital for every student, regardless of their background or their "academic ability". High achievers need it if they are going to cope with the demands of their academic/vocational pursuits beyond school. And low achievers need it even more, because without these dispositions, they are condemned to stay in the slow lane of learning.

We need to help children become *ready* and *willing* to learn on their own, and not just *able* to. We want them to be keen to learn, as well as capable of learning. It is not enough to train children in learning or thinking "skills", because a skill is just something you *can* do, not something you are *inclined* to do. And we want children to be inclined to be resourceful, creative, and cooperative, not just able to be when prodded. Earlier work on teaching thinking skills often found that, while children enjoyed their thinking skills lessons, and were indeed able to think better in the classroom, as soon as they found themselves in a different setting these skills seemed to go inert. They didn't appear when they would have been useful, and they didn't transfer to new situations.[1]

The next string of words – *choose, design, research, pursue, troubleshoot, and evaluate* – begins to unpack what it means to be a powerful learner. In a traditional classroom it is the teacher who does most of the choosing, designing, troubleshooting, and evaluating of learning, thus depriving the children of the necessity – and the opportunity – to learn how to do these things for themselves. The "Mission: Possible" of the LPA teacher – should you choose to accept it – is to teach in such a way that they gradually do less and less managing and organising of learning, and the children become more and more confident and capable of doing it for themselves.

Alone and with others stresses the importance of being able to take charge of learning both on your own and in collaboration. In the adult and out-of-school worlds – in a project team, a special-interest chat room, or a friendly staffroom – groups of people naturally get together to figure things out for themselves, so learning to be a good team player, a skilled conversationalist, and a respectful sounding board are as important as knowing how to wrestle with a difficult book on your own.

In school and out reminds us that the whole point of the LPA is to prepare children not just for the next stage of their formal education, but to give them a broad, positive orientation to learning – to grappling with things that are hard or confusing – whenever and wherever this may occur, for the rest of their lives. So we have to not only try to cultivate these attitudes, but also help children to appreciate their relevance to any of the widespread tricky stuff that life throws at them.

And *for grades and for life* tells us not to see "life skills" and "good grades" as in competition with each other. The LPA wants the two side by side, and the research

---

1   See Raymond S. Nickerson, David N. Perkins and Edward E. Smith (eds), *The Teaching of Thinking* (Hillsdale, NJ: Lawrence Erlbaum, 1985).

shows that we can indeed have both – if we design our classrooms in a particular way.[2]

How Does the LPA Work?

There are lots of ways in which schools can try to incubate the attitudes that underpin powerful learning. Some of them involve changing the content of the curriculum – for example, by having more thematic or cross-curricular topics. Some involve changes to the structure of the timetable; giving children more opportunity to figure things out for themselves may work better if lessons are longer, for instance. Some may need a shift in policy about the use of smartphones or tablets in the classroom, as children are encouraged to find their own answers on the Internet when faced with a challenging question.

But none of these changes work reliably without the presence of a flesh and blood teacher who lives and breathes the ideals of the LPA. Indeed, such a teacher can breathe new life into quite traditional-looking lessons. You do not need half-day sessions, a roomful of tablets, or a maths teacher and a geography teacher working together to create a learning-power classroom. At the heart of the LPA is an understanding of how to develop children's resourcefulness and independence through the creation of a particular classroom culture. Many small details in the way in which a teacher designs their classroom turn out to have an impact on the way the children behave and grow as learners. It is these details – all of them under every teacher's control – that this book is going to tell you about. Many of them can be implemented right now, without any major

> Many small details in the way in which a teacher designs their classroom turn out to have an impact on the way the children behave and grow as learners.

---

2   This research is reviewed in detail in the first book in this series, *The Learning Power Approach*.

upheaval, and without any risk to the conventional "standards" of achievement and progress against which schools are regularly judged.

The Strands of the LPA

The LPA is unusually coherent as a philosophy of education. It tightly knits together a clear *vision* of the purposes of 21st century education, a coherent *scientific rationale* for the approach, a set of teaching methods or *pedagogies*, and a view of *assessment*. The LPA is also underpinned by a well-founded *psychology of learning*, more of which in the next section. Here is a summary of what these strands look like.

The *vision* is to give all young people the knowledge, expertise, and especially the attitudes and dispositions towards learning that are needed to thrive economically, socially, and personally in complex, fast-changing, multicultural societies. Individuals need to know a lot of things in order to function well in their culture, and they clearly need a variety of skills or literacies: literary, mathematical, scientific, digital, graphic, and visual, for example. But more than that, they need to be good at discovering, critiquing, customising, and creating things. In the era of social media and fake news, everyone now needs to be not just a knowledge-*consumer* but a knowledge-*critic*, and a knowledge-*maker* as well.

The *scientific rationale* for the LPA rests on recent changes in our understanding of the make-up of the mind, and especially of what we mean by intelligence. Research shows that the intelligent mind comprises – in addition to some basic structures and constraints – a set of malleable habits that are picked up from the families, friendship groups, and schools to which children belong. Our personalities and mental aptitudes are not set in stone. They change and develop over our lifespan, meaning that teachers have the opportunity to deliberately influence the development of these habits and dispositions in positive directions.[3]

---

3 For a review of this research, see: Bill Lucas and Guy Claxton, *New Kinds of Smart: How the Science of Learnable Intelligence is Changing Education* (Maidenhead: Open University Press, 2010). For a more erudite treatment, see: Cecilia Heyes, *Cognitive Gadgets: The Cultural Evolution of Thinking* (Cambridge, MA: Harvard University Press, 2018).

The LPA *pedagogy* comprises a set of powerful design principles that create a classroom environment in which young people naturally strengthen a spirit of adventurousness, determination, imagination, reflectiveness, criticality, and sociability when faced with difficulties and uncertainties. Adopting this teaching style does not prevent teachers from expressing their personalities and interests in a whole variety of ways. We don't want to turn teachers into robots or inhibit their creativity – far from it. But there are some tried-and-tested ground rules that will steer children in the direction of becoming more independent and resourceful.

The LPA approach to *assessment* combines a concern with sound knowledge and important literacies with the ability to evidence the growth of children's learning capacities and dispositions. In particular, there is a focus on evidencing improvement and progress, rather than just achievement.

The LPA Psychology of Learning

This is how the LPA sees classroom learning. In every classroom there are three different kinds of learning going on: knowledge is being accumulated; specific skills and techniques are being acquired; and more general attitudes and habits of mind are being formed. We find it useful to think of these as different levels or layers in a flowing river.

On the surface, quite fast moving and most visible, are the subjects of the curriculum – the knowledge. As you sit on the riverbank, you can watch the different topics floating by. There go the Vikings. Close behind comes adding fractions. Ah, here comes the difference between prepositions and conjunctions. And so on.

> In every classroom there are three different kinds of learning going on: knowledge is being accumulated; specific skills and techniques are being acquired; and more general attitudes and habits of mind are being formed.

Then just below the surface of the river come the forms of expertise that enable students to acquire and make sense of that content – linguistic, numerical, and digital literacies, the skills and disciplines of mathematical and historical thinking, the ability to read musical notation, and so on. Both of these layers are very familiar to teachers, and of great concern.

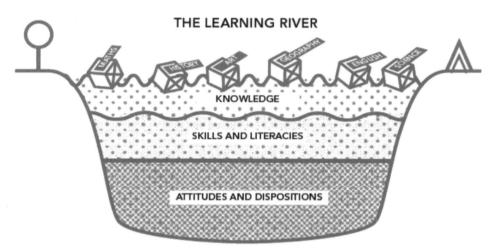

Figure 1.1: The Layers of Learning in the Classroom
Source: By kind permission of Juan and Becky Carlzon

But lower down in the depths of the river, slower moving and less easy to see, the attitudes that shape children's engagement with learning more generally are being formed. Questions we might ask ourselves about these attitudes include:

+ Are children becoming more able to sort things out for themselves as they go through school, or less?

+ Are they becoming more imaginative in their thinking, or more literal-minded?

+ Are they learning to question what they read, or becoming more uncritical?

+ Are they learning to enjoy digging deeper into questions and problems, or becoming more focused only on the marks they get on tests?

- Are they becoming more subtle in their thinking – and able to handle more complex material – or are they only interested in the "right answer"?

- Are they learning to appraise their own and each other's work in an honest and respectful way, or becoming more fragile in the face of feedback?

Learning at each of these layers is going on all the time. They don't compete for time and attention. You don't have to stop practising spelling in order to work on your resilience. Resilience is being strengthened – or weakened – by the way in which the teacher is "doing spelling" with the children. Some ways of doing spelling encourage the children to be more tolerant of mistakes, and more able to spot and fix them for themselves. And other ways of doing spelling make the children more passive and dependent on the teacher. As a teacher – or as a parent, come to that – you can't *not* be affecting the habits of mind that are slowly developing at layer 3 in the river – for good or ill.

> Some people think they can't do things and give up. But the man who created the light bulb, he never gave up. Learning powers help me try and help others to do well too.

What Does the LPA Ask of Teachers?

Different aspects of teaching are important at each of the three layers of learning. Whether children are developing secure and accurate understanding at layer 1 depends on the quality of the teacher's knowledge; we have to "know our stuff". And we have to explain things clearly and make sure that the children have understood them by marking their work carefully and asking good diagnostic questions. At layer 2, where we are building skills, the activities we design for the children are obviously the most important. Just as an expert coach designs practical exercises that will develop the skills of an electrician, a chef, or a guitarist, so we design activities that stretch and extend our children's literacy and numeracy. A good activity starts from where the children are and moves them on.

But down at layer 3, where more general attitudes and habits of mind are being developed, it is not the telling or training that matters so much as the *culture of practices* and *expectations* we create – the atmosphere of our classrooms. You can't just tell someone to be more resilient or creative – though, as we will see, a little explicit instruction does help. A child might be able to tell you what resilience is, or even write a good essay about it, while not becoming any more resilient in the face of real difficulty. And you can't just train creativity. There are a few techniques that can help you to generate ideas, but being creative-minded depends on attitudes such as curiosity, playfulness, and determination, not just on a bit of brainstorming.

Small details in the way in which classrooms and schools operate cumulatively impact on the development of these critical attitudes and habits of mind. How we teach slowly shapes the way children respond to the unknown – to change, challenge, complexity, and uncertainty. As a teacher, you are always creating these undercurrents – through your words, your reactions to the children, the activities you design, the choice of what to display on your walls, the things you notice as you mark the children's work, and dozens of other details that contribute to their experience in school.

> How we teach slowly shapes the way children respond to the unknown – to change, challenge, complexity, and uncertainty.

This shaping is not inevitable – some children are "bent" more than others by routines and expectations, and some resist being shaped at all. But the culture that a teacher creates acts like a magnetic field that attracts, stimulates, and rewards certain habits of mind and not others.

You can teach the history of the First World War, for example, in a way that engages the children's scepticism of historical accounts, their ability to research independently, their collaborative skills, and their empathy. You could get them to assess the reliability of different accounts, to research new information for themselves, and to write about the Battle of the Somme through the eyes of three contrasting participants. Or you could use the same material as an "exercise machine" to develop the inclination to accept what you are told without thinking, to depend on others to tell you "the truth", and to believe that there is always going to be one right answer. All you have to do to achieve the second effect is to get your learners, day after day, to copy down pages of notes mindlessly from the whiteboard, plough through prescribed pages of a textbook on their own, and sit tests that focus only on the right/wrong recall of factual information.

Different lessons will, intentionally or not, affect different dispositions at layer 3. Learning to remember and recall things accurately is useful, so you might sometimes focus on helping the children to develop good memories. But accurate retention is just one mental capacity among many, and we should not work that mental muscle monotonously day in, day out. Just as important are the readiness to question knowledge claims, the ability to stay focused despite distractions, or the ability to put yourself in someone else's shoes and consider their side of the story. You might be aiming to develop the disposition of collaboration in one lesson and reflection in another. Over time, if your children have a good mixture of learning experiences at layer 3, they will get a thorough all-round mental workout. You will help them become mind-fit for life.

As we say, every teacher's classroom conveys messages about the kinds of learning dispositions that are expected; you can't avoid influencing at layer 3. What you can do is be conscious and intentional about what you want to be happening down in the lower layers of the learning river – and that is what the LPA asks you to be. What habits of mind would you wish for your learners to develop? Which ones will stand them in good stead, not just for their Key Stage 2 SATs[4] but for life beyond school? And are they the ones that are being implicitly invited and exercised in your room – by the way in which you lay out the chairs and tables, the language you use as you help a child who is struggling, or the written comments you make on their work? The LPA asks you to take a careful look at the climate you create, and to make sure that there is a good alignment between the values you espouse and the messages that the children are getting.

> Every teacher's classroom conveys messages about the kinds of learning dispositions that are expected.

---

4   National tests that all children in England take at the end of primary school.

There is widespread recognition of the vital importance of the third layer of learning – the development of learning dispositions. Research shows that success in life and personal fulfilment depend upon those mental habits.[5] However, many current approaches to teaching either make the mistake of just assuming that good traditional teaching automatically builds positive attitudes toward learning – which it doesn't – or they simply ignore it in practice. The LPA builds teachers' awareness of what is going on at the third layer in their classrooms, and offers practical advice about how to strengthen and direct dispositional learning.

> We'll need maths and English but learning powers are even more important because we need to persevere. If you don't get the job you want, you need to be determined. You need to empathise. My sister always makes us look at things from the other person's shoes. You use them so much but you don't realise it and they are some of the most important things you will need.

Where Does the LPA Come From?

The LPA forms a kind of middle way between the extremes of "traditional" and "progressive" teaching. It preserves the traditionalists' focus on the importance of knowledge and understanding, and on helping all children achieve the grades of which they are capable. But it combines this with the progressives' concern with the development of the whole child, especially with helping them to build a set of positive attitudes and mindsets towards dealing with challenge and uncertainty.

---

5   For an accessible overview, see: Paul Tough, *How Children Succeed: Grit, Curiosity, and the Hidden Power of Character* (New York: Houghton Mifflin Harcourt, 2012).

Over the last twenty years or so, a number of groups have been homing in on this possibility, refining its specification, and researching practical ways of making it a reality in today's busy classrooms. Though they each have a distinct flavour, they agree about much more than they argue about. The LPA aims to distil the essence of this emerging school of thought. Its principal architects include:

- The Expeditionary Learning – now called EL Education – schools, built around Ron Berger's view that all children, with the right support, are capable of developing an attitude of "craftsmanship" towards their studies, and producing high-quality work.

- Ron Ritchhart's work on classrooms as "cultures of thinking", and the development of intellectual character.

- The Habits of Mind school of thought, with its complementary idea of "dispositional teaching", developed over many years by Art Costa and Bena Kallick.

- The highly successful International Baccalaureate (IB) programmes used in thousands of schools around the world.

- The New Pedagogies for Deep Learning work of Michael Fullan and his colleagues.

- The Learning without Limits approach of Susan Hart, Alison Peacock, and colleagues.

- Guy and his colleagues' development of the approach known as Building Learning Power (BLP), now in use in many schools around the UK as well as in Ireland, Poland, South-east Asia, Australia, New Zealand, South Africa, and various countries in South America.

> The LPA ... preserves the traditionalists' focus on the importance of knowledge and understanding ... but it combines this with the progressives' concern with the development of the whole child.

References to the work of these groups can be found in the Further Reading and Resources sections at the end of the book. There are many more contributors to this school of thought, both contemporary and historical, that are covered in more detail in *The Learning Power Approach*.[6] From the pioneering work of great educators such as Maria Montessori and John Dewey, to contemporary scholars such as Carol Dweck and David Perkins, there is a long tradition of rigorous thinking and research that leads in the direction of the LPA.

What Does the LPA Offer?

As well as providing a rationale for a certain kind of teaching, the LPA offers teachers a variety of tools for growing an LPA culture in their classrooms. There are what we call *seeds*: small tweaks or techniques which convey the spirit of the LPA, and which teachers can insert into any lesson. You'll find these mostly in the "dipping your toes in" sections of the following chapters. *Routines* are small, well-defined procedures that teachers can use to get children to stretch their minds in a variety of different ways, across a wide range of subject matter. Well-known routines are Edward de Bono's Plus-Minus-Interesting (PMI)

> *If we didn't have learning powers we wouldn't have all the skills and muscles to help stretch our brains and to understand our learning in a lot more depth. It helps us understand what we're doing.*

– used to explore the pros, cons, and points of interest of an idea – and Ron Ritchhart's Think-Pair-Share that sequences children thinking on their own, then talking with a partner, and finally sharing thoughts with the whole class.

Then there are *protocols*, which are general templates for designing lessons. You will meet EL Education's protocol called "Speed Dating". BLP has a protocol called

---

6   Guy Claxton, *The Learning Power Approach: Teaching Learners to Teach Themselves* (Carmarthen: Crown House Publishing, 2018).

"Split-Screen Teaching" that designs lessons explicitly with two ends in mind: mastery of particular content *and* the stretching of a specific learning muscle.

And then there are our own personal *habits*, which may also need bringing a little more into line with the aims of the LPA. We are all creatures of habit – we couldn't get through the day without them! But sometimes we may need to expend a bit of effort to become aware of those habits and adjust them. For example, some teachers have a strong impulse to rescue and reassure children who are on the brink of getting upset by their inability to do or understand something. But if we jump in too quickly we may be depriving children of a vital opportunity to build up their learning stamina, and to feel the pride that comes with having wrestled with something hard and worked it out for yourself. That impulse to rescue may be a habit that could be retrained a little.

Finally, there are two important frameworks that we use for organising thoughts and intentions about the design of teaching and learning. The first is called *the elements of learning power*, and it is a fairly detailed description of the habits of mind, attitudes, and dispositions – or learning muscles – that underpin someone's capacity and appetite for engaging productively with tricky matters. Chapter 6 in The *Learning Power Approach* talks you through these in some detail. They are summarised in Figure 1.2. This framework enables you to keep in mind the big picture of learning power, so you are less likely to neglect some of the important, but maybe less obvious, details.

Curiosity:	Having an inquisitive attitude to life.
	Wondering: Being alive to puzzles and incongruities.
	Questioning: Seeking deeper understanding.
	Exploring: Actively and adventurously investigating.
	Experimenting and Tinkering: Trying things out to see what happens.
Attention:	Locking your mind onto learning.
	Noticing: Being attentive to details and patterns.
	Concentrating: Maintaining focus despite distractions.

	Contemplating: Letting perception unfold.
	Immersing: Being engrossed in learning.
Determination:	Sticking with challenges that matter to you.
	Persevering: Staying intelligently engaged with difficult things.
	Recovering: Bouncing back quickly from frustration or failure.
	Practising: Mastering the hard parts through repetition.
Imagination:	Creatively exploring possibilities.
	Connecting: Using metaphor and association to leverage new ideas from what you know.
	Playing with Ideas: Allowing the mind to bubble with possibilities.
	Visualising: Using mental rehearsal to refine skills and explore consequences.
	Intuiting: Tapping into bodily based hunches and inklings.
Thinking:	Working things out with clarity and accuracy.
	Analysing: Reasoning with logic and precision.
	Deducing: Drawing inferences from explanations.
	Critiquing: Questioning the validity of knowledge claims.
	Systems Thinking: Thinking about complex states of affairs.
Socialising:	Benefiting from and contributing to the social world of learning.
	Collaborating: Being an effective and supportive team member.
	Accepting: Being open to ideas and feedback.
	Imitating: Being permeable to other people's good habits.
	Empathising: Adopting multiple perspectives.

	Leading: Playing a role in guiding and developing groups and teams.
Reflection:	Standing back and taking stock of learning. *Evaluating*: Appraising the quality of your own work. *Self-evaluating*: Knowing yourself as a learner. *Thinkering*: Blending doing and thinking together. *Witnessing*: Quietly watching the flow of your own experience.
Organisation:	Managing and controlling your own learning. *Learning Designing*: Creating your own learning activities. *Planning*: Anticipating needs and pitfalls of the learning journey. *Resourcing*: Building your bank of learning resources. *Adapting*: Being able to change tack when needed.

Figure 1.2: The Elements of Learning Power[7]

The second framework is what we call *the design principles for learning power teaching*. These are general guidelines that identify the aspects of teachers' styles and methods that we have found to have the greatest impact on the development of positive learning dispositions. They will help to steer the development of your pedagogy, so that your classroom becomes an ever more effective incubator of children's attitudes and habits as learners. The design principles that underpin the ethos of a learning-powered classroom are listed in Figure 1.3. Of course the list is not exhaustive, but it should serve as good guidance as you think about experimenting with your style and practice as a teacher.

As stated in the introduction, this book is structured around these design principles, but we will tackle them thematically rather than in strict numerical order. Each

---

7   The keen-eyed reader will have spotted some small changes to this list from the one that appears in *The Learning Power Approach* and we have revised the wording of some of the design principles too. We have also added a few words to our definition of the approach. Apologies: we are inveterate thinkerers! And we hope you will be too.

chapter will give hints and tips on how to get started with some of the design principles, as well as describing more in-depth examples which will challenge you to adapt your lessons and day-to-day practice to boost your children's learning power.

1. Create a feeling of safety.

2. Distinguish between learning mode and performance mode.

3. Organise compelling things to learn.

4. Make ample time for collaboration and conversation.

5. Create challenge.

6. Make difficulty adjustable.

7. Talk about and demonstrate the innards of learning.

8. Make use of protocols, templates, and routines.

9. Use the environment.

10. Develop craftsmanship.

11. Allow increasing amounts of independence.

12. Give students more responsibility.

13. Focus on improvement, not achievement.

14. Lead by example.

Figure 1.3: The Design Principles for Learning Power Teaching

Why Does the LPA Matter?

We would like to conclude this overview chapter by summarising ten reasons why the LPA is so important. Again, these reasons are explained and explored in more detail in Chapter 5 of *The Learning Power Approach*. It is important to keep remembering why the LPA matters, so we can overcome the inertia of habit and resist the demands of people who have a more superficial or antiquated view of education. Tinkering with "what works" to make it even better is effortful; it takes time and awareness. Understanding the point of doing so keeps us going. So, the LPA matters because:

1. Today's world is complicated, fast-changing, and cognitively demanding. We are bombarded by choice, opportunity, and (fake) news; expected to keep up with social media and suss out scams; and master new technology and work out what new gadgets are worth buying. Everyone needs to be a powerful learner these days.

2. In the face of all this complexity, it is tempting to opt in to a simpler world of fundamentalism. People can replace the messy uncertainties of reality with the comforting black-and-white image provided by a fanatical religious sect, violent political nationalism, or social tribalism, such as following a football team or a particular dress code. But this escapism and factionalism can further destabilise society. Learning power makes the world a safer place.

    > [We need learning powers] to help us in the future, and to help generally. You use them on a daily basis. We reflect, concentrate, and we collaborate a lot – in school, at home, on holiday – so it's there to help you improve in life.

3. Alternatively, people may stay with complexity but feel overwhelmed and defeated by it. Major surveys show how many young people suffer from stress and a variety of mental health issues, drowning in a sea of responsibility for

which they feel unprepared and ill-equipped.[8] Learning power helps to grow the resources needed to avoid depression and anxiety.

4. In adult life, nobody is followed round by a caring tutor or a guardian angel, telling them what to learn or how to make choices. We all have to decide our learning lives for ourselves. So it just seems common sense that teachers should teach in a way that prepares children to organise their learning for themselves.

5. Large-scale studies have shown that traits such as curiosity, perseverance, self-discipline, imagination, concentration, and empathy correlate significantly with how stable, successful, and satisfied people are with their lives as they grow up and into adulthood. They also show that these attributes are affected by early experience – at home, with friends, and in school.[9]

6. Time and again, surveys show that employers value these kinds of attributes highly – often more highly than qualifications. Some big firms like Google and PricewaterhouseCoopers hire people who can think on their feet in preference to those with impressive degrees. Learning power makes you more employable.[10]

7. Research also shows that traits like curiosity, resilience, grit, and growth mindset predict rates of learning and levels of achievement in school, as well as beyond. Even the ability to think and talk about your learning – being well-versed

> It is important to keep remembering why the LPA matters, so we can overcome the inertia of habit and resist the demands of people who have a more superficial or antiquated view of education.

---

8 For example, Stephan Collishaw, Barbara Maughan, Robert Goodman, and Andrew Pickles, Time trends in adolescent mental health. *Journal of Child Psychology and Psychiatry* (2004), 45(8): 1350–1362.

9 Tim Kautz, James Heckman, Ron Diris, Bas ter Weel, and Lex Borghans, *Fostering and Measuring Skills: Improving Cognitive and Non-Cognitive Skills to Promote Lifetime Success* (Paris: OECD, 2017).

10 University of Birmingham, What employers want: what attributes are most valued by employers? Available at: https://hub.birmingham.ac.uk/news/soft-skills-attributes-employers-value-most.

in the elements of learning power – predicts better performance in high-stakes examinations.[11]

8. Students – especially students from poorer backgrounds – who have learning power are much less likely to drop out of college, university, or an apprenticeship.[12]

9. Learning power doesn't just benefit the learners themselves; it makes life easier and more interesting for teachers as well. Children who are more curious – open to being engaged and intrigued by things – and more determined to work things out for themselves – more likely to relish a challenge than be floored by it – are more fun to teach. (Who knew?)

10. Finally, powerful learners are just plain happier, more of the time. People who have discovered difficult, worthwhile things that they want to accomplish, and who feel empowered to pursue those goals with all their hearts, have access to a world of unselfconscious absorption, wrestling with challenges and making progress in overcoming them, in which – they report in retrospect – they feel happy.[13]

So, what's not to like about learning power?

With that brief introduction to the whats, hows and whys of the LPA under our belts, let's now dive in to the practicalities.

---

11 Chris Watkins, *Learning, Performance and Improvement*, Jane Reed (ed.), Research Matters series no. 34 (London: International Network for School Improvement, 2010).

12 See Tough, *How Children Succeed*.

13 See Mihaly Csikszentmihalyi, *Flow: The Psychology of Happiness* (London: Rider, 2002).

Chapter 2

The Learning Power Approach in Action

After that overview, we now want to throw you straight into some LPA classrooms, so you can get a feel for what the LPA looks, sounds, and feels like. We are going to describe three lessons in different subjects, with children of different ages, so you can see how flexible the LPA can be, but also get a sense of what is common to them all. We will describe the lessons, offer you some reflections about what is going on, and what the teachers' intentions are, and then pose some questions for you to wonder about. At the end of the chapter we will tie the threads together using the design principles that we outlined in Chapter 1.

Remember that the three teachers you will meet in this chapter are quite experienced practitioners of the LPA, so you will see a lot of subtlety and flexibility in their use of the approach. Over time they have learned how to think on their feet so they can capitalise on what is going on in the classroom, and customise their comments and directions accordingly. As with the formation of any new habit, this level of fluent expertise takes time to develop – so if the LPA is new to you, don't expect to be able to do what these teachers are doing overnight. In the rest of the book we are going to slow the journey down and take it step by step. This chapter is just to orient you to the potential of the approach, and give a sense of where we are heading.

What Does the LPA Actually Look Like?

Our first example comes from Becky's Year 1 classroom in Christ Church Infants School in Bristol in the UK. Here is a description of the lesson. We have written it from the standpoint of an observer, so you can imagine yourself being in the room, watching what is going on.

It is near the beginning of the year and the children need to consolidate their knowledge about ordering the numbers from 1 to 10. Of course, as in any class, there is a wide range of understanding. Some children can already order the numbers up to 10 very easily; others struggle to get beyond 5. The key challenge is to engage and stretch all children and, in the process, help them to learn that they can independently stretch themselves without the "OK" from their teacher. Since it's the beginning of the year, the children are still in the early stages of exploring what makes a good learner. For example, they have been getting used to collaborating with a range of different children for a good few weeks, and they are also beginning to understand what it means to challenge themselves.

In order to deepen the children's understanding of ordering numbers from 1 to 10, Becky has gathered a range of resources that could be ordered in that way. These include standard primary school mathematical equipment, such as Numicon, felt number tiles, Multilink cubes, clocks, and also some natural objects like leaves, sticks, and stones. In fact, Becky asked a classroom assistant to go outside with some children with special needs before the lesson and count and collect sets of natural objects to use in the lesson. After a few warm-up activities, such as simply practising counting forwards and backwards, Becky asks the children to find a "learning partner" to sit next to, and then arrange themselves in a big circle. She reminds them that good learning partners are not necessarily their best friends, but are children who they know will help them to concentrate and learn. She tells them that it is always good to challenge yourself and be brave enough to learn with someone new.

Once the children are in a circle, she asks them to discuss with their partner how many different ways they could use the resources to build a number line from 1 to 10. She asks them if they can develop a plan to build a number line from 1 to 10 in as many different ways as they can think of. During the discussion Becky circulates, listening to and extending the children's ideas and facilitating talk. She makes comments and asks questions like:

"I wonder if you can think of another way to do that."

"How could you make that even trickier for yourselves?"

"What steps might you take to make that number line?"

"What could you do if you have finished?"

"What would you do if someone else wanted to use those resources?"

After the talk in pairs, the children share their ideas with the whole circle. Becky makes it clear to them that this is a really important time to listen as they might want to borrow good ideas from their friends, or they might pick up ideas that they can add to their own plan. She asks a few children to share their ideas, carefully picking some more basic examples and more in-depth, tricky ones. For example, one pair say they would like to order number tiles from 1 to 10 and another adds to that by saying they could count out objects on top of the tiles to match the numerals. Another pair say they really want to challenge themselves to see if they can make times on the clocks and order them!

Once a few ideas have been shared, Becky lets the children go off to put their plans into action. She circulates around pairs of children, commenting on, questioning, and nudging them to develop their ideas. She is also acting as an "idea fertiliser", sharing ideas between groups of children and sometimes with the whole class. For example, when children think they have completed the task, she makes comments like, "I wonder if you can spot any ideas other children are using and use them to make yours even better ..." As she wanders round, she takes photos of the children learning, planning to use them in the review at the end of the lesson.

The children's ideas range from making towers of Multilink cubes and ordering them, chalking numbers and matching the correct amount of sticks to each number, ordering the cardboard clocks by moving the hands to make different times, and using an abacus to "make a number line that goes back and forwards". The children are already getting into the spirit of the LPA because you can hear them saying things like:

"We chose the clocks because they were the trickiest, didn't we?"

"I know! I'll get us a number line to check the numbers!"

"Let's write the numbers and count out some objects. What should we use to count?"

For the last ten minutes of the lesson, the children gather round the interactive whiteboard. Becky chooses some photos to focus on and discuss in more detail. Again, she values simpler ideas alongside ideas where the children have really extended themselves – for example, by ordering times on the clocks, the children eventually made a number line, ordering clocks by the hour, and then extended themselves to make some of the clocks say half past, quarter past, and quarter to. One child suggests making a display of all of their ideas, so after the lesson Becky prints some of the photos and displays them with the title, "How many ways could you make a number line from 1 to 10?"

There are many aspects of this lesson that illustrate the philosophy and practice of the LPA. The aim is to teach in a way that encourages the children to learn how to "do it for themselves". Why? Because if they learn how to take risks and push themselves in their learning, and to recognise and enjoy the buzz of learning something new, they will become more proactive and robust and will no longer need someone else to either push or reassure them. Not only does this mean the children progress more quickly, it also makes the teacher's job easier as the children start to drive their own learning.

Getting the children to choose their own learning partners, and to keep daring to find new ones, is a deliberate ploy to strengthen their ability – and willingness – to collaborate well with each other. In many classrooms, children are encouraged to gain a feeling of security by sitting in the same place, and always working with a chosen partner – their best friend perhaps – with whom they feel comfortable. But this security makes children vulnerable to change, so Becky continually encourages them to discover ways of working well with new partners, and to consider for themselves the benefit of working with a wide range of other learners with different views and habits to their own.

> The aim is to teach in a way that encourages the children to learn how to "do it for themselves".

This kind of steady, "drip, drip" stretching of habits develops throughout the year. To begin with, some children find learning with new partners difficult – because it's unfamiliar and "risky". But the ones who find it difficult are the ones who need it most, as they are typically the ones with weak socialising muscles that need exercising. If we avoid this difficulty, or don't plan to provide these children with opportunities to learn with new friends, we are doing them a disservice as those learning muscles will stay weak, although of course this doesn't mean they will instantly enjoy the experience of changing partners. By encouraging children to constantly seek out new partnerships, they are learning how to make new friends, to gain confidence, and to explore the value of learning with lots of different children.

> In an LPA classroom, borrowing or even stealing each other's ideas, customising and enriching them in the process, is actively encouraged!

Notice also the kinds of open-ended questions and comments that Becky uses, continually nudging the children towards thinking for themselves, exploring different pathways and possibilities, and taking greater responsibility for their own learning. Her use of "I wonder …" invites children to wonder along with her; it stretches their curiosity. When she says "I wonder if you can spot any ideas other children are using and use them to make yours even better …" their noticing and mimicking muscles are being stretched by being asked to adopt useful ideas from others as well as making use of what's going on in their own heads. In an LPA classroom, borrowing or even stealing each other's ideas, customising and enriching them in the process, is actively encouraged! There is always something useful to learn from others, and imitation – provided it is not mindless copying – remains a useful resource for all of us throughout our lives.[1]

> When you're curious you explore, experiment, question, or wonder something. It means you want to find out something.

---

1 In *Cognitive Gadgets*, Cecilia Heyes argues that this kind of "social learning" is one of the most important learning strengths anyone can have.

Other questions nudge children, pushing them to think about the problem in a different way, or to extend their thinking. When Becky asks, "How many different ways could you use these resources?" she is deliberately using language that pushes the children towards a more imaginative and creative engagement with maths. Using and modelling this language demonstrates that there is not one correct answer but various avenues of thought to be explored. This is not only good for their understanding of maths, but also for getting them used to dealing with a complex world.

By her manner, Becky is trying to ensure that children who differ widely in their current levels of confidence and ability all feel welcomed and valued in her classroom. When children are feeding back their ideas in the big circle, she is deliberately choosing some simple ideas and some more complex ones. This allows a safety net for less-confident learners and also models how all the children can really challenge and extend themselves. Getting some of the children with special needs to go and help an adult forage for useful resources for the lesson gives those who might find it harder to engage some extra time and encouragement to warm up and practise their thinking. It also gives those children a feeling of contributing to the lesson and gives Becky a chance to praise them in front of the class for being helpful.

You can see many ways in which these subtle, or not so subtle, hints and nudges are paying off in terms of the children's attitudes towards their learning. Children who say, "We chose the clocks because they were the trickiest, didn't we?" are clearly learning to relish challenge. The child who says, "I know! I'll get us a number line to check the numbers" is demonstrating their resourcefulness. The child who suggests making a public display of all their ideas is beginning to think like a teacher. And Becky

> In an LPA classroom there are thirty brains generating and sharing ideas about how to make learning better, not just one!

encourages this sense of ownership and participation by picking up the children's ideas and running with them. In an LPA classroom there are thirty brains generating and sharing ideas about how to make learning better, not just one!

Wondering

What learning-power teaching do you think has happened in the few weeks before this lesson? What could the children have spoken about? How might the teacher have helped the children begin to build an idea of what good learning looks like?

Since the children choose their pairs, they are mixed up in a way the teacher couldn't have planned. What do you think the advantages of this could be? What could some of the sticking points be? How might you try to overcome these?

Can you see similarities to Becky's teaching in your own practice? What are they? What ideas are new? Can you see the value in them?

How might you adapt a lesson this week to encompass some of the elements of this example? Is there another context in which you could start the learning off with a question and allow the children to collaboratively investigate?

Our second example comes from Michelle Worthington's Year 3 class in St Bernard's RC Primary School near Chester in the UK. Here is the description of a lesson which combines English and history, as well as the development of the children's learning power.

The children have been learning about the history of Pompeii for a few weeks. Michelle has planned a series of lessons that will lead up to some detailed descriptive writing and storytelling. She begins the lesson by telling the children that they will be going on a journey in space and time, far away from their classroom to the city of Pompeii. A few children grab each other at the mere thought!

Michelle shows the children a list of the different learning muscles and asks them, "If we are going to Pompeii, what learning muscles might we use?" The children have a discussion with their learning partners. These learning partners were chosen at random at the beginning of the week. When they gather together to discuss as a class, the children offer ideas such as using their noticing muscles to look for clues and their imagination muscles to explore what they see.

The children close their eyes, and Michelle leads them through a short guided visualisation of their journey to Pompeii. When they open their eyes again, there is a detailed illustration of Pompeii projected on the interactive whiteboard. Michelle prompts the children, "What do you notice? See if you can look really closely and notice something no one else will see." Again, the children share ideas. They really do go into detail! One notices tiny thin cracks up the walls of some of the buildings, another notices a bird cage, rocking from side to side. Michelle draws the children in to using their other senses, "What do you smell? How does it feel to be here?" As the children begin to picture and feel the scene, they start fanning themselves from the heat, scratching from the imaginary ash, and coughing on the imaginary smoke.

She then asks the children to put themselves in the shoes of the people in the scene, "You are now one of those people. What might you do?" The children offer ideas about hiding, running, and escaping in boats. She nudges them further. "How are you feeling?" The children agree that they are terrified. They decide that, even though they will be running in the direction of the trouble, they must run for the boats to try to escape. The children get up and run for cover! The tables become boats and they all get inside. Children are beckoning their friends to join them. One child is hanging from the rafters, looking forlorn, jumper pulled over her head as protection from the ash raining down. They are really in role! Michelle ends the role play element by telling the children to cover themselves in blankets and sleep.

As they "wake up", she asks them, "What are you wondering?" and hands out pieces of sugar paper cut into speech bubble shapes. The children collaborate in pairs or small groups to write down all of their wonderings. They are now invested in role and are writing heartfelt questions, like "What has happened to my family?" and "Has the city survived?" There is a focused buzz in the room. Michelle circulates, discussing ideas with the children and opening up the story and dialogue further.

The children are finally shown a video of an exploding volcano, followed by another detailed illustration of Pompeii, this time from the point of view of a boat at sea, looking back at the destruction of the city. She hands out photocopies of the same picture with magnifying glasses, which will help the children notice the tiniest of details. They are asked to write their own noun phrases to describe the scene. Michelle reminds them to make links to previous lessons, in which they have explored descriptive language, and draws their attention to the anchor charts that they created as a class. Again, Michelle circulates, supporting children who need it and extending ideas and descriptions. Once the children have had a chance to write down some ideas or sentences, she nudges them further, saying, "I'm going to challenge your noticing skills even further. You're getting really good at noticing details in pictures, but one area you find it trickier to use your noticing muscle in is your own writing. Can you try to challenge yourself to notice your own mistakes? Perhaps you can share your writing with your learning partner and see if you can help each other improve?" Children look back at their writing and several pairs take up her suggestion.

The lesson ends with the children sharing their best noun phrases. Michelle also reflects back on the learning muscles that have been used. She points out that they have really stretched their noticing muscles, but have also been using their immersing, imagining, and empathising muscles. As the children go to lunch, Michelle leaves them on a cliffhanger, letting them know that they do survive the volcano, but that is all she can tell them for now.

Again, let's take a closer look at what Michelle is up to in this lesson, and why. She starts by engaging the children's interest by telling them that they are going on a journey. Hooking their attention with something that intrigues them is not special to the LPA, of course; it is just good teaching. But Michelle quickly goes on to get the children thinking about the kinds of learning that such a journey might require, or make possible. She prompts them with a list of the learning muscles, which they are already familiar with, and gets them to try to anticipate which ones they think they might need – or which might be stretched – on the journey. They are primed to be thinking about learning as well as about Pompeii.

> You think you're in a different world, you can imagine what you want to do, you can empathise when you imagine. You can be different people.

By saying "Which muscles might we use?" rather than, for example, "Which muscles will you need?" she is inviting the children's curiosity about the learning they might be doing. She wants them to think, not to be told. She is signalling that this isn't a "right answer" type of question, but one to be investigated. And by saying "we" rather than "you", she is including herself as an explorer and "wonderer", along with the children. The linguistic tone itself encourages the children to use their imaginations – as does her use of the guided visualisation, to get the children's imagining muscles warmed up. Notice too that Michelle, like Becky in the first example, is encouraging the children to develop their confidence and ability to think and learn well with an expanding variety of different partners. Their collaborating muscles are getting a workout too.

The illustration of Pompeii is used as a stimulus for the children to stretch their noticing muscles. Michelle challenges them to look so carefully that they might even spot something that no one else has noticed. Handing out some magnifying glasses later on reinforces the idea that their job is to be meticulous detectives, alert to the tiniest of clues as to what is going on in the illustrations. And she links this physical attentiveness to the pictures in front of the children to their developing ability to imaginatively embellish the scenes for themselves – can they enrich their mental pictures with sounds, smells, and, especially, their feelings? Incidentally, this skilled ability to reinforce perception with imagination is a key tool that many creative adults such as engineers and poets talk about.[2] Not only are the children viscerally engaged, but their minds are being stretched in a variety of increasingly useful and sophisticated ways.

Then Michelle invites the children – again in pairs or small groups – to represent some of this rich harvest of wondering and imagining in words and phrases. She prompts them to draw on their memories of previous learning about descriptive language, and to make use of their own self-generated anchor chart – a display on the classroom wall with suggestions about how to talk productively to each other when exercising their collaborating muscles. And she challenges them to swivel their attention and apply their noticing muscles to their own writing, so that

> It is an important element of the LPA that children are helped to become not just more accomplished learners, but also more articulate and aware of their own learning.

they can help each other to detect mistakes and polish phrases. You may have noticed that not all the children are ready for this next stretch of their ability to collaborate

---

2   See, for example, Bill Lucas, Janet Hanson, Lynne Bianchi, and Jonathan Chippindall, *Learning to Be an Engineer: Implications for the Education System* (London: Royal Academy of Engineering, 2017); and Anne McCrary Sullivan, Notes from a marine biologist's daughter: on the art and science of attention. *Harvard Educational Review* (2000), 70(2): 211–227.

and reflect well together – but some are, and over time this mood of self-help is likely to become contagious in the classroom.

Michelle ends with a feeling of accomplishment as the children share the noun phrases of which they are most proud. They then reflect on the lesson, and the kinds of learning that have been going on. They review the learning muscles they have been using – noticing, collaborating, imagining, self-evaluating, and practising, for example – and discuss how the lesson has helped them to refine and sharpen those learning dispositions. It is an important element of the LPA that children are helped to become not just more accomplished learners, but also more articulate and aware of their own learning, so that they are better able to transfer what they have learned to other contexts and situations.

Wondering

What basics of learning and behaviour does Michelle need to have in place in order to be able to teach this lesson? How might she have established those basics?

The children in this lesson have gone beyond mere engagement; they have become deeply invested in their learning experience. How has Michelle actively created this investment? What did she use to draw the children in?

This lesson focuses on developing children's noticing skills. How do you think this important skill could be developed in and out of school? Can you think of other lessons or contexts in which you could develop this learning muscle?

Could you adapt this lesson to develop or focus on different learning muscles? Concentrating? Empathising? Critiquing?

Our third and final example takes us to Mariyam Seedat's Year 6 classroom in Sandringham Primary School in East London. The class is in the middle of a series of geography lessons, exploring the topic of environmental damage. The topic will conclude with the children making animated videos of environmental change. The children are working in groups of four. Mariyam has designed the groups carefully so that they have equal numbers of boys and girls, and also so the children in each group have varied current levels of attainment. The groups have already decided on an environmental topic they would like to explore and have collaboratively researched their topic both in school and as homework. One group is looking at the environmental impact of urbanisation. Another is researching deforestation. A third is finding out about water pollution. In this lesson, the children are planning how they are going to put together their animations and thinking about what resources they will need.

Mariyam brings her Year 6s to the carpet and they discuss a slide she has projected onto the interactive whiteboard. On the slide, she has outlined the stages of the geography project. The children discuss what they have done so far and what they might need to do next. They discuss the meaning of some key words, such as "props". When the children explain their ideas, Mariyam asks them to stand up, express their ideas articulately, and project their voices. When one less-confident child struggles, she warmly encourages him to rethink and try again. There are sentence starters stuck onto the bottom of the interactive whiteboard, which the children naturally use to expand on ideas in discussion. For example, one child defines props as "extra objects that have a part in this story" and another child adds, "I agree with you, and you also use props in plays and theatres." Mariyam stretches the children's descriptions by asking them to add detail, give examples, and be specific.

After discussing the overall plan and coming to a shared understanding of their next steps, the children go off in their groups to plan how they are going to create their animation and what resources they are going to need. The class is immediately abuzz with chatter and action! To begin with, the children excitedly – and very naturally – discuss how they are going to organise themselves. All the groups organise themselves in quite different, but efficient, ways. One group works as a whole team, discussing ideas, then writing them down on the large sheets of sugar paper they have each been given to record their planning. They explain, "We all have creative ideas and we want to share them." Another group assigns roles, "Two of us are writing down the ideas and two of us are adding to the resources list as we go. It means we don't forget anything." One group splits into two pairs, "We've done it like this so everyone gets a part and no one is doing nothing." When asked how they make sure they are all thinking along the same lines, at first they look confused, then later solve the problem, "When we write an idea, we make sure we say it out loud so it's not repeated."

With the groups organised, they get on with collaborating to plan their ideas. Again, each group's approaches are different. Some draw sketches of ordered scenes, others describe what they are going to do. Many label and annotate their ideas. Different children take on different roles. Some are writers, some draw, some generate ideas, and many children swap and take turns. They understand their roles and the thinking behind them. Roles continue to grow and change as the task goes on. Some children take on the role of overseer, pushing their group to think of new ideas and solutions. They ask questions like, "So, what's going to happen in this bit?", "We've done these bits, but what's next?", and "I like this idea, but how are we going to do that?" They play around with different ideas by asking questions like, "What will happen if …?" This all stems quite naturally from the children.

When the children have had a good amount of time to brainstorm and think through their plans, Mariyam provides each group with a writing scaffold to formalise and present their plans. The children transfer their ideas onto this A3 sheet, filtering out ideas they no longer need, and refining what they have already written. Since the sheet is smaller than the sugar paper, now only one child can write at a time. The children are quite quick to pick up on this and reorganise themselves accordingly. One girl says, "While they write, we can add to our plan." Other children explain how they have planned to take turns so that everyone gets a go.

At the end of the lesson, Mariyam explains that she will have a look through the plans and double-check that they are "doable". It might mean that next lesson some of the plans will need a few tweaks to bring the children's ideas into reality, but that's fine because it's all part of the process.

In this series of lessons, the teacher is stretching the children's ability to choose, design, and carry out an extended project. They are being introduced to new levels of responsibility, but not in a way that threatens to overwhelm them. Mariyam is carefully scaffolding the lessons so that the challenges are manageable, and the children will create a successful product in the end. Her use of the slide that summarises the stages of the project, for example, helps the children to keep the big picture in mind as they delve into the details and different steps, and also builds their capacity to think strategically. She is simultaneously coaching their communication skills as she gets them to stand up and speak as clearly as they can. Her commentary makes them aware of the skills needed to be a confident and effective speaker. The visible array of sentence starters – such as, "I agree with you and …" – help to train the children in the ways of productive communication.

Mariyam is also upping the ante by getting the children to work together in groups that vary both in individual levels of achievement and in gender mix. It is clear that she has thought carefully about which children to put together so that the resulting varied groups will be manageable and productive – although she is always ready to step in when the children seem unable to sort things out for themselves. The fact that they are able to start self-organising, and come up with different but effective ways of doing so by themselves, is a testament to the coaching work that has gone on before.

I never used to ask questions in class but now I am more involved and I ask questions all the time.

Mariyam encourages this autonomy, but is also ready to nudge or challenge the children – for example, to "be more specific" – with a well-judged question.

These children's ability to slip in and out of different roles in the group is also a reflection of the way in which they have been taught. At this stage they are able to adopt and assign these roles fluently and spontaneously; however, previously these roles will have been discussed and assigned by the teacher to make sure that every child gains experience of taking responsibility and developing leadership qualities. At Sandringham School, all the teachers are skilled at making sure different children – and, importantly, shyer children – take on different roles within a group at different times.

Notice that Mariyam doesn't provide a template for the children to write up their plans until after they have had plenty of time to develop their own ways of thinking. In a traditional classroom, the teacher might have given out this template at the beginning of the process, and thus channelled the children into being compliant rather than creative in their thinking. By collaboratively sharing ideas beforehand, the children have experienced a rich planning process, which could be quite similar to a brainstorming session in real life – in a business meeting, perhaps. The LPA constantly seeks to design learning activities that stretch those capabilities which will be genuinely useful to the children later in life. And the children clearly enjoy this creative process.

Wondering

Some teachers see this kind of lesson and say, "I wish my children could do that but I've tried and they just can't work together." What do you think Mariyam has done before this lesson, slowly and continuously, to enable the children to collaborate effectively and positively in this way? Incidentally, it is worth mentioning that Sandringham is in one of the most deprived boroughs in London, yet they refuse to use their children's, admittedly very challenging, backgrounds as an excuse for lowering their expectations of what they can achieve. If they can develop this kind of disciplined learning power in their learners, we think anyone can!

Designing a series of lessons in this way works well with geography or history research projects. Can you think of a way in which you could extend this design to other subjects and topics? How about for extended writing projects in English or maths investigations?

We didn't say much about what the teacher is doing while the children are getting on with planning their projects. What do you think her role is? What kinds of questions might she ask?

Mariyam purposefully mixes the children into groups of four, with two girls and two boys. In what other ways could you group your children? How could you go about it? What could be the advantages and disadvantages of each?

What kind of "learning language" is being used in this lesson, by both the children and their teacher? How could you highlight this language so that the children could capitalise on it and use it again?

If your class isn't used to collaborating yet, what small steps could you take to acclimatise them to learning with different children in different contexts? What could the sticking points be? How could you pre-empt and plan for them?

What are the benefits of gradually teaching children to learn together in this way? In school? Out of school? For life?

Summary

We hope that these examples have sparked your interest and given you a taste of the LPA in action. We are especially keen that you start to notice some of the subtle ways in which LPA teaching differs from some more familiar, more traditional approaches – approaches that may work well for building knowledge and expertise at layers 1 and 2 of the learning river, but which may neglect, or even have adverse effects on, what is going on down at layer 3, where longer-lasting attitudes and dispositions towards learning itself are being shaped. We've seen how LPA teachers are alert to opportunities to give their children manageable amounts of responsibility for their own learning. We've also seen

> Quite subtle shifts in teachers' use of language can create corresponding shifts in the children's attitudes towards difficulty.

how quite subtle shifts in teachers' use of language can create corresponding shifts in the children's attitudes towards difficulty, and how a variety of hints, prompts, and visual tools can support the development of learning power. We've even got a sense of how long-term dispositional goals can be woven into the practical life of the classroom. And we hope that you are reassured that all this can be done alongside the development of accurate knowledge, robust understanding, literacy and numeracy, and intellectual expertise.

Now that we have, hopefully, whetted your appetite – and affirmed some of the approaches you may already be using with your children – let's zoom in on the different aspects of LPA teaching, and show you how you might deepen your practice in each of these areas.

Chapter 3

Setting the Scene: Making Your Classroom a Safe and Interesting Place to Be a Learner

In this chapter we start to dig deeper into the details of the LPA design principles. As we have warned you, some of our ideas and suggestions may well already be a familiar part of your practice. If so, you might just want to check to see if you could embed them more thoroughly, or push them a bit further. Other suggestions might seem a bit too much of a challenge right now. And some – we hope not too many – might seem pointless or unappealing. As you go through the chapters, you might like to make a note about our suggestions like so:

4 = I already do it intuitively and flexibly.

3 = I do it sometimes, but could do it more.

2 = I don't do it, but I'd like to.

1 = I don't want to do it.

This might help you make decisions about how you want to develop your practice, and also help you to identify the ideas you want to implement as you flick back through the book. Perhaps you could focus on implementing ideas you have ranked as a 2 or a 3. Take time to pat yourself on the back for your 4s and reflect on what's making you opposed to your 1s. The final process is particularly important to try to unearth any potential barriers or thought processes that might be stopping you from implementing certain aspects of the LPA. Try to look at these ideas from the point of view of the learners in your classroom and imagine how they might benefit their learning. It might be worth coming back to your 1s after trying out some other ideas and seeing if you'd rank them differently.

We have included in Table 3.1 what we hope will be a useful reflection tool to illustrate what each of these scores might look like in practice and to help you decide the areas in which you might like to start developing further:

Table 3.1: Reflecting on the LPA Principles in Practice

Design principle	1	2	3	4
Learning environment	Displays relate only to classroom rules, curriculum content, and students' best work. All decisions are made by the teacher.	Displays tend to be static and to refer to learning habits, growth mindset, and so on, but do not play any active part in the learning lives of the children. The teacher decides the content.	Displays refer to the process of learning as well as its content. For example, they encourage a positive attitude to making mistakes. Anchor charts are created with the children and used to develop learning habits.	Displays aim to strengthen learning habits in a variety of ways. Some displays are interactive and the children have ownership of them. The children are involved in designing, making, and improving displays to strengthen their learning capacities. Some displays show work in progress, not just the final product.

Language	The teacher's language focuses on discipline and the accurate comprehension of content.	The children are familiar with some learning-focused frameworks and are able to parrot back key terms. However, understanding is skin-deep and use of language is not spontaneous.	The children and adults are beginning to use learning-focused language more naturally in the classroom and it is becoming part of the ethos. Attitudes and habits are noticeably changing alongside this language change.	The children and adults in the classroom talk fluently and spontaneously about the process of learning. They naturally use a range of phrases and words to encourage, stretch, and broaden learning. This language is effortlessly threaded into every second of every day.

Design principle	1	2	3	4
Collaboration	There may be a little collaborative learning. When group work does happen, formats are repetitive and grouping decisions are made by the teacher.	The children are sometimes in varied groups or pairs – for example, during topic work or PE lessons – but they do not reflect on the purpose or success of their group work.	Groups and pairings are fluid and changed regularly according to the task. Collaboration is central to the classroom ethos. The children are relaxed about working with a variety of peers, in a range of groupings.	The children are increasingly responsible for choosing their own partners and groups. They can articulate when it is best for them to learn independently or with others and are sometimes given the space to make this decision. The children can take on a variety of roles within a group. They are also given the chance to reflect on their collaboration skills and continually improve them.

Conversation	Most interactions are between individual children and the teacher. The teacher's questioning aims to elicit textbook answers.	The children are given a chance to share ideas – for example, by using thinking routines like Think-Pair-Share.	Talk is seen as central to learning, and exploratory talk is common. Quality conversations are developed through the regular use of anchor charts and protocols.	The children are taught how to become aware of, reflect on, and improve their conversation skills in a variety of ways and in a variety of contexts. They easily move in and out of the roles of "teacher" and "learner" in their interactions with each other.
Challenge	Activities are predetermined by the teacher, with little regard to whether they are sufficiently challenging for all children.	The children are beginning to understand the value of challenge and the teacher has techniques for checking who is being challenged by the work.	The teacher designs tasks with different degrees of difficulty. The children regularly use visual tools like the learning ladder and the learning pit to visualise, discuss, and reflect on challenge.	Split-screen lessons create challenge both in terms of lesson content and use of learning muscles. Tasks are designed so that the children learn how to adjust the level for themselves.

Design principle	1	2	3	4
Classroom responsibility	The children take very little responsibility for what happens in the classroom. They are predominantly passive and compliant in their approach to learning.	Selected children are involved in some relatively superficial classroom responsibilities, such as looking after particular areas and resources, handing out books, or running errands.	The children are given choice over some aspects of their learning, such as how to present their work, who to work with, or to determine the size and composition of groups for collaborative learning.	The children are involved in every aspect of their learning, from designing their own tasks to identifying and practising their next steps. They are involved in larger-scale projects like writing, planning for, and performing their own plays and teaching parts of lessons.

	Reflection, improvement, and craftsmanship
	Tasks and tests are mostly one-offs, and the children have little opportunity or encouragement to reflect on and improve their own performance.
	The children are beginning to develop a habit of self-improvement by reflecting on their work. They are beginning to have a positive attitude to learning from their mistakes.
	The children are regularly given a chance to reflect on and improve their learning, using rubrics to aid understanding. They are able to give precise, useful, and respectful feedback to each other. The children have a positive attitude to self-improvement.
	The children are regularly given a chance to reflect on and improve their learning across the curriculum. They frequently practise and revise through successive drafts. In each and every lesson, the children are purposefully strengthening their learning muscles, and reflecting on this process.

To begin with we are going to look in more detail at the first three LPA design principles. They are:

1. Create a feeling of safety.

2. Distinguish between learning mode and performance mode.

3. Organise compelling things to learn.

It is a rare kind of learning that proceeds smoothly and quickly from ignorance to comprehension, from clumsiness to expertise. Mostly it involves periods of feeling confused and uncertain; trial and error, and making mistakes; practising until you can reliably "get it right"; accepting and acting on critique and feedback; and reflecting on and redrafting your efforts. Learning is a feelingful business, and it is often difficult. So it's hard to be a learner if you are constantly being distracted, are unsure what you are supposed to be doing or being, or if you are frightened that you will be laughed at if you venture your ideas.

The first step in the LPA, therefore, is to make the classroom a place in which it is normal and safe to experience the ups and downs of the learning journey – and in which there are interesting things to explore and discover. This chapter is full of ideas about how to get these "basics" right.

From the LPA point of view, however, the calm, well-managed classroom is not the gold standard of "good teaching". Establishing orderliness, clarity of purpose, and engagement is just the beginning. Once learners have built the basic habits of concentration, self-reliance, and respect for others, the classroom can become a much more lively and variegated place that incubates *self*-discipline – rather than obedience – and cultivates creativity and collaboration as well as diligence. So the old-fashioned virtues of traditional good teaching have their place in the LPA, but only as the launch pad for developing a much broader and richer set of learning strengths. This is yet another example of how the sterile "either/

> It is a rare kind of learning that proceeds smoothly and quickly from ignorance to comprehension, from clumsiness to expertise.

or" debate between the traditionalists and progressives gets turned into a much more powerful "both/and" construction within the LPA.

It is the teacher's job – especially with younger children, or those who haven't already mastered the basic habits of sitting still, paying attention, playing nicely, and tidying up – to gently instil these essential behaviours. And there are many aspects of the way in which you design your classroom that can help facilitate this. They include:

> The old-fashioned virtues of traditional good teaching have their place in the LPA, but only as the launch pad for developing a much broader and richer set of learning strengths.

+ The ways in which you interact with the children.

+ The ways in which they see you interacting with other adults.

+ How you talk about the ground rules of the classroom, and the extent to which the children are involved in creating and monitoring these rules for themselves.

+ How you organise the furniture and the seating plan.

+ The ways in which they see you dealing with small upsets and interruptions.

All of these facets help to convey the cultural messages that you want the children to internalise. Most children will quite readily accept "the way we do things round here", provided the messages are clear and consistent. Above all, they need to get the message that "we are in this together"; that they – and you as their coach – are in a cooperative, challenging, and engaging learning community. You need to help them see for themselves that the classroom works best when everyone feels clear about the expectations and safe enough to be a learner. Figure 3.1, redrawn from Costa and Kallick's Habits of Mind series, brings to life the idea of a shared, purposeful direction in classroom ethos and learning.

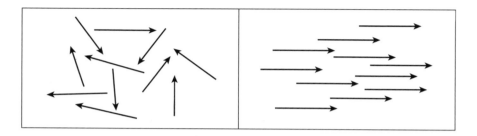

Figure 3.1: Two Types of Organisational Alignment

Source: Adapted from Arthur L. Costa and Bena Kallick, Habits of Mind series

Most courses of initial teacher training tell you what you need to do in order to build this orderly culture, so we will simply add a few hints and tips that suggest how you might do this in the LPA spirit.

Prerequisites for a Learning-Powered Classroom

✓ Model respect, understanding, and kindness.
✓ Create a calm, orderly, and accessible classroom.
✓ Have clear expectations, focusing behaviour around learning.
✓ Make it socially safe to be a learner.
✓ Build trust.
✓ Make learning intriguing, engaging, and purposeful.
✓ Distinguish between learning mode and performance mode.

Dipping Your Toes In

Model respect, understanding, and kindness

Through our modeling, we have the opportunity to nurture the very attitudes, values, and behaviors we want to see in our students.

Ron Ritchhart, *Creating Cultures of Thinking*, p. 127

The ways we behave as adults in the classroom send messages to the children about what we think and what we value. This goes for all learning behaviours – the more we model the behaviours we wish to see in the children, the more they will pick up on and begin to reflect these behavioural expectations. At the most basic level, this involves finding ways to value, listen to, and include every member of your class or school community. Simply saying "please" and "thank you" to both children and adults is a good start. Modelling patience, forgiveness, and an openness to ideas will begin to set the tone in your classroom and, most importantly, make the children feel safe – which is a prerequisite to taking risks in learning. As teachers, we need to aim to be relentlessly and endlessly patient in staying true to this attitude. This is especially important for our most vulnerable learners.

If you need further convincing of the impact that patient, understanding teachers can have on individual children, you might like to watch Jaz Ampaw-Farr's TED Talk.[1] It is an uplifting and moving story of how a "broken little girl" was saved by "ordinary teachers" – everyday heroes, she calls them – who rebuilt her resilience by refusing to accept that she "couldn't do it".

https://www.youtube.com/watch?v=q3xoZXSW5yc

---

1   Jaz Ampaw-Farr, "The Power of Everyday Heroes", *TEDxNorwichED* [video] (30 March 2017). Available at: https://www.youtube.com/watch?v=q3xoZXSW5yc.

You can deepen this ethos of inclusion and understanding in several ways. One is simply to build adults and children up, rather than put them down. Notice and comment on everybody's strengths, rather than focusing on what they didn't or couldn't do. Value children's contributions, and make a habit of noticing – and commenting – when they are making an effort to get things right. Jo, a teacher at Wroxham Primary School in Hertfordshire in the UK, which was taken from Ofsted's "special measures" category to "outstanding" – the journey of which is described in *Creating Learning without Limits* – describes how the children taught her "the importance of treating their work as a gift" by responding to their contributions and efforts with awareness and care.[2] Time pressures often make giving this kind of attention feel difficult, but, whenever you can, bringing this kind of warm presence into the attention you give the children and their contributions will inevitably make them feel valued and, over time, raise their self-esteem and confidence.

Include adults in the classroom by valuing their input and ideas. Becky makes a point of doing this by telling the children about discussions she's had with her learning support assistants – or "learning coaches", as they are called in some LPA schools – showing how she values their expertise and input, and modelling being a good collaborator. Develop relationships with other adults in the classroom – and, of course, with the children – that are non-threatening and accepting, modelling the belief that everyone makes mistakes and deserves a second chance. Steve Jenkins, a case study teacher featured in *Learning That Lasts*, has created this kind of environment, which Ron Berger and colleagues describe as, "a 'be easy on the people, tough on the ideas' classroom".[3]

Try to find moments to have informal chats with the children to find out about their interests and what makes them tick. Be interested in the person they are, not just who you want them to be. It doesn't have to be anything big; perhaps just having a quick chat about something personal to individual children as they come into class, or taking time to celebrate some learning they are particularly proud of. In her excellent book *Hopeful Schools*, Mary Myatt talks about children's – and adults' – need to be noticed and acknowledged, stressing the right of every child to make a

---

2   Mandy Swann, Alison Peacock, Susan Hart, and Mary Jane Drummond, *Creating Learning without Limits* (Maidenhead: Open University Press, 2012), p. 59.

3   Ron Berger, Libby Woodfin, and Anne Vilen, *Learning That Lasts: Challenging, Engaging, and Empowering Students with Deeper Instruction* (San Francisco, CA: Jossey-Bass, 2016), p. 208.

contribution.[4] Find time during the day or week to give each child this opportunity. This is what Dame Alison Peacock and her colleagues at Wroxham School refer to as "the ethic of everybody" – the trust they place in all children's power as learners and contributors to the class community.[5] Sometimes, if you listen carefully, you will be able to use informal chats with the children to improve your teaching, even regarding simple choices like which book you select as class reading. You will find more on incorporating the children's ideas into your planning in Chapter 8.

Julian Swindale, an early years teacher at Sefton Park School in Bristol, makes a point of recording children's positive learning behaviours by writing them up on a large whiteboard and taking photos of fantastic learning. The learning behaviour and the effect this has on individual and collective growth becomes part of whole-class storytelling at the end of the day. Before home time the children gather around the whiteboard to review and discuss what has been recorded that day. They love this time and are proud to recognise their own contributions; and this is a way of constantly building up a picture of "how we do things round here". Here are some examples of what Julian might say:

> "Freddy looked after the classroom by making sure there were enough pencils, pens, and paper for everyone to use – and now we are ready for tomorrow. Thanks, Freddy, good job."

> "Kenny and James collaborated to figure out how many bricks are in the tower – 5,400 – and they have a calculation tip that will help others. In fact, if someone builds a tower tomorrow could Kenny and James teach and support them?"

> "Jess came up with a new way to get unstuck when reading – rereading the sentence to get a feel for what the unknown word might be. Would you explain further, Jess? Using her strategy, Jess has read an entire book! Well done, Jess: you are widening your skills in reading and teaching us at the same time!"

> "Charlie looked after Polly when she fell over and, look, Polly is feeling better and, Charlie, you made a big contribution to that … not me … you did that, Charlie."

---

4   Mary Myatt, *Hopeful Schools: Building Humane Communities* (Mary Myatt Learning Ltd, 2016).
5   Swann et al., *Creating Learning without Limits*, p. 5.

Julian commented:

> Sharing these observations at the end of the day shows children that you value their contributions and efforts partly by the very fact that you remembered them and that they were important enough to broadcast to others. It puts the focus on their own learning behaviours. And it underpins the important fact that school is about the children's achievements – what they are doing, thinking, and achieving. I found that often, by the end of the day, very young children would have forgotten what they did in the morning, so reminding them of their achievements means they spring out of the classroom and share what they have done with their parents. It all contributes to the message that school is an exciting place where children are the players – where they can grow, find themselves, and feel part of a community with social learning at its epicentre. I often start the day with a review of the previous day's successes as an awakening to set us all up for the day to come. The resultant learning is always better because of this. If I am one of the pack leaders in the classroom, I want to lead by heading in the right direction.

Julian also cultivates the virtue of kindness by having a "kind hands" display at child height on the wall. On one side of the display he sticks photos of every person in the class, including the adults. On the other side are images that depict kindness. In Julian's display, the children have made prints of their hands with paint, and these are laminated and velcroed to the board. When they spot someone being kind, the children can move their photo onto one of the kind hands. By constantly making use of and referring to this interactive display, the children build up a picture of what kindness looks and sounds like, and become ready to recognise and value what it feels like. They just naturally become more aware that being supportive of one another is central to the classroom culture.

How do you create a feeling of inclusion and togetherness in your class? One idea we've seen in several classrooms is creating a "family tree" display at the beginning of the year, for which children bring in photos of their family to share with the class and add to the display. It's a simple idea that sends the message that you value the children's wider worlds, not just their lives within the school walls. One Year 5 classroom we visited had a "shout out" board, on which teachers', parents', and children's contributions were recognised and celebrated on a regular basis. The key is to find a way to keep revisiting kindness and inclusion, and to integrate them into day-to-day learning, so the children understand that it is highly valued and can't help but feel safe, included, and welcome in the classroom.

Most humans want to feel secure, supported, validated, and to be given opportunities to reach their full potential.

Nathan Armstrong, quoted in Ron Ritchhart, *Creating Cultures of Thinking*, p. 96

Create a calm, orderly, and accessible classroom

Calm, orderly classrooms create a feeling of safety and help children lock onto learning. This is not to say that all learning will be neat and tidy or that, at times, the classroom won't be abuzz with collaborative chatter. But, as a prerequisite for deeper learning experiences, children need to understand and follow classroom routines. Building a repertoire of fine-tuned routines will help to create a calm classroom. Additionally, your manner as a teacher will have a huge effect on the energy in the room. Have you noticed that when you start the day in a flurry and a rush the children begin to behave in a more flustered and erratic way too? So purposefully take the time to approach learning calmly. Equally, when you want to create excitement and buzz, make sure to reflect that excitement in your manner, attitude, and behaviour.

Furthermore, children need to know how to access resources quickly and effectively. By taking the time to organise your classroom and clearly label resources and the areas in which they can be found – and making them accessible to the children – you are ensuring that they can find the tools they need to assist their learning without having to wait for your attention. Spend time teaching the children to take responsibility for these areas. It is worth thinking about how you will make this a productive and positive experience so that the children take pride in their classroom, rather than regarding keeping it tidy as a chore. For example, with her Year 1s, Becky had a cheeky puppet, Trixie the Pixie (see photo on page 61), who would "mess up" the areas of the classroom which the children needed to pay a bit more attention to looking after. Photos of the puppet's misdemeanours, and taking time to discuss what the problem was in these photos, stopped the children feeling blamed and enabled them to have grown-up conversations about keeping their classroom tidy.

For older children, you could raise the profile of looking after the classroom by discussing regular classroom "jobs" and requiring the children to "apply" for the classroom responsibility they would most like. This creates a shared responsibility for looking after the classroom and gets buy-in from the children. It turns what could be a rather mundane task into something to strive for and take pride in.

Have clear expectations, focusing behaviour around learning

Making sure that all your expectations, procedures, and instructions are really clear and appropriate also contributes to a calm, orderly, and learning-focused classroom. You can't focus on *learning* if you don't know what you are supposed to be *doing*.

It is a good idea to involve the children in the process of creating class rules and expectations for behaviour. Talk to them about what behaviours they think are conducive to effective learning and why they are important to maintain. Take time to review and build on these expectations and help the children gain a clear understanding of how they can create an effective learning community.

Ask them who is responsible for maintaining these rules: the teacher, their parents, themselves? Ask them how they could go about positively supporting themselves and their classmates to make good decisions about their learning. Creating shared

> The essence of an LPA classroom is in getting the balance between safety and challenge right.

expectations of class behaviour should pre-empt a lot of behaviour management issues, and avoid situations in which you feel harassed or have to raise your voice and therefore become punitive.

When they are invited to become part of a shared understanding of positive learning behaviours, children can become quite astute at recognising what is helping themselves and others to learn. For example, when reviewing how the learning went in one writing lesson, Becky asked her children, "What did you notice about how we were learning today?" One child responded, "I could become really absorbed in my learning today because everyone was so quiet and focused."

Make it socially safe to be a learner

The essence of an LPA classroom is in getting the balance between safety and challenge right. Feeling safe doesn't mean not being challenged or being allowed to stay in your comfort zone. It means that you dare to be a learner because everyone else is being a learner too. It means knowing that no one will laugh at you or disparage you if you make a mistake or don't know something. Not being able to do something doesn't mean you are stupid; it means you haven't learned to do it *yet*. There is a world of difference between "I can't do it" and "I can't do it yet". Carol Dweck's TED Talk on the power of yet sums up the theory.[6] And there's also a cute *Sesame Street* song on this theme which is worth watching.[7]

https://www.youtube.com/watch?v=J-swZaKN2Ic

---

6   Carol S. Dweck, "The power of yet", *TEDxNorrköping* [video] (12 September 2014). Available at: https://www.youtube.com/watch?v=J-swZaKN2Ic. We will discuss the "power of yet" in a little more detail in Chapter 5.

7   *Sesame Street* and Janelle Monae, "Power of yet" [video] (10 September 2014). Available at: https://www.youtube.com/watch?v=XLeUvZvuvAs.

https://www.youtube.com/watch?v=XLeUvZvuvAs

So it is part of your job to make sure that nobody is ever rude or nasty to anybody else for not being good at something, *yet*. If children laugh at others for not possessing the same knowledge or skills, don't let it pass – and reinforce that this is not the kind of attitude we have about mistake-making. Use this as an opportunity to remind them that it is the very essence of learning to be vulnerable, and that we all need those around us to cut us some slack when we are wrestling with something we find hard – even if most of the other people in the room can do it already. So, no groaning or rolling of eyes, or whispering "*Everybody* knows that". We support each other's struggles, and celebrate each other's successes – because we are all going to be in the position of not-knower or can't-doer sooner or later. You could open up discussions about these attitudes in a non-threatening way by sharing videos of famous sportspeople, pop stars, or scientists talking about their struggles and successes. Here are a couple that some LPA teachers have used successfully, to get you started:

> *I have used leading when I am captain of the football team. I tell the team what to do, but not in a mean way. I support them. If they score an own goal I tell them that I have done it too and they are just unlucky.*

https://www.youtube.com/watch?v=x0m4Xc5zXr0

International high jumper Isobel Pooley discusses learning dispositions, including perseverance.

https://www.redbull.com/gb-en/danny-macaskill-s-wee-day-out-the-gopro-edit

The behind-the-scenes edit of mountain biker Danny MacAskill's "Wee day out" could also be used to discuss perseverance and mistake-making.

Build trust

Alongside creating a feeling of belonging and safety, you also want to build trust within your class – between you and the children and between the children themselves. Trust has several dimensions. First, trust means doing what you said you would do – keeping your word. Children are very sensitive to broken promises. For example, in the famous "marshmallow experiments", children are much more likely to scoff the single marshmallow – instead of waiting for the adult to come back and give them a second one – if the adult in the experiment has previously failed to honour a promise.[8] (Wouldn't you do the same?)

> While children have to understand that your job is to expand their capabilities by stretching them, they also need to know that you will not throw them in at the deep end of the swimming pool and walk away.

---

8   Celeste Kidd, Holly Palmeri, and Richard Aslin, Rational snacking: young children's decision-making on the marshmallow test is moderated by environmental reliability. *Cognition* (2013), 126(1): 109–114.

Second, children are also very sensitive to unfairness. They need to see that your response to making mistakes, for example, is the same for all children – or if there is a good reason why it is not, they need you to explain. They generally accept, for example, that it may not be right to hold children with special needs to the same standards of behaviour or accountability as the rest of the class.

Third, the children need to trust you not to let them drown in the challenges and difficulties you are asking them to grapple with. While they have to understand that your job is to expand their capabilities by stretching them, they also need to know that you will not throw them in at the deep end of the swimming pool and walk away. There is a balance to be struck, and where and how you strike it will vary with different children, and with any individual child as their moods and needs fluctuate across the hours and days.

To get this balance right, more often than not, you need to learn how different children signal when they are ready to be pushed, and when they really do need you to dial down the pressure or simply tell them the right answer. You will get better at reading these signals as you gain more experience, both with a particular class and with the LPA in general. Of course, to build robust independent learners, you will want to gradually reduce their reliance on you as the safety net. By getting to know your children and their levels of independence and confidence, you can learn how to gradually nudge them to seek out support for themselves when they need it. As you build a more collaborative classroom – as we explore in more detail in Chapter 6 – you will find that children become more ready, willing, and able to help each other out, and their reliance on you will decrease. However, to begin with, it's important for children to know that your support will be there if and when they really need it.

If in doubt, we recommend that you talk about this issue with the children. Tell them that everyone sometimes needs to wind down and do easy, fun, or routine things rather than challenging themselves the whole time. And, if still in doubt, ask them whether – at this moment – it is OK for you to push them, or whether they are getting to the end of their tether. You could ask, "Would it be OK to see if you can struggle on for a few minutes before I help you … or do you really need me to rescue you right now?"

To build your own ability to get the balance between challenge and support right, it can help to become more aware of how quickly you are inclined to jump in and save children when they are struggling.

Wondering

Are you more inclined to jump in with some children than others? Some teachers, without even being aware of it, tend to rescue girls more quickly than they do boys. Why do you think that is?

What happens when you step back a little and begin to give children the space to grapple with and struggle through their learning?

How good are you at finding the right way to just nudge children to get them back on track?

Digging Deeper

Make learning intriguing, engaging, and purposeful

What does a big-hearted classroom look like? Well it is robust for a start, because difficult, demanding work goes on here. There is no watering down, no soft options, everyone is working hard, struggling but persevering. But now and then there is a heartfelt laugh ... And in a big-hearted classroom, the feedback, critique and analysis is robust and kind in equal measure.

Mary Myatt, *Hopeful Schools*, p. 30

Creating a learning-power classroom isn't just about creating a feeling of safety and belonging. It's about purposefully cultivating an ethos that is focused around pushing yourself, self-improving, and enjoying the struggle of learning. Obviously, you want to make the learning challenges as relevant and meaningful as possible for the age of children you are teaching. Some children will respond obediently to, "Do it because I say so." But many more will sign up if the learning connects with things that they are likely to find interesting, are authentic, and which have a bearing on their lives — whether they be 5-, 8-, or 11-year-olds. We will say much more about creating a culture of challenge in Chapter 7.

When learning has relevance and purpose, children can see how it feeds into their lives outside of the school walls and how it empowers them to have an impact on the world around them. As Ron Ritchhart points out in *Creating Cultures of Thinking*, authentic learning often starts from children seeing themselves as members of a club, a gang, or a community with shared interests, who enjoy grappling with the same kinds of challenges. By creating learning that is — in the nice phrase the *Creating Learning without Limits* folk use — "endlessly enticing", children will be hungry to learn and find out more, and take pride in their final product.[9]

> Creating a learning-power classroom isn't just about creating a feeling of safety and belonging. It's about purposefully cultivating an ethos that is focused around pushing yourself, self-improving, and enjoying the struggle of learning.

There are many ways to create this learning culture, some of which are listed below. We are sure you will have plenty of ideas of your own too.

+ Make links with the local community. Think about what makes your community unique and find ways to create learning experiences that involve making connections outside the school. For example, one of the teachers at Wroxham Primary School got older learners to collaboratively plan museum visits for younger children with staff at their local museum.

+ Turn your classroom or school into a museum and invite parents to visit.

+ Connect learning with current global issues.

---

9 Swann et al., *Creating Learning without Limits*, p. 42.

- Organise school performances, shows, concerts, and galleries. Be creative in finding different ways to make this meaningful and motivating for the children.

- Create opportunities for older children to teach younger children or vice versa, or for the children to learn from one another in the classroom.

- Use puppets and characters. Think up creative scenarios in which the characters and their stories give the children reasons for learning.

- Involve the children in developing the school grounds – for example, by gardening, looking after animals, or designing outdoor areas to suit their needs and interests.

- Plan authentic experiences in which the children can become immersed in their topic or inquiry.

- Invite parents in to spark particular interests or share special skills.

- Plan learning around real-life problems.

- Build on children's interests and engage with their identities.

Here we explore a couple of ideas in a little more detail.

Discovery-based lessons

Ron Berger, Libby Woodfin, and Anne Vilen's *Learning That Lasts* is a mine of ideas for inspiring, challenging, and empowering children. The first chapter in the book explores the uses of different lesson formats designed to spark interest, encourage grappling and questioning, and cut down on teacher talk – and their advantages. One of these formats is discovery-based lessons. They suggest that you might use this lesson structure when children have some prior knowledge, as well as the sufficient desire and motivation to tackle a problem with little instruction.[10] Children would also need to be well-versed in classroom routines and expectations, as well as being used to exploring problems by themselves or with their peers.

---

10 Berger, Woodfin, and Vilen, *Learning That Lasts*, p. 35.

Here is an example of a discovery-based lesson in a mixed first-, second- and third-grade science class. Bill Simmons is aiming to develop his 6–8-year-old learners' observation skills, as well as their ability to take care of animals and their habitats. In order to pique the children's interest, he has set up a large glass aquarium filled with dirt, moss, and plants in the middle of the classroom. Beside the aquarium are various bits of scientific equipment, including magnifying glasses, rulers, and notebooks, as well as smaller individual aquaria which the children are going to use.

As the children gather round, Bill explains that, sharing responsibility with a partner, they will create a home for two snails and then look after them. They are briefly shown how to handle the snails carefully and are assigned partners – in this case, an older child with a younger child. The children are asked to:

- Pay close attention to the model environment, and recreate that environment using the resources provided.

- Choose two snails from the large aquarium to adopt into their new habitat.

- Observe the snails closely, adding notes and drawings to their science journals. They should note what they notice about the snails' bodies and behaviour, as well as any questions they have about the snails.

The children excitedly go about their task, full of questions, ideas, and observations about the snails. Bill makes sure they are on track, reminding them when necessary to stay calmly focused.

At the end of the lesson, the class gathers round to share their ideas. Although the children are very excited to share their observations, Bill aims to keep the discussion centred on the children's questions, writing them on the board as they arise.

This lesson follows a format that the EL Education schools call the "Five Es". It starts with *engagement* – grabbing the children's attention with live snails. This is followed by *exploration* – of the snails and their environment. The next two Es – *explain* and *extend* – come through Bill's nudging and questioning during the lesson. The final E is *evaluate* – when the class come together to share their ideas and the questions they have moving forward. This lesson activates and stretches many of the children's learning muscles – for example, by noticing details, developing curiosity through questioning, and collaborating effectively with a partner. It also invites the children to take on the mindset of inquisitive, attentive scientists, rather than just "learning about science".

It is easy to imagine how deeply engaged and enthused the children would have been during this lesson. Bringing live creatures into the classroom for the children to observe and take care of suddenly makes learning more "real" and gives it a context. Sourcing the snails would have taken prior planning and thought, but this initial effort would have paid dividends during the series of lessons that followed.

Lessons like this are not unusual in primary schools. A lot of children are tasked with looking after mini-beasts. But what we would like you to focus on is the precision with which the lesson format is designed to activate and stretch specific learning muscles. Having fun and being engaged are means to a longer-term end – the growth of children's learning power – not ends in themselves. As we often say, having a roomful of busy, happy, engaged children is not the point. The point is the learning and stretching that can go on when children are busy, happy, and engaged.

Here is another example of a series of engaging lessons, adapted from Becky's blog.[11]

Singing for songbirds – St Bernard's RC Primary School

The staff at St Bernard's are working alongside the staff at Chester Zoo to develop a very engaging and pioneering curriculum. The curriculum capitalises on ongoing work at the zoo that touches on wider ecological issues. It also blends the LPA's focus on developing children's strengths as learners with an approach called dilemma-led learning, which has been pioneered by Hywel Roberts and Debra Kidd.

To begin to build this curriculum, St Bernard's had piloted a songbirds project the previous year. The project had engaged children across the whole school in thinking about the depletion of songbirds in Indonesia. Put in a wider context, the children were learning about the interplay between traditional cultural practices – such as trapping and selling the songbirds – and conservation.

---

11 See Becky Carlzon, Investment + learning power = learning dynamite. *Learning Power Kids* [blog] (5 December 2017). Available at: http://learningpowerkids.com/colearning/investment-learning-power-dynamite/.

Together, teachers and zoo staff created a cross-curricular project in which different subject-specific skills were taught in the context of the songbird crisis. They carefully planned engaging activities with the children to communicate the plight of the songbirds. For example, Years 4–6 wrote and choreographed a song that they performed in the middle of a local shopping centre. As staff stood out of the way, the flash mob took place, grabbing the attention of shoppers. Children had prepared leaflets about the songbird crisis beforehand and were organised in campaign teams which marched through the shopping centre, explaining to shoppers why they should care. Alongside this, they were taught valuable speaking and listening skills, including how to approach people, what to do if their "targets" weren't interested, and how to capture their interest – thus stretching their socialising muscles. Younger children held a "demonstration" in the playground for parents at the end of the day, while Year 3 prepared and presented an assembly to other schools in the local area. The children's passionate engagement with the plight of the birds meant that the knowledge and skills that teachers exposed them to were quickly absorbed and firmly retained. When we went to visit the school again, four months after the songbirds project had taken place, children were still excitedly sharing their learning about the project.

The children's understanding of the problem was deepened through activities that required them to step into the shoes of different people: the trappers, the conservationists, the customers buying the songbirds, and so on. In doing this, they were not only learning that there are many valid viewpoints on a problem, but they were also developing empathy, and an understanding of those different viewpoints. And this richer under-standing meant that their proposed courses of action became wiser and more practical. They learned how to write persuasive, heartfelt letters and design eye-catching leaflets to draw the issue to the public's attention. Being so strongly invested in the project raised

> Creating learning that raises expectations of the children's potential is what LPA teachers constantly strive for – a curriculum that empowers and excites children rather than controls them.

the stakes for the children in all the right ways. It meant they *had* to make the letters persuasive; they *had* to draw in their readers. The songbirds were depending on it. The children now care passionately about birds and have mastered many national curriculum requirements effortlessly because of their commitment to the cause. You can see how they shared the culmination of this work with the world on YouTube.[12]

There is a trade-off here that you have probably noticed. Setting up projects like these two examples takes time, effort, and resources. But the set-up costs seem to be more than handsomely repaid by the energy, intelligence, and commitment which are unleashed in the children. Well-designed, the project requires them to learn many things that are "on the syllabus", but they are learned easily and enthusiastically because they become a means to a genuinely valued end, rather than being seen as – often quite mysterious – ends in their own right. Highly engaged and motivated children learn things fast, and they stick. Cognitive science has confirmed what we all know: that memories are stronger and more persistent when they are imbued with personal significance. And, in addition, fired-up children are generally a pleasure to teach.

---

12 "St Bernard's songbird project with Chester Zoo" [video] (22 June 2017). Available at: https://www.youtube.com/watch?v=LfN--DWm5Zo&feature=youtu.be.

Incidentally, we have noticed something curious. A few people seem to object to the idea of making children's learning activities "relevant" in this way. Perhaps they think that harnessing children's natural enthusiasms and interests is a kind of "dumbing down"; that they won't be learning anything new and that they would be far better off simply being made to study subjects that are mandated by the national curriculum. We think differently. We think you can train children's minds to be stronger and smarter by getting them to dig deeply into things that strike a chord with them. Some schools and some teachers manage to arouse that passionate interest through Latin or chess. If it works, all well and good. But if learning about endangered species of songbirds helps children to build the knowledge, skills, and attitudes towards learning that will stand them in good stead for the rest of their lives, then we don't see a problem with this either. In fact, creating learning that raises expectations of the children's potential is what LPA teachers constantly strive for — a curriculum that empowers and excites children rather than controls them.

Distinguish between learning mode and performance mode

If you buy a new soundbar for your television, you will probably find that it has several different presets that give you the optimal sound for different types of programmes — sports, drama, music, documentary, and so on. When you select one of these, the detailed profile of amplitudes and frequencies is changed. Children have a range of different presets which determine the variety of ways in which they respond to what is going on in the classroom. One of these is learning mode. Another is performance mode. A third is defence mode. You can see all the different settings laid out in Table 3.2. Let's explain them briefly.

In learning mode, your goal is to get better at understanding and mastering things. Your focus is on expanding your competence, so naturally you zoom in on the things you are not sure about, or the places where there is room for improvement — you put yourself in the learning zone. In the learning zone you expect to make mistakes and to learn from them. You engage in trial and error, and you treat the errors as informative. Often you are happy to join forces with others who are engaged in similar explorations; support and feedback from other people is welcome.

In performance mode, your job is to be as successful and impressive as you can. You want to look good and get it right. Flawless execution is your goal. In this mode, you are trying to avoid mistakes, and when they do come – or when someone else points them out – they can be very unwelcome. If the cost of mistakes – whether social or material – is high, your fear of failure can be high as well, making you quite anxious. You don't try out new things if you aren't sure you can pull them off, and if you do make mistakes you try to cover them up and carry on. Eduardo Briceño has given a good TED Talk called "How to get better at the things you care about" which explains these first two modes very clearly.[13]

In defence mode, you aren't trying to learn or to perform, you are just trying to survive – especially to protect your self-esteem. You may feel miserable and vulnerable, and just want the earth to swallow you up – or someone to come along and scoop you up and make you feel safe. Or you may get angry and lash out at anyone who seems to threaten you.

Table 3.2: Beyond Growth or Fixed Mindset: Valuing Learning, Performance, and Defence Modes

	Learning mode	**Performance mode**	**Defence mode**
Goal is to	Improve	Impress/ succeed	Self-protect
Benefits your	Long-term growth/future	Immediate performance	Survival

---

13 Eduardo Briceño, "How to get better at the things you care about", *TEDxManhattanBeach* [video] (November 2016). Available at: https://www.ted.com/talks/eduardo_briceno_how_to_get_better_at_ the_things_you_care_about. The model we are presenting here is our development of Briceño's line of thinking.

	Learning mode	Performance mode	Defence mode
Focus is on	Areas for improvement	Flawless execution	Avoiding threat
Resources used to	Expand	Optimise	Preserve
Errors are	Informative	Invalidating	Injurious
Failure is	Expected	Avoided	An insult
Perceived cost of error is	Low	High	Fatal
You are feeling	Open/ interested	Controlled	Fearful/ aggressive
Experimentation/ trial and error is	Constant	Minimal	Desperate
Feedback is	Supportive/ welcome	Judicial/ unwelcome	Rejected
Cheating is	Pointless	An option	Necessary

Source: Adapted from Eduardo Briceño, "How to get better at the things you care about"

The vital thing to understand about these three modes is that we need each of them at different times. Sometimes children, as well as adults, do need to go into that self-protective mode, and just need to be reassured and comforted. Trying to learn when you are in defence mode just makes you feel worse. Sometimes we all need to be in performance mode. We need to look our best and strive to pass the test. When children are facing high-stakes examinations – for example, the Key Stage 2

SATs in England – they really do need to do as well as they can and avoid mistakes as much as possible. On stage, whether playing in the school concert or acting in the play, or in the final of a football tournament, you want to get it right. You don't try out a piece that you've never rehearsed, or try out

> It is best if your default mode is learning mode – because that is the zone in which your competence and confidence grow the most.

the new moves that you haven't nailed yet. We want to help children learn how to be in performance mode without suffering from stage fright; how to develop what sportspeople call mental toughness or big match temperament.

But, all other things being equal, it is best if your default mode is learning mode – because that is the zone in which your competence and confidence grow the most. High performers, when they come off stage, or finish the match, quickly drop back from performance mode into learning mode. They are eager to explore the little things that didn't go according to plan, or to try out a new idea that has just occurred to them.

So as teachers, we want to make our classrooms places where learning mode predominates. We want to avoid creating an atmosphere – or allowing one to develop – in which every mistake is treated as a bad thing, costly in terms of a child's final grade, or the esteem in which they are held by their classmates. We want to help children gradually develop their confidence in performance mode, so they don't go to pieces when it matters or when they are "on show". And we also want to recognise and respond appropriately when any child really has dipped into defence mode and needs our comfort and reassurance.

We think this way of looking at the different modes improves on the popular distinction between growth and fixed mindsets, which has got into a bit of trouble recently. Though the originator of growth mindset theory, Professor Carol Dweck, didn't intend it, some teachers have developed a bit of a fixed mindset about growth mindset, you might say. They think that growth mindset is always good and fixed mindset is always bad, and this misrepresents the situation. In our view, having a fixed mindset is what happens when you have got stuck in performance mode, and you forget to slip back into learning mode when you are "off stage". Having a growth mindset simply means that learning mode is your default. It is a matter of balance and appropriateness, not one good and the other bad.

Wondering

How do you signal to the children in your class that you want them – most of the time – to be in learning mode, not in performance mode?

What is it about the way you present a task or an activity that might swing the children in one direction or the other?

When you are teaching, are you yourself mostly in learning or performance mode? How could you be in learning mode a little more? Do you think it would be good for the children to see you when you are in learning mode?

Summary

In this chapter we have shared ideas about how to create strong, safe, and stimulating foundations for learning in your classroom. We want to achieve this classroom culture partly because we want our children to grow up with good manners and consideration for others, but also because learning is inhibited if those foundations are not in place. Where there is a lack of trust or kindness, of order or calm, then learning is impeded. Where mistakes are always seen as costly – if your academic or social success depends upon not making mistakes – learning is suppressed. And where invitations to learning do not capture children's interests and sympathies, and do not engage their intelligence wholeheartedly, again learning suffers. Get these foundations right, however, and children will willingly bring their minds to school, and be ready to stretch and develop their learning capabilities as they go along.

Chapter 4

Designing the Environment

> The constructed environment sets up and facilitates certain ways of acting and interacting. It sends messages about what is valued, important, expected, and encouraged. As a student walks into a classroom, the physical space is part of the hidden curriculum, conveying messages about how learning will happen.
>
> Ron Ritchhart, *Creating Cultures of Thinking*, p. 230

The previous chapter was about ensuring that the brakes of learning are off and that we are confident with using the clutch to change gears – shifting between learning and performance mode as needed. Now it is time to talk about the accelerator. Once the children are happily and enthusiastically learning, how do we go about helping them to become better and better at it – strengthening their ability to be good learners? How do we configure our classrooms so that they are effective incubators of children's learning power? That's what the next few chapters are about.

The design principles we are going to focus on in this chapter are:

8. Make use of protocols, templates, and routines.

9. Use the environment.

We will start with the environment. Take a look around. What is your environment like right now, as you read this book? Are you reading on a computer or tablet? If so, does that make it easier to look things up – references to research, the meaning of unfamiliar words, and suchlike – as you go along? Does the Internet challenge your concentration by making an alluring little noise when an email arrives? Are there other distractions? Are you too hot or too cold? Are there books within reach? Are there other people around to talk to about ideas that spark your interest? Does your environment provoke thought and stimulate thinking? Or does it interfere with your learning?

Wherever we are, our physical environment impacts on our learning through the distractions and resources which it contains. And this is especially true of classrooms.

Many features of the classroom affect the kinds of learning that the children will engage in, and the kinds of learning strengths and behaviours which they will draw on. For example, some classroom layouts facilitate collaborative conversation, while others inhibit it. Some classrooms have displays and anchor charts that act as reminders to the children to continuously work on and strengthen themselves as learners. Some invite imagination and concentration. Some invite silent reading or encourage competition. Some encourage the children to be resourceful and independent, while others encourage dependency and helplessness.

When teachers realise that they are inevitably in the "cultivating attitudes" business, they have to pay attention to every element of the classroom that carries messages about learning, and about the kinds of learners that the children are expected to be. In this chapter we will look at a variety of environmental factors which you probably have — at least some — control over, and which steer your learners' development in one direction or another. We will look at many aspects of the physical set-up in the classroom, and suggest how they can be tweaked so that more learning happens, and better learning habits are grown.

We will illustrate how the environment affects a number of the elements of learning power, especially determination, collaboration, organisation, and reflection. How can the classroom itself encourage learners to be resilient, to have good learning conversations, to be methodical and resourceful, or to be more reflective and self-aware?

Before we get into the *how*, let's take a moment to talk about the *why*. There are a number of good reasons why purposefully designing the learning environment is a good idea:

• The early childhood teachers behind the famous Reggio Emilia approach describe the learning environment as the "third teacher" — the other two being the actual teacher and the relationships and interactions between the children. If this is true, then obviously we want to configure the environment to make the third teacher as effective as possible.

• You can use the environment to reinforce the specific learning dispositions and habits you are trying to teach. Displays and anchor charts serve to remind the children of good learning habits, and can be referred to during teaching and reflection times.

- Displays can be interactive and developed in collaboration with the children, which gives them a greater feeling of ownership over their classroom, and also encourages them to become more thoughtful about what is going on in it. It gets them thinking about how they learn and how their surroundings make a difference.

- Furniture can be arranged purposefully to foster the kind of learning you want, and to develop the learning muscles which you are targeting. For example, you can think about how to arrange the tables for group learning, paired learning, individual learning, or a mix of all three.

- When children understand how to use resources to support their learning, and those resources are readily available, they gain independence and ownership over their learning, and thus build resourcefulness and initiative.

Designing the Environment with Learning Power in Mind

✓ Think about the layout and use of the furniture.
✓ Assess the provision of resources.
✓ Source inspirational quotes that reflect positive learning habits.
✓ Make anchor charts.
✓ Create a wonder wall.
✓ Create a personal best wall.
✓ Show works in progress.
✓ Build interactive displays that strengthen learning muscles.

Dipping Your Toes In

Now to the how. We'll begin by offering some simple hints and tips about how to tweak the physical layout of your classroom, and move on to examples of what you could put on the walls to reflect and embed the learning habits you are trying to build. In the final section of the chapter, we dive deeper and explore how you can use your classroom to really strengthen children's learning muscles by creating interactive displays which can be used during the learning process. We suggest delving into these deeper ideas once you and your children are in the rhythm and flow of developing learning power, otherwise they might fall flat or not have the impact you would hope for.

Think about the layout and use of the furniture

Take a moment to reflect on how your classroom is laid out at the moment. Think about what kinds of learning behaviours are made easier or more difficult by this layout. What implicit messages does the classroom send to the children about how responsible and independent you want them to be?

Wondering

Are the tables in rows facing the front, or are children in groups around tables? What effect do you think this has on the learning in your classroom?

Who decides who sits where? Do the seating arrangements change or do the children always sit in the same place? What are the pros and cons of you deciding, or of the children having a say?

Is the layout variable – do you rearrange the furniture in order to facilitate different kinds of learning? If so, when? Why? How often? Could the children be involved in thinking about this?

Do you tend to group children according to ability? Do you try to disguise this by inventing what you think are neutral names for the groups – for example, the Yellow Table, the Elephants, and so on? Do you think the children see through this? How can you tell whether they do or not? What effect do you think it has on the children's attitudes to learning if they know they are in the top, bottom, or middle group?

Do you have your own desk? Do you tend to hide behind it when you are anxious? What message do you think this sends to the children?

When you have considered these questions, think about what might happen if you changed things around. Do a PMI on each idea. As we explained in Chapter 1, this is a thinking routine that asks you to separate out the *pluses* – the positive effects, the *minuses* – the risks or disadvantages, and any *interesting* questions that arise in your mind. Once you have reflected, why not try out some new ideas? See what happens when you put all the chairs in a big circle, or put the chairs to one side so children have to stand, sit on the floor, or lie down. What happens when you move your own desk, say from the front to the back of the room – or get rid of it completely? Could you create a classroom layout that is easily adaptable to individual learning, group learning, and paired learning without causing too much of a fuss?

Here are some examples we've seen in practice:

+ In St Bernard's RC Primary School the children often arrange two tables to make an L shape when they are working in pairs. This means that two pairs can comfortably learn side by side, and that each pair can easily ask the other questions when they need to. If the teacher needs to talk to both pairs, they can move to the inside corner of the L and thus easily give feedback and make eye contact with all four children.

- At West Thornton Academy, they have planned their learning environment so that children can choose to learn in a variety of spaces. Some might decide to learn sitting at a table, some on bean bags by themselves, and some in groups lying on the floor. There are nooks and cosy corners where the children can focus by themselves or have quiet conversations. There are open outdoor spaces they can retreat to if they like. They have invested time and thought as a whole school to ensure that all classrooms have the space and resources to do this, but you could think carefully about how to make the most of the space you have in your classroom. Do you have different areas that are inviting or intriguing? Spaces where children can wonder and let their imaginations run wild? Quieter, cosy areas for children to retreat to? Areas that invite collaboration or group learning? With a few simple furniture changes, and some cheap props, a whole new "thought-full" learning environment can be created.

- At a school in Milton Keynes, a Year 2 teacher[1] engaged her class of reluctant writers in a research project on the question, "Where do we write best, and

---

1   We need to apologise as we can't remember the names of all of the teachers and schools we mention. Some of these examples go back a few years. We are nonetheless grateful to them for sharing their great practice.

does our location affect the quality or nature of what we write?" She had them writing outside, in the staffroom (when the other teachers weren't using it), lying on the floor on their tummies, and so on. She was delighted to find that this simple "ploy" had a massively positive effect on the children's – the boys' in particular – willingness to write, and on the length and quality of their work. It also provoked some really thoughtful conversations among the children about the effect of their environment, and their posture, on their learning.

• A Year 1 teacher, Victoria Scale-Constantinou at Roath Park Primary School in Cardiff, made an intriguing tent-like hideaway in one corner of the classroom out of a black sheet and some broom handles. She told the children it was the "Creativity Corner". As one child said to Guy, it's a space where, "We can go and be quiet for a bit, before we start working on a new project like a painting or a poem, so our brains can cool down and then they can bubble up with new ideas." This change of environment had a marked effect on the quality and originality of children's work.

In all these examples, the children are encouraged to think about how and where they learn best, and to become more aware of how they can regulate and customise their surroundings to maximise their learning. Of course, the children have been trained over time to value these privileges and not use them as an opportunity to slack off or mess about. They know that their teacher is keeping a wary eye out, and if they abuse the freedom they are given it can be quickly withdrawn, so they take their responsibilities seriously.

Assess the provision of resources

Again, we invite you to take some time to reflect on the provision of resources in your classroom. See if these wonderings prompt any interesting thoughts.

Wondering

What resources are under the children's control? Do they have to ask you to provide them, or request permission to get what they need?

Where are resources stored? Are they on the tables? In labelled drawers? Put away in a cupboard?

How explicit are you about when and where you want the children to organise and assemble their own resources without asking you? Do you trust them, or do you perhaps tend to supervise and suggest a bit too much?

How do you respond to the "helpless" child who seems incapable of deciding for themselves what they need? What different things could you say?

In order to be resourceful learners, children need to:

a. understand what resources can help them learn at any given time, and

b. be able to easily access those resources.

Is your classroom currently enabling the children to do this? If not, how can you encourage them to be more resourceful by gradually increasing the demand that they select and collect their own resources?

Alongside making resources more accessible to the children, you could create "unstuck" posters as a class by discussing different ways in which they could solve problems in their learning without having to rely on an adult.

> I am more resourceful. If I don't have a pen or something, I don't just sit and wait for the teacher to get me one; I go to the back of the room and get it myself.

Source inspirational quotes that reflect positive learning habits

Inspirational quotes can emphasise the learning habits you are aiming to develop and create opportunities for you to structure class discussions about them. West Thornton Academy and Miriam Lord School have covered their walls in inspiring quotes, using a range of wall stickers, posters, and framed pictures. By taking care in presenting them and giving them pride of place, the message is sent to the children that these ideas are important. Here are some other points to consider when finding and using inspirational quotes to support learning powers:

+ Do they cover the full range of learning powers?

+ Who sources them – you or the children?

+ How often do the displays change, and who decides?

+ How often do you refer to them?

+ Where are they positioned? Who can read them?

There are lots of quotations on the Internet, attributed to various famous people, that emphasise the necessity and importance of making mistakes if you are trying to achieve anything novel or worthwhile. For example:

"Ever tried. Ever failed. No matter. Try again. Fail again. Fail better." Samuel Beckett

"Success does not consist in never making mistakes, but in never making the same one a second time." George Bernard Shaw

"The minute I stop making mistakes is the minute I stop learning." Miley Cyrus

"I look on losing not as failure but as research." Billie Jean King

"Once you accept that we're all imperfect, it's the most liberating thing in the world. Then you can go around making mistakes and saying the wrong thing and tripping over in the street and all that, and not feel worried." Paloma Faith

"I can accept failure. Everyone fails at something. But I can't accept not trying." Michael Jordan

"I have not failed. I've just found 10,000 ways that won't work." Thomas Edison

See if the children can find new ones to display. Alternatively, ask them to make up good quotes about the power of failure.

Another way to make mistakes sound positive rather than negative is to create a display which celebrates the most interesting or intelligent mistake made that week – by a child or an adult. The one in Becky's classroom is titled "Mistake of the Week". See if you can talk the children into volunteering their own mistakes for consideration, or ask them to nominate each other. Make this the most exciting display in your classroom by talking about it regularly and building anticipation with the children by saying things like, "I wonder who will make it onto the Mistake of the Week wall this week?!"

Make anchor charts

An anchor chart is a visual display that prompts children to push or stretch one of the learning muscles, and is commonly used to list the kinds of phrases that help children frame discussions about learning.[2] For example, each classroom in Sandringham School has a display with lots of ideas about how the children can start productive sentences. In Mariyam Seedat's classroom there is a prominent whiteboard display featuring these sentence starters:

"I agree with …"

"Building on …"

"I disagree with …"

In each lesson at Sandringham School you can hear the children justifying their answers and politely adding to each other's ideas using these frames for learning talk. Teachers constantly refer to these during discussions, and won't let the children get

---

2   There are lots of examples of anchor charts on the web. See, for example: All about anchor charts. *Common Core Writing Academy* [blog] (8 October 2014). Available at: http://commoncorewritingacademy.com/2014/10/08/all-about-anchor-charts/.

away with saying things that are tactless, unhelpful, or unclear. They are constantly being trained in the art of being a good conversationalist.

In Becky's class, good examples of children's language for learning are captured as they emerge. She listens carefully to what the children are saying and when they use effective language for learning she adds it to a display titled "Superpower Learners Say ..." The children love the display because the ideas come from them and are displayed in a speech bubble beside their photo. Here are some of the phrases children have naturally used in Becky's classroom which have been featured on the display:

"I wonder how I can help my friends ..."

"I'm not the best at this, but I'll try ..."

"I wonder how I could make this even better ..."

Each phrase demonstrates the attitudes to learning that Becky is cultivating in her classroom — for example, creating a culture of *supportive* learners who *persevere* and have an attitude of *craftsmanship* towards their work. She refers back to each of these phrases as and when they are relevant — which is quite often! Having naturally come from the children, they are even more powerful than they would be if they had come from an adult.

In general, it is best if the children are involved in creating the anchor charts. This is especially useful when you are introducing them to a new learning muscle, and getting them to realise what that muscle looks, sounds, and feels like when it is being used. So ask the children to make — with your help and guidance — their own anchor charts to remind them, for example, how to maintain their concentration despite distractions, or how to anticipate resources needed and pitfalls to be avoided as they embark on a new task. If the children don't have much experience of a particular learning habit yet, you might want to paint a picture for them before you start working with them to create the anchor chart. You could do this by taking photos of them demonstrating that learning habit and discussing the images, or by showing them videos of famous people doing so — examples of which can be found in Chapter 3. Don't hesitate to challenge them to keep on track during a task: it's your job to teach them what each disposition looks like and why it is valuable. And, again, don't let this display just become wallpaper. Refer back to your anchor charts and use them to keep deepening and broadening the children's appreciation of those learning muscles.

When Becky talked to her Year 1s at the beginning of the year about what makes a good collaborator, the children came up with the following ideas:

"If someone wants to do the same thing as you, let them join in."

"You can take turns."

"You need to be kind."

"You should say 'please' and 'thank you'."

"You can let other people use your ideas."

"You can be a teacher!"

With these ideas to guide them, they were able to generate really helpful examples of the kinds of speech that would bring those attitudes to life in a discussion. For example:

"Would you like me to show you how to …?"

"Could someone please help me to …?"

"Would you like to join our group?"

"I'd like to have a turn, if that's alright."

"Can I help you?"

"What do you think?"

"Are you OK?"

Later on in the year, and as they progress through school, the children can build on this and come up with more subtle ideas, thus producing much more sophisticated anchor charts. Learning to be an excellent discussant or facilitator is a lifelong project!

Create a wonder wall

Curiosity is the lifeblood of learning. The disposition to be interested in new things – and excited by things you can't do yet – is one of the most important of the learning muscles. So anything we can do to strengthen children's willingness to bring their innate curiosity into the classroom has to be worthwhile. One display that can help to strengthen children's curiosity is the wonder wall. It is a big sheet of paper – put on the wall at the right height for your age group – on which the children are urged to post their own questions. They are encouraged to write on sticky notes and add ideas about things that are puzzling or intriguing them. You could refer to the wonder wall to stimulate class discussions, or welcome the children back after a weekend or holiday by inviting them to post juicy questions that occurred to them while they were away. As a small reward – at the end of the day, say – you could invite a child to choose their favourite question and have everyone help them wonder about it.

> Your job is ... to stimulate the children's thinking, and to help them strengthen their tolerance for intelligent pondering, wondering, and researching.

Patricia Calmels D'Artensac, primary French teacher at Bangkok Patana International School, has adapted the wonder wall, labelling one of her walls with the title 'Burning Questions'. While she is working with a group, children can independently add questions about their French learning to the wall. This encourages them to ask questions whenever they want, not just when they are guided to do so, and has developed independence and confidence within the class.

It is important to keep in mind that it is not the answer that matters here but the fact that the processes of thinking and questioning are stimulated. Your job is not to *know* the "right answer", nor to *steer* the class in this direction – as teachers are often used to doing – but to stimulate the children's thinking, and to help them strengthen their tolerance for intelligent pondering, wondering, and researching. The best questions may take years to answer, or they may have no answer at all ... At times, you could take some of the children's wonderings as starting points for deeper whole-class investigations. Other times, you can just leave the questions hanging.

Create a personal best wall

Gather photos or examples of work that represent the children's personal bests – a PB – not necessarily in writing or maths, but in developing their learning muscles. For example, you could display photos of children persevering, collaborating with a new partner, paying attention to detail, or reflecting on their learning. Such images act as tangible symbols and reminders to the whole class, as well as to the children pictured, of what aspects of powerful learning look like. A PB is like a hook of ambition thrown into the future. It tells children "Look! You did this once. So you can do it again, do it in a different context, or do it more often." It is both an achievement and a target to improve upon, so it offers them a trajectory in their own development that they can realistically aspire to.

Professor Margaret Carr, a noted early childhood educator from New Zealand, told us the story of Katy, a 4-year-old in a kindergarten, who had got used to the idea of having her personal bests celebrated. One day she got to the top of the climbing frame by herself for the first time. Teetering rather unsteadily, she looked wildly around until she spotted Margaret across the playground. "Quick, Margaret," she yelled at the top of her voice, "get the camera."

PBs are good conversation starters. You can pick apart why this is a personal best for a child, and how they might build on it. This, in turn, makes the processes of learning and commitment visible to the children. And over time, you can increasingly hand over control of the PB display to the children, as they become ready to choose and add their own examples.

Show works in progress

Let's begin this section, as we often do, with some questions:

> # Wondering
>
> How do you currently choose examples of the children's work to display?
>
> Do you only select the best examples of the "finished product", or do you also proudly display the multiple drafts that show determination, revision, and progress?
>
> Can you think of a project in which you could pull apart the learning for the children and display the drafts and works in progress rather than just the finished product?

Teachers sometimes assume without thinking that it is their job to decide which bits of children's work to display on the walls – and they usually just choose the best ones. But what if we let the children choose? Or what if we displayed not just the finished product, but a range of drafts to show the progress they have made? Perhaps we could progressively involve the children in being our co-curators of the displays and exhibitions that adorn the classroom. Instead of seeing it as our job to select what goes up on the walls, we can open this up for discussion with the children, and see what they want to contribute. They could offer their own ideas about the kinds of inspirational words and images that might work well for them – to emphasise the importance of reflection, organisation, or collaboration, for example. And they could have a hand in selecting the pieces of work that they would like to put on display, perhaps because they are genuinely proud of all the thinking, planning, and imagining that went in to their creation. You could invite them to annotate their favourite piece of work with the reasons why they have selected it, or they could explain their choice to the rest of the class. As Ron Ritchhart has pointed out, it is a pretty feeble kind of pride to feel good just because your work is up on the wall along with everyone else's. Much better to feel proud of the genuine "blood, toil, tears and sweat" – as Winston Churchill famously put it – that went into it. You can get the children used to not always having their work up on the wall, and build their understanding about the different meanings behind this changing selection.

Lots of schools encourage children to display not only the finished piece of work of which they are most proud, but also some earlier drafts or photos alongside it that capture something of the learning journey. Such a display invites them to be proud of not just one but two things: the quality they have managed to achieve, and the process that they have gone through in order to achieve it. By displaying the stages and difficulties of learning, as well as the finished products, you are encouraging the children to understand and value the process of learning and the effort that has gone into their drafting, redrafting, and improving. You are also making their learning processes visible and "talk-about-able", so that they build up a realistic picture of what lies behind the production of high-quality work.

Below is a simple display from West Thornton Academy, showing children commenting on and redrafting work. The title of the display is "Practice Makes Progress" – a subtle but important shift in language!

Diving Deeper

Build interactive displays that strengthen learning muscles

Some of the physical tools we can use in the classroom are designed to tackle the core learning muscles head-on, and to introduce the children to the overall framework of the LPA. In this section we introduce some of these tools. Many of them are used interactively by the children to guide their growth as learners. They can be used as an integral part of the learning process, during whole-class or small group sessions, and in reviews at the end of lessons or at the end of the day. They are better introduced when you are already into the spirit of the LPA – when the children are already in the habit of being supportive of each other's learning, are used to talking about learning muscles and understand that they can strengthen them, and when the culture of the classroom is starting to focus around learning and self-improvement.

Learning ladders and riskometers

You could make – or get the children to help you make – a learning ladder or a riskometer, both of which are the brainchildren of Julian Swindale, a primary school teacher in Bristol. They offer children a way to picture how challenging their learning is going to be, or has been. Each rung of the learning ladder represents a different level of challenge, from low – when the learning has been too easy – through medium – when the learning has really pushed that child's thinking – to high – when the learning really was too difficult or dispiriting for a child. The riskometer represents degrees of challenge as different temperatures on a thermometer. Children can place a laminated photo of themselves on the rung of the ladder or level on the thermometer that represents the degree of challenge they have chosen, or which they anticipate they will encounter that lesson or that day. Having a physical representation of challenge is a way of showing the "guts of learning" to the children.

By using a learning ladder or riskometer, children begin to understand that effort, confusion, and frustration are just natural parts of learning, not things to be frightened of or feel ashamed about, and they therefore begin to take more responsibility for pushing themselves in their learning. Since moving between the levels is fluid, children can think about how to challenge themselves further – how to make their learning harder – or, if it is too hard, how to get unstuck or how to make their learning easier.

We suggest explicitly teaching the children how to use these tools effectively. You might begin with a discussion about the feelings of learning. For example, when learning is too easy, you can feel bored and distracted. Equally, if it is too tricky, you can feel frustrated or anxious. However, you can feel excited and gripped if the level of challenge is "just right". It is also important to discuss with children how they might find themselves at different temperatures – or on different rungs of the ladder – at different times, in different subjects, and on different days. Explain that we can't challenge ourselves every second of every day as we would burn out! Equally, we can't take things easy all the time as we wouldn't learn anything new and we would be bored. You could ask them about the things they choose to do for fun that are challenging, but which make them feel alive and absorbed.

These simple visual tools can be used for planning, reviewing, or tracking learning as it progresses. For example, you could explain an activity and ask the children to discuss in pairs where they would put their photo to correspond to the level of risk or difficulty that they anticipate. As they do the activity they could track how they are feeling, and move their photo accordingly. And at the end they could review the level of riskiness they experienced, and how it made them feel.

As the children become more confident and comfortable with using these tools, you can begin to hand the control over to them. As well as purposefully planning to use these tools at set points, you can allow the children to use them as integral parts of the learning process. In Becky's class, it isn't unusual to see children suddenly jump up to move themselves on the learning ladder when they've finally cracked a challenge. This approach to capturing that feeling of

> *I like to use the learning ladder because it helps me to be brave and try out tricky learning.*

excitement is a powerful way to value resilience, helping the children to think, "This is what it feels like when I stick with my learning! It's worth it in the end!"

The learning pit

Another way to depict the ups and downs of the learning journey is by using James Nottingham's learning pit. The learning pit is a useful visual and interactive tool that takes children through the journey of constructing new knowledge. It is interactive because the children use the image of the pit to "scaffold" their experience of grappling with a new challenge, and as something to refer to in their discussions with each other. They begin with a challenging idea or stimulus – this could be a maths problem that requires prior knowledge to solve, a stimulus from the media, or a Philosophy for Children (P4C) style question, some examples of which are explored further in Chapter 5. Being in the pit means experiencing uncertainty, confusion, and frustration. Their journey through the pit is a process of creating new meaning and working things out for themselves. As children gain clarity and construct new understanding, they begin to exit the pit. Finally, once on the other side, children reflect on the learning process they used to get themselves out. Using the learning pit as a tool to support learning can build an appreciation of and tolerance for being in learning mode. It also helps to create class cohesion, build collaborative skills, and strengthen the learning muscles of self-evaluating and persevering.

Here are some examples of ways in which we have seen the learning pit being used to deepen children's understanding of their learning:

- At West Thornton Academy, they have the learning pit printed onto a large whiteboard. This way children can plot their bespoke journey, according to each lesson or series of lessons. It might be difficult to find the space to dedicate a whole whiteboard to the learning pit, but you could easily save one as an interactive whiteboard slide to refer to during a lesson.

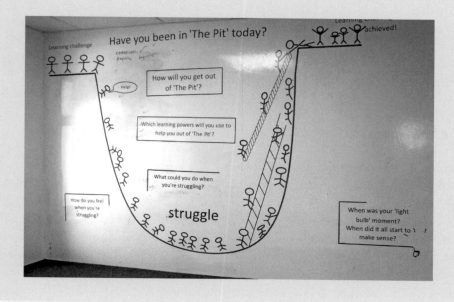

✦ Carlogie Primary School in Angus, Scotland, involved their children in a competition to redesign the learning pit. Children entered all sorts of interesting and exciting ideas – for example, steps up to a slide which you went down when you finally "got it". The photos below show this slide, and the winning entry, which represents the learning pit through emojis. How much more meaningful the image will be for their children now that they have gone through the process of designing their own versions.

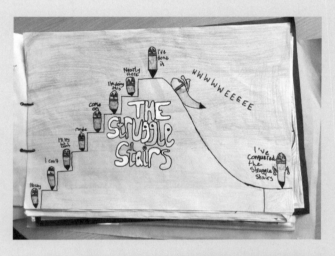

+ As well as using learning pits in their classrooms, Sandringham School has one displayed in the corridor showing teachers as learners. As you can see in the photos below, the teachers are not afraid to make fools of themselves and – crucially – they are laughing and joking and looking like they are having a good time! What a powerful way to demonstrate that teachers also enjoy the struggle of learning!

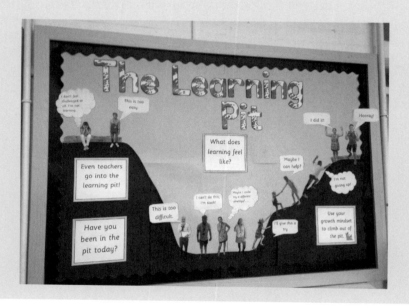

You can find other examples of teachers and children using the learning pit on James Nottingham's website.[3]

Displays of the learning muscles

Many schools have a display of the set of learning muscles in their classrooms, as well as in the staffroom, the foyer, and so on. You can see a fairly detailed version of the

---

3   https://www.jamesnottingham.co.uk/learning-pit/.

elements of learning power on pages 22–24. Obviously this may be too complicated for younger children, or those who are completely new to the framework, so we encourage you to make a display that picks out the dispositions you think are the most important, or the ones that you would like the children to concentrate on first. You can always expand the display with older children or as your class gets more familiar with the idea of learning power.

As the children get used to thinking and talking about themselves as developing learners, you can involve them in thinking more deeply about what the learning muscles mean, and even whether they have identified any new ones they would like to add. The following photo shows the work of Year 4 children from Prospect Primary School in Adelaide, Australia, critiquing and customising the BLP framework, and Table 4.1 shows the version that they produced for themselves. Pretty impressive work, we think you will agree!

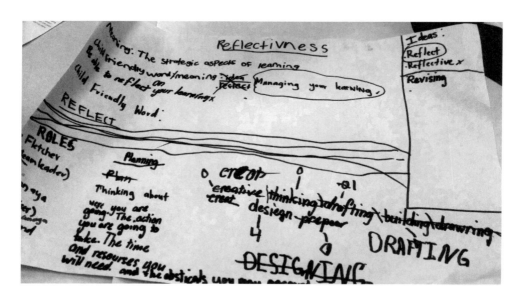

Table 4.1: Building Learning Power Framework

EMOTIONS Being nervacited about your learning	ORGANISATION Being organised in a way that helps you learn and think	TACTICS Getting ready for the challenges you may face in the near future	TEAMWORK Being in a team helps progress your learning
Fusion You are so absorbed in your learning that you cannot focus on anything else apart from your work. You are being at one with your learning.	**Asking** Asking questions helps give you a better understanding of learning. Being curious helps get better ideas.	**Planning** Writing down future events in order by the due date in your diary/calendar. Set out your work times on a piece of paper.	**Trusting** Knowing when it's the right time to work with someone or by yourself.
Concentrating You block out any distractions heading your way. You know when to move seats so you can focus, creating your own space so you	**Connections** Working with other people gets a better understanding and gets more ideas. **Thinking** Thinking of learning outside of the box to explore new ideas.	**Looking back** You've gone through the pit and you're now on top of the hill, then you see what you've done well and improve on the things you haven't done well.	**Cooperation** Being there for someone. Helping them to understand the task. **Helping** Showing someone how to understand the task. **Copying** Getting ideas and habits from people you see.

can stay on task and finish your work on time. **Awareness** You know what you need to do in your task. If you are in trouble, go ask for help. Read the task over and over again to see if you made any mistakes. **Persistence** You always try your best and you never give up when you are in the learning pit. Use our learning strategies: solve problems, focus, persist, teamwork, high expectations, set goals, and practice. Also when you are in the pit you are resilient so you don't get sad and start crying.	**Give reasons** Asking why or how after someone gives an instruction. Try to persuade people with your ideas by giving strong reasons. Give feedback by giving two medals and a mission. **Resources** Being adventurous with resources and options.	**Sifting** You know how to do something because you know from your past experiences. **Learning to learn** You can explain your work to other people, you use strategies to get out of the pit and you think of other people's learning while thinking of yours.	**Checking understanding** Ask your teammates for help and offer help to other people. **Relationship with the teacher** The teacher must trust us with our own learning. The teacher must know what learning is all about.

Source: Prospect Primary School

At Miriam Lord School, in a deprived area of Bradford in the UK, the children are getting quite adept at stretching and using their learning muscles, so, with support from staff, they have discussed how to break down each learning muscle into smaller elements. In some classrooms, a display is dedicated to exploring the learning muscle which the children are particularly focusing on that term. Children move laminated photos of themselves onto the display when they have been exercising that learning muscle.

Table prompts

St Bernard's have devised table prompts to equip the children to talk about how and when they have used their learning muscles. Each learning muscle is accompanied by a set of sentence starters that the children can use to reflect on and explain how they have been exercised. They also use table prompts when they record entries in their diary room, which is explored in Chapter 9.

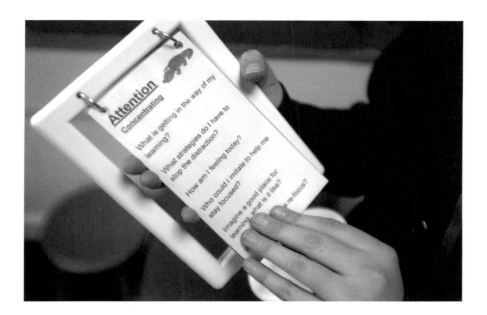

Wondering

Which of these ideas appeal to you? Which feel risky or impractical?

Which ideas do you already do in some form? How do you find they support learning?

Which ideas could you try out tomorrow? This week? This term?

Which ideas have changed your thinking?

Which ideas could be "quick wins"? Which could take a bit more thought and planning?

Have you tried out any of the ideas already? What went well? What didn't go so well?

How could you make sure these display ideas don't become wallpaper and are integral to your classroom?

Bumps Along the Way

In this section, Becky unpicks some of the potential pitfalls you might encounter as you implement new ideas, based on her experience in the classroom. Here the focus is on setting up and using displays in the classroom.

What if ...	Try this ...
The children don't come up with ideas when discussing learning muscles.	Children can only talk about ideas once they have experienced them. If you want to discuss a learning habit and they have no experience of what that looks like, they are likely to get stuck and your discussion will fall flat. Make sure the children have some experience of a learning habit before you discuss it with them. Also, be ready to give them prompts or nudge them in the right direction if they get stuck. This is why I like to start building children's learning power around empathy and kindness – all children have some understanding of what this looks like, or doesn't look like! You can also use

What if …	Try this …
	books and videos to spark a discussion about learning muscles, and how and why they might be useful. There are some great cartoons on YouTube and some super books to use as a starting point – for example, *Rosie Revere, Engineer* for persevering, and also for positive female role models![4]
You make a learning ladder or riskometer and the children don't use it properly. How can you ensure it doesn't disrupt lessons and become more of a hindrance than a help?	This can happen! Children are curious, they love photos of themselves, and they like to push the boundaries! This would be a good opportunity to pause and take stock. In what way are they using it incorrectly? When is it interrupting learning? Are there times when you want them to use the learning ladder, and other times when you'd prefer them to focus on their learning? Have you made this clear to them? Once you have digested these questions, try talking again with the whole class. This has happened to me a few times at the beginning of the school year. When I've opened up the discussion again with the children, they have understood that there need to be rules around using interactive displays in the classroom – just like there are rules about when to go to the toilet! Just a word of caution here though – make sure it's not too rule-heavy! The temptation is to take control, but this would result in the children losing ownership. You need a few ground rules, but also for the children to know that they can use the interactive tools for their learning. I personally love it when children jump up mid-lesson, saying, "I've got it! I'm moving myself

4   Andrea Beaty, *Rosie Revere, Engineer* (New York: Abrams Books for Young Readers, 2013).

What if ...	Try this ...
	up the learning ladder!" I want to bottle more of those moments! And the children need ownership for that to happen.
You move the tables around but the children then can't settle into their learning and are too distracted.	If children are used to their classroom being set up in a certain way, they are bound to behave differently when everything is changed. Having a discussion about this beforehand might help. Let them know that the tables are going to be in a different place when they next come into the classroom and explain why this is happening. Go even further and involve the children in the planning process. Ask them how we could set up the classroom to encourage learning. Ask them to come up with ideas for behavioural expectations and take the time to remind them about these expectations before they start learning. Review how the learning went in the new classroom layout afterwards and discuss tweaks that could be made to make the learning even better. Involving the children as much as possible will take a bit more time, but it will pay dividends in the future and will give them an understanding of the thinking behind the process.

Summary

In this chapter we have thrown a lot of ideas at you about how to configure the physical environment in your classroom to support the development of the children's learning power. There were ideas about altering the physical layout of tables and other furniture, about how to develop accessible resources – so the children can become more resourceful – about different ways of selecting inspirational quotes that focus not just on success but on the process of becoming successful, about the kinds of visual tools and displays – such as anchor charts, learning ladders, and the learning pit – that help children think about themselves as burgeoning learners, and about ways to vary the displays of children's work – to highlight their efforts and their progress, as well as their achievements. Don't underestimate the effect of such apparently small adjustments; they all help. And, finally, don't forget to keep using the 4-3-2-1 ranking tool we suggested at the start of Chapter 3, to note whether you do these things regularly already, could do them more, would like to start doing them, or just don't want to. We hope that engaging actively and critically in this way will help you get the most out of the ideas.

Chapter 5
The Languages of Learning

This chapter focuses on the vital role of language – including body language – in the cultivation of learning power. We will zoom in on these design principles:

7.   Talk about and demonstrate the innards of learning.

14.   Lead by example.

Two of the most important aspects that influence the learning-power classroom are how teachers speak – the messages about learning that are carried by the vocabulary we use, for example – and the way we behave, especially when there is tricky learning to be done by both the children and the adults. Through our words and our actions we convey messages to the children about what learning is like – that mistakes and effort are normal and inevitable, for example – and how we expect them to be as learners – such as cheerful explorers rather than timid passengers.

People's beliefs, attitudes, values, and dispositions are contagious. Children pick them up unwittingly from everyone around them, especially those they trust and/or admire – parents, siblings, friends, and, of course, their teachers.[1] And these messages are conveyed principally by the way in which we put things in language, and by the kinds of things we model in our spontaneous behaviour. How we speak and behave in the presence of children matters. Some of the most important things they learn, especially down at layer 3 in the river, they pick up intuitively through what they hear us saying and see us doing. When toddlers are faced with something novel or strange, they will look at a parent to see how they are reacting, and will take cues from their facial expression, body language, and words of encouragement or warning. Psychologists call this "social referencing". But it doesn't just apply to little children; we all do it.[2]

---

1   See Heyes, *Cognitive Gadgets*.
2   Tedra A. Walden and Tamra A. Ogan, The development of social referencing. *Child Development* (1988), 59(5): 1230–1240.

For example, consider the difference between asking a class, "What do we think might be happening in this picture?" and saying, "What does this picture show?" At first glance they seem to be asking more or less the same thing. But the changes, though subtle, are not innocuous. In the first example, "we" makes this sound like a collaborative activity, one in which the teacher is involved as well as the children. And "might be" is more open-ended than "does"; it invites the children to be speculative, to use their imaginations. The two questions convey different moods. The first is collective, inclusive, and tentative. The second strongly suggests there are right answers which the children are expected to provide. Over time, these kinds of subtle cues steer children towards either learning or performance mode, and build their sense of school's expectations of them. In this chapter we will explore the effects of some of these cues, communicated both verbally and through everyday behaviours.[3]

> Through our words and our actions we convey messages to the children about what learning is like – that mistakes and effort are normal and inevitable, for example – and how we expect them to be as learners – such as cheerful explorers rather than timid passengers.

But changing our language and our spontaneous behaviour isn't as easy as just putting up some new displays or rearranging the furniture. These things are more personal. To be honest, in this chapter we are asking you to think about changing some of your unconscious habits. And habit change requires effort and takes time. It doesn't happen overnight, or just by thinking "Oh, that sounds like a good idea." Just like learning any language, it takes time to build up a new vocabulary and you will need to practise for a while before you can speak it fluently with the children.

Tweaking the routine ways in which you speak and behave in the classroom takes conscious awareness. Habits are things we do without thinking, and to change them we have to become aware of when and how they manifest in our actions. You may well find that a new way of speaking or behaving feels a bit "clunky" to begin with, like it isn't really you – yet. But it is the same with all habit change. When a tennis coach tells you to try a new way of gripping the racket, it feels unnatural to start with. But

---

3   See Ritchhart, *Creating Cultures of Thinking*, p. 64, for a similar discussion.

with a bit of perseverance, you get used to it – and then feel the benefit of it as your backhand gets stronger. In the classroom, the benefit will come when the children's behaviour starts to change in response to yours. So it is worth persisting. The effort will quickly pay off and you will reap the rewards.

As the children in Becky's class started to respond to her changes, and to adopt some of her new language habits as their own, other teachers began to notice the positive effect on the children's approach to learning. These language habits then started to spread through the school. For example, teachers started using the word "collaboration" more regularly in the classroom, and commenting on it when the children were collaborating well, so they then understood more deeply that collaboration was a valuable learning tool and it became a more natural part of the classroom ethos.

Or take making mistakes. Many children, even when they are as young as four and just starting at school, have developed an aversion to "making mistakes".[4] In some cultures, getting things wrong is even seen as bringing shame on the family, or meaning you've "lost face". Getting the children to accept that making mistakes is a natural and necessary stage on the road to learning can be hard. So you could try not using the word "mistake" and instead talk more about "improvement". Rather than "correcting mistakes", talk about how we could "improve what we have done"; how we could "make it even better". Australian teacher Birgitta Car tried this with her 11-year-olds in a school in Thailand, and managed to boost their learning power considerably just by the change of a word. Becky uses positive language when talking to her children, such as, "I love the way you noticed for yourself that that spelling wasn't quite right, and found a way to improve it." As we mentioned in Chapter 4, West Thornton Academy have a display in their foyer with the title, "Practice Makes Progress". Please don't underestimate the effect that such seemingly small changes can have. Try them and see!

> You explore in your head and you don't imagine anyone else – you do it in your own way.

---

4   For the research, see Carol S. Dweck, *Self-Theories: Their Role in Motivation, Personality and Development* (Philadelphia, PA: Psychology Press, 2000).

Language is ultimately the backbone of the learning culture in a classroom. It is perhaps the hardest tool to master in an LPA teacher's toolkit, because it takes time and requires awareness, but it will reap the biggest rewards.

The Languages of Learning

✓ Refer to "learning" rather than "work".
✓ Capitalise on the power of "yet".
✓ Invite the children to use their imaginations with "Let's say ..."
✓ Use "could be" language.
✓ Make use of "wonder".
✓ Rethink your language around "ability".
✓ Talk about the innards of learning.
✓ Open up a dialogue about making mistakes.
✓ Informally notice the effective use of learning muscles.
✓ Model fallibility.
✓ Model metacognition.
✓ Examine the underlying values.
✓ Get everyone speaking learnish.
✓ Learn by example.

Dipping Your Toes In

To begin, let's reflect on the types of language structures you are already using in your classroom. See if you can build up your awareness of how you talk, and become interested in the effect your language has on the children. You might want to read through the questions that follow, and then take a few days or a week to practise paying attention to your language in class and its impact on the children.

Wondering

Pay attention to your questioning. Are you signalling to the children that you are looking for one answer? Do you make space for children to give multiple answers? How are you doing that?

What kinds of answers do you value? The "right" answer? Interesting ideas and different ways of thinking? How do you show which answers are valued?

When children are struggling, what do you say? Do you dive in and rescue them with some comforting words? Do you immediately show them how to do it so the struggle goes away? Or do you encourage them to grapple and enjoy the struggle of learning? What kinds of things do you usually say? Can you think of any additional alternatives you might try out?

Do you wonder openly with the children? Do you make your thinking visible when you are trying to solve a problem or model how writers think when they are writing, for example?

How do you use praise? Is it general? Specific? What do you praise children for? When and how often do you praise them?

What language do you use around mistake-making? Are the children scared of making mistakes or excited by them? Why do you think that might be?

Do you draw attention to the learning habits the children are using and developing? When? How? What impact do you think this has?

So, now you've stirred up your thinking around language, we can dive into some ideas to tweak your vocabulary to develop a learning-power classroom. Let's start with some little words that pack a big punch – some to use for good, and some to be avoided. Ask yourself when and how often you use these words in the classroom – and whether they are having the effect you would wish.

Refer to "learning" rather than "work"

Many teachers use the word "work" a lot. "Have you finished your *work?*" "Get on with your *work*." "How's your *work* coming on?" "Finish it off for home*work*." But stop and ponder for a moment what the word "work" means. It is usually used to refer either to a finished product – "a good piece of work" – or to a more or less disagreeable activity undertaken not for its own sake – for the inherent pleasure or interest of it – but to achieve an outcome for which you get rewarded, with a mark, a star, some "golden time", or, when you are a grown-up, a pay slip.

We think it is fine to talk about work in the first sense, but not in the second. In LPA classrooms we don't want children to race through their tasks simply in order to get them done, or just to get a star or to please their teachers. We want children to take what they are doing as an invitation to think and wonder and experiment – and the word "work" doesn't support that. All too often "work" is what feels like drudgery. So we advise you to stop using the term. To start with, try to cut it out completely and replace it, where appropriate, with the word "learning". And then, after a while, you could allow yourself to use it to refer to the product, but not to the activity of producing it.

If talking about "work" is a deeply engrained habit, you might need some help to notice when you do, and to pause and find a different term. So here's a suggestion. Pop into a pound shop and buy yourself a money box. This is your "swear box" – but the bad language you are trying to avoid is that which limits learning. Every time you use the forbidden word "work", you put a coin into the box, and this helps you break the habit. Take the box into your classroom and explain to the children that you are trying to stop using the word "work" – by all means

> We want children who take what they are doing as an invitation to think and wonder and experiment.

explain why if you think they will get it. Every time you inadvertently say "work", you want them to point it out – politely, obviously – and you will put ten pence, say, in the box.

We have found that most children enjoy the process of being their teacher's coach. At the end of the first week there will likely be a healthy haul in the box, and everyone can get a small present. At the end of the second, there might be much less in the box, as you become better able to spot when you are about to say work and find a different word to use instead. By the third, you should be ready to see if this small change has had any effect on the children. Depending on the substitutes you have started to use, you will probably find a healthy increase in their engagement, and in their willingness to see "learning" as an interesting activity, rather than as merely the means to the end of completing the assignment or getting a good mark.

Capitalise on the power of "yet"

As mentioned in Chapter 3, Carol Dweck has given a TED Talk on the power of yet. She starts by talking about a school where students don't get a fail grade; they get a *not yet*. When you "fail" it is easy to feel that you have been tested and found wanting. The word emphasises your inability to do something, and, often, alongside that comes the feeling that that's just the way it is. You just can't do it. But if your grade is not yet, this very language – to use Dweck's evocative phrase – "opens a path into the future". Not "I can't do it (full stop)", but "I can't do it – yet". The use of that little word raises not just the possibility that you will eventually be able to do it, but the expectation that you can – and will.

Of course, the word by itself doesn't make that expectation come true all by itself. It is possible to use any of these linguistic shifts in a way that is tokenistic. If the culture you create doesn't follow up on the possibility that your children will indeed "get it" eventually, they won't be fooled. But if your teaching style constantly allows and encourages them to have another go – to keep at it till they have got it – then the little word "yet" does indeed hold a promise that can be fulfilled.

Invite the children to use their imaginations with "Let's say …"

Both of us were at a conference recently with a wonderful pair of educators called Hywel Roberts and Debra Kidd. We'd recommend having a look at their book *Uncharted Territories*; it's full of really great ideas.[5] Their "thing" is hooking children into learning through their imagination muscles. They are always saying, "Let's say …" With young children, they might begin, "Let's say we all go into a forest and we meet the Fairy King, who tells us there is a thief in the forest who is stealing children and leaving only their sad, lonely shadows behind …" Immediately the children start wondering about what is in the forest and where the thief might be hiding. They could create a map. They might start thinking about what shadows are, how they are made, and whether they could really be detached from the people or objects that made them. Enthusiastic exploring and experimenting are triggered, and off they go.

With older children, Hywel and Debra might say, "Let's say you live near a forest which is the last one left in the world, and it is your job to take care of it. How could we find out about all the plants and animals in it? How many tourists should we allow to come and visit the last forest? How can we balance the income that we need to look after the forest with the possible damage that hordes of tourists could create?" And again, off the children go, learning about ecology, animal husbandry, tourism, and climate change, and enthusiastically stretching their noticing, their analysing, their collaborating, and of course their imagining muscles.

Incidentally, don't make the mistake of thinking that such imaginative contexts are only for little kids. Bringing your learning muscles to bear on imaginary worlds is just as much the domain of scientists and mathematicians, economists and psychologists, artists and designers, and poets and performers, as it is of children.

> Bringing your learning muscles to bear on imaginary worlds is just as much the domain of scientists and mathematicians, economists and psychologists, artists and designers, and poets and performers, as it is of children.

---

5 Hywel Roberts and Debra Kidd, *Uncharted Territories: Adventures in Learning* (Carmarthen: Independent Thinking Press, 2018).

120

You can read more about Hywel and Debra's dilemma-led learning and how it can be blended with the LPA in Becky's blog on the topic.[6]

Use "could be" language

"Could be" is the more thoughtful cousin of "let's say". It is more about the imaginary worlds of possibility inside your head than in the outside, real world.

Take a moment to ponder the difference between saying "is" and "could be". Think about these contrasting examples:

> "What is the solution to this problem?"
>
> *"What solutions could there be to this problem?"*

> "What word is needed here?"
>
> *"Can you think of some words that might work well here?"*

> "What are our class rules?"
>
> *"What could our class rules be?"*

What do you notice? You might see that "is" language shuts off thinking. It suggests that there is only one solution, or that further thought is not needed. "Could be" language opens possibilities. It invites children to offer multiple solutions and to engage in reflection. Harvard psychology professor Ellen Langer has shown that learners engage much more of their critical and creative thinking when problems are couched in "could be" rather than "is" language.[7] Try shifting some of your language from is to could be and pay attention to how the children respond. You might find that some usually passive children become more inclined to join in. You might also find that their answers to questions are more varied and more thoughtful.

Maths teachers, pay attention! Don't think you are off the hook just because maths questions do only have one right answer. There is plenty of scope for could be in maths. It's true that 6 times 4 *is* 24 ... but what *could* six fours be? Half of 48? 444,444?

---

6   Carlzon, Investment + learning power.

7   Ellen J. Langer, *The Power of Mindful Learning* (Cambridge, MA: Perseus Books, 1997).

The number of limbs on three octopuses? Or take 2.58 divided by 6: there are lots of ways to go about it. How *could* you do it? Are some ways better than others? Better how? More efficient? More resistant to careless mistakes? Becky used this approach to build a number line with her Year 1s at the beginning of the year, asking, "What could 2 (or 5 or 12) be?" The children came up with all sorts of imaginative ideas, including a pair of shoes, five animals, and a dozen eggs. Engaging the children in this way proved to be a great problem-solving activity; it stretched the children's understanding of number and drew their attention to using the number line.

Science teachers, you can join in too. Don't teach the children what the colours of the rainbow *are*. There aren't really seven colours in nature. Isaac Newton just made that up one day, and he chose seven because that was a magical number for him; he thought the rainbow was analogous with a seven-note musical scale. Indigo? Really? Why not purple, or mauve, or

> Try shifting some of your language from is to could be and pay attention to how the children respond. You might find that some usually passive children become more inclined to join in.

lilac? Get the kids to look afresh at a photo of a rainbow and decide for themselves how many colours they can see, and what names they are going to give them. They'll soon be learning like real scientists; not just remembering something they were taught that isn't real anyway!

English and art teachers, listen up. As a writing assignment, ask the children to write a description of a picture. Get them to work in threes to compare their pieces, and think about the pros and cons of different ways of describing things. "You could say … but also you could say … What difference does it make?" Or show them an unusual object and ask them to write down their ideas about what it "could be".

You can see, of course, that *let's say* and *could be* language – as well as *what if, how come*, and *I wonder* – are not at all incompatible with hard thinking, factual recall, and meticulous observation.

Make use of "wonder"

Wonder is another good word for getting children into learning mode. Like *let's say* and *could be*, it invites them into the realm of speculation – of *thinking* – rather than into the cut and dried world of right/wrong answers. Wonder can be used in several ways and in a variety of contexts:

+ When you are discussing something, ask the children, "What does that make you wonder?"

+ When reading a book, or discussing a topic, you could say, "I wonder what it would be like to …" Gather children's wonderings, or just leave the idea hanging in the air.

+ Take some time to ask children what they wonder about. This could be linked to using the wonder wall mentioned in Chapter 4.

+ "I wonder …" can be used to model your own curiosity and open up possibilities for the children – for example, model your thinking out loud by saying, "Oh, I wonder how I could go about this problem …?" or "I wonder what I might do first to plan this story …?"

+ You can also model using "I wonder …" when thinking about possibilities: "I wonder what would happen if …" This can be used to stimulate children's scientific or mathematical thinking.

+ Your wondering can also be used to stretch learning muscles, such as persevering, collaborating or imagination. For example, "I wonder if you can find a way to make sure everyone has a chance to speak in your groups."

In all of these ways, wonder guides children to discover new ideas and ways of approaching a problem for themselves, without directly giving them an answer.

Rethink your language around "ability"

"Improve"

As we mentioned in the introduction to this chapter, learning is all about improving – whether it's expanding your French vocabulary, making your free kicks more bendy, or getting better at checking your sums before you hand them in. So – like Birgitta Car, who we mentioned earlier – try swapping the language of "correcting mistakes" for "improving your ability to" and "getting better at". It is more positive and encouraging.

> Evaluating helps us because I learn from one bit of feedback and I have learnt to always check back on things because I know I can always make it better.

This is especially important when we come to think about assessment and marking, which we will talk more about later. The research shows that children find it much more motivating to judge their performance in terms of how much improvement they have made over time, than to be compared with the rest of the class or with some external standard.[8] So try to shift your focus from attainment to improvement – and see the effect this has on their attainment!

"Able"

Train yourself to stop talking about children as if you know what their "ability" is. This is something that many teachers are very used to doing – making judgements about a child's potential on the basis of their current performance. But it implants a very unhelpful idea in the children's minds: that if they get things right quickly then they are "bright", and if they make lots of mistakes then they "lack ability". Both of these constructs get in the way of learning. Obviously, if the reason I didn't do well is because I "lack ability", then it would be a waste of my time and effort to bother trying,

---

8   Gwyneth Hughes, Ipsative assessment: motivation through marking progress. *British Journal of Educational Studies* (2015), 63(2): 246–248.

wouldn't it? I'd just be banging my head pointlessly against a brick wall, and getting a headache as a result.

On the other hand, if the reason I did well is because I'm "bright", or "high ability", or "gifted", then I ought to *always* get things right and look as if it is easy, shouldn't I? The label becomes a standard I feel I have to live up to. So when the inevitable happens, and I find myself struggling with something, I feel as if something has gone wrong. I'm bright – so I ought to be understanding this quickly. And if I'm confused and don't get it, well, that means I may not be as bright as I'm supposed to be after all. And that causes an uncomfortable feeling of having let myself down, of not having been good enough. So I get upset and become a super-striver, terrified of not living up to expectations. Or I get a tummy-ache or feel sick. Or I start cheating, to keep up the pretence of being "bright". And all of these are defensive strategies, not learning strategies.

It is perfectly all right, by the way, to talk about different current levels of achievement or performance – CLAPs, we call them. Children know perfectly well that they are currently better than their classmates at some things and worse at others. That's just a fact of life: no point in getting upset about it, or trying to pretend it isn't so. The problem only arises when teachers and parents talk as if those CLAPs are a strong predictor of future success – and they aren't. Or at least they aren't unless we cause them to become self-fulfilling prophecies by talking about ability.

There are all kinds of reasons, other than "lack of ability", why children might sometimes struggle with their learning. They may have other preoccupations and anxieties, or they may lack confidence, or just not be interested. And we probably know

> We want to let children surprise us by surpassing our, and their, expectations

little or nothing about these other factors. We want to let children surprise us by surpassing our, and their, expectations – don't we? So let's stop talking as if we know, reliably and accurately, what they are capable of. We don't. And it's damaging to suppose otherwise.

Instead of talking about ability, we need to build our conversations with children around the strategies or attitudes they are bringing to their learning that may be behind their – relative – successes and failures. We should be focusing these conversations on things that the children can try to strengthen, rather than on "ability" – something which they could seem to be stuck with. Carol Dweck suggests saying things like:

"I like the way you wrote those summaries to help you remember."

"Well done for concentrating through all those distractions."

"Wow – how did you come up with so many creative ideas?"

"Let's try to figure out what it is that is making this hard for you to learn, and what might help you get the hang of it."

"I know you used to love being the one who knew all the answers ... But I'm really excited about how you are pushing yourself more now ... choosing things you are not so good at, and really sticking at them ..."[9]

You might like to try using a few of these phrases to see how the children react. Remember, anything new may feel clunky at first – but don't let that put you off trying to get used to it.

Children don't develop a fluid view of their ability just by being told to "have a growth mindset". When teachers first got excited by Carol Dweck's research, some of them fell into the trap of thinking that just telling children about growth mindset, or putting up some posters, would do the job. It won't. If they have already picked up the idea that someone's "ability" or "intelligence" is fixed, this has become a habitual way of thinking, and, as we've said, you can't change your habits just by being told to. To build growth mindsets, we have to change the messages of the medium – the "cultural practices" – in our classrooms. We have to act and talk *as if* we believe that all children can – and will – get smarter, and set them challenging tasks accordingly. That's the way to grow growth mindsets; not by tacking a set of new, rather cheesy slogans onto business as usual.

---

9   See Carol S. Dweck, *Mindset: The New Psychology of Success* (New York: Ballantine Books, 2007), pp. 177–179.

Talk about the innards of learning

We want to get children interested in the process of learning – the feelings and strategies that are involved – and not just in the end result. We want them to understand that learning is full of ups and downs, trial and error, feelings of frustration and confusion, as well as moments of pride or delight at having finally mastered a tricky skill or understood a difficult idea. We want them to be resourceful enough to come up with new strategies or possibilities that will help them out of their difficulties, without having to rely on us to rescue them, or getting upset. So we need to talk to them about the innards of learning, and get them used to talking about these with each other. Here are some examples of the kinds of things we should get used to saying, routinely, as we wander round our classrooms and chat with the children:

"What's your plan for tackling this?"

"What do you know that might help?"

"What could you try?"

"What exactly is it you don't understand?"

"What have you tried in the past that has helped?"

"What resources do we have in the classroom that might help?"

"Are you OK to keep going for a bit?"

"Are you feeling frustrated/confused/fed up?"

"What do you need to do to get back into learning mode?"

"How did you do that?"

"How else could you have done that?"

"Which are the tricky bits? What's tricky about them?"

"What could you do when you are stuck on that?"

"How could you help someone else understand that?"

"How could I have taught that better?"

"Where else could you use that?"

"How could you make that harder for yourself?"

These are examples of little nudges that encourage the children to be more self-aware, and more creative in solving problems for themselves. Nudging is a way to wean children off dependence on an adult. We suggest keeping an imaginary thought bubble above your head, constantly saying to you, "What's the least amount I can do here to get this child back on track and back into learning mode?"

You know your children and will know when to step in and nudge them in the right direction. Some children may need this kind of scaffolding more than others – and to begin with, more children are likely to need this guidance. In time, as your learning-powered classroom develops, children will gain more independence in knowing how to save themselves, and guide and develop their own learning.

> When we started using curiosity we got deeper with our questions.

To further wean children off the addiction of seeking right answers, you could respond in a way that shows interest in children's methods and ideas without giving away whether or not you "approve" of the answer. For example, by asking questions like:

"What makes you say that?"

"Very interesting. What brought you to that solution?"

"How did you get to that?"

"Why did you solve the problem in that way?"

Questioning in this way homes in on methods, gives children a chance to verbalise and explain strategies, and gives the message that you are just as interested in the process of reaching an answer as the answer itself. This makes thinking visible and demonstrates to children that answers don't just pop into your head – there's a process involved in reaching them. When making thinking visible in this way with the whole class, you might also find that they pay closer attention because they're not sure whether the answer is right or wrong and are mentally grappling with the process of solving the problem themselves.

Sometimes it is as much about what you *don't* say as what you do say; you need to allow children the time and space to ponder. You can gradually build this kind of thoughtful, reflective thinking through the regular use of thinking routines such as Think-Pair-Share and Give One, Get One. A fuller list and description of some of these can be found in Table 5.1. Costa and Kallick suggest foregrounding this kind of thinking:

> Tell children that you are looking for thoughtful, reflective answers and you will wait a minute or so before calling on anyone.
>
> Arthur L. Costa and Bena Kallick, Teaching habits of mind, p. 41

This sends the message that sometimes it takes a while to come up with your answer – that pondering for a while is a valuable process – and that sometimes the first answer that pops into your head isn't your best one. It helps the children become less impulsive and encourages a deeper level of thinking. By requesting and exploring multiple answers, you are also teaching flexibility and acceptance, as well as dealing with ambiguity. Both Ron Berger and Art Costa suggest sometimes not providing the "right" answer when teaching maths, but rather discussing with the children which methods are more or less effective, thereby encouraging them to enjoy the process of exploring, and to become comfortable with "not knowing" all of the time.

Table 5.1: Thinking Routines

Thinking routine	Description	Learning muscles strengthened
Think-Pair-Share	Children take time to ponder a question or idea, then share their thinking with a partner before sharing ideas with the class.	Playing with ideas Wondering Questioning Collaborating
Plus-Minus-Interesting (PMI)	Children discuss a question or idea, focusing on the positives, negatives, and interesting points that come to mind.	Noticing Analysing Critiquing
See-Think-Wonder	Children describe what they can see or notice, what they think about it, and what it makes them wonder. Great for scientific thinking and wondering, it can also be used for thinking about writing passages, to develop mathematical thinking, or to critique art.	Noticing Contemplating Wondering
I used to think … now I think …	Children reflect on what they have learned. This could be used at the end of a lesson or topic. It could also be used to reflect on behaviours and actions, such as a growth in learning muscles. For example, "I used to give up easily, but now I stick with my learning."	Self-evaluating

Thinking routine	Description	Learning muscles strengthened
What's happening here? What makes you say that?	Children describe what it going on in a scene, picture, description, maths problem, and so on, and back up their thinking with evidence. Great for developing inference skills.	Noticing Analysing Critiquing
Circle of viewpoints	Children brainstorm a list of viewpoints about a topic or during a discussion, by putting themselves in the shoes of a different person or character. They can also think of questions from this character's point of view.	Empathising Questioning
Claim-Support-Question	One child makes a claim and the others – or that child themselves – are encouraged to find evidence to support the claim and to question it.	Analysing Deducing Critiquing
Give One, Get One	Children generate a list of ideas related to the topic or lesson, then find a partner with whom to share these. They get one idea from their partner and give one to them in return. The children can then find new partners and do the same. A great way to build on and share ideas as a class, and can lead to discussions to reason why certain ideas are the most useful to get.	Concentrating Playing with ideas Collaborating Accepting

Open up a dialogue about making mistakes

We have found it very useful to talk with the children directly about making mistakes. Ask them, "Do you think mistakes can be a good thing or a bad thing?" You could open up a discussion around "smart mistakes" – mistakes made when taking a risk in learning – and "sloppy mistakes" – mistakes made when you're just being careless. Show positive interest when the children make smart mistakes and encourage them to learn from them. When the children are ready, highlight smart mistakes with the class and discuss the learning that is happening because of them – often these mistakes boost learning for the whole class.

Create an excitement around making and learning from mistakes. Children in Becky's class will often exclaim, "Yes! I made a mistake! My brain just grew!" Cultivating this kind of attitude takes the shame away from mistake-making and invites children to open up and learn when they have made mistakes, instead of shutting down in embarrassment.

Informally notice the effective use of learning muscles

Commentating is another way in which you can develop the types of learning behaviours you are aiming for in the classroom. Become familiar with the elements of learning power outlined in Chapter 1 and begin to notice the children using them. You might want to start with one or two that you think would have the most impact on the learning culture in your class. Alongside talking to the children about what each of these learning muscles looks like in action, and planning learning that will stretch these capacities, you can start to really pay attention to and highlight when these are being used well. For example, you might say things like:

> "I am noticing how absorbed everyone is in their learning today. We are helping each other to stay focused and are learning a lot."

> "I like the way you have chosen to practise your spelling today. That will really help you when you come to your next writing piece and will make your writing easier to read."

"That's a really imaginative idea! I've never thought of it that way …"

"You really pushed yourself today, challenging yourself to try something you'd never tried before, and you stuck with it until the end of class. You should be really proud of yourself."

"It was so kind the way you included X in your group. How do you think that made them feel?"

"I love that you're going back and checking your work to see if you can improve it. That's what real writers/mathematicians/artists/scientists do."

You can quietly make such comments to individual children or make this commentary more public. If it suits the mood of your class, it can be really impactful to stop everyone mid-learning to share an excellent example of a child stretching their learning muscles. This says, "I value what you are doing so much, I'm going to stop everything so that we can all celebrate your efforts and learn from them." It raises the profile of the learning habits you are aiming to develop, and, as a result, using and applying these habits will become more widespread.

Model fallibility

By modelling your own fallibility to the children, you are showing them that it is OK not to know, that even adults don't always know, and that everyone needs to be resourceful when finding things out. You can model that you are willing to stick with a problem, to research it, and to spend some time thinking about it and distilling the information you already have. This can be achieved by thinking out loud with the children while you are teaching. You could say things like, "I might be wrong about this …" You could perhaps use this before delving into a tricky mathematical problem or before researching historical or scientific facts.

You could also use phrases like, "I'm not quite sure about that at the moment. I might have to go away and think about it and come back to you." This models to the children that sometimes it's good not to just accept the first idea that comes into your head; that sometimes thinking and finding out takes time and that, depending on the problem, it can be wise to step away from learning for a while and come back to it later. You can model risk-taking to the children by saying things like, "Let's try it!" This creates a contagious sense of excitement about diving into the unknown.

Sharing your own experiences as a learner can also be hugely powerful for boosting learning power in your classroom. There is something about talking about your life outside of school that has the children on tenterhooks! Children will be fascinated to hear that you go through the same struggles as they do when learning and they will also see that learning is a lifelong adventure.

What are you learning at the moment? Are you training for a run? Learning to play an instrument? Learning to cook new recipes? Improving an area of your teaching practice? Going to a Pilates class? Share your journey with the children – especially the bits that are tricky and frustrating, and how you are tackling those. You can refer back to these experiences when children are struggling in their own learning. For example, "Remember I told you I was learning to play the guitar and there was one part of a song I just couldn't quite get right? What did I do? How was I feeling then? How did I get through it?"

Model metacognition

To really get the children thinking about thinking, you can show them what it looks and sounds like by "thinking aloud". This can help children to become more aware of the thought processes they might have running through their heads while they are learning. Through your modelling you will be developing in them a kind of built-in self-reflection tool, as well as a greater awareness of themselves as learners. You can also model the way "experts" think, such as how a scientist, writer, or artist might approach a task or problem.

Gemma Goldenberg, assistant head in charge of curriculum and professional development at Sandringham School, used this technique in a series of assemblies in which she wanted to target children's skills at reporting back to the whole class on their small group discussions. She had posed a series of P4C-style questions for the children to discuss in small groups and then asked individual children to feed back the ideas from their groups. Below are some example questions, taken from Sandringham's "Thinking Fridays", some of which were conjured up by their Year 5s:

"Should you trust someone if they don't trust you?"

"What qualities make a good teammate?"

"Should you always keep a secret?"

"Why do people risk their lives for love?"

During one assembly on Martin Luther King Jr. Day, the Year 4s were pondering the question, "Should you always speak out when you see something unfair happening?" Gemma had noticed that some of the rapporteurs were more adept at reporting back than others, and had designed the assemblies to highlight some of the sticking points. She shared a slide with the children to stimulate discussion and self-awareness, shown in Figure 5.1. On one side was a list of some of the things that the children were saying; on the other Gemma revealed the kinds of things she was thinking when they offered such comments.

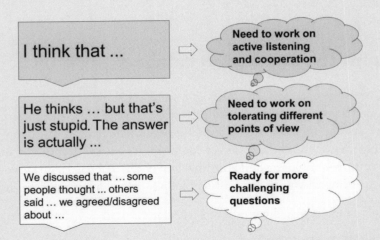

Figure 5.1: Modelling Thinking

Source: Gemma Goldenberg, Sandringham School

By making her thought processes transparent, she enabled the children to see how they could improve upon the accuracy and fairness of their reporting. This also provided the children with more challenging language stems to use when feeding back on their group's thinking.

Diving Deeper

We have just shown you some of the ways in which the language you use, and the things you model, can help the children develop as powerful, reflective learners. Now all you have to do is use these terms regularly and thread them seamlessly into the everyday language of your classroom! This, as we've said, will take patience, time, practice, and attention. It is a journey from consciously trying out something new to unselfconsciously talking in a different dialect. Some phrases and ideas will come easily to you, and some will take a bit more picking apart and practice to embed. When you get to the point where talking and thinking in learnish – the language of learning – is as natural as breathing, you will be having the deepest possible impact on classroom culture.

Examine the underlying values

Behind your language lurk attitudes and mindsets about learning. If your mindset doesn't match your language, the children will probably sense the disparity between how you talk and other aspects of your behaviour which may be "leaking" a different underlying message, and they will get confused. As you go deeper, you may need to unpack your own mindsets and attitudes, and check that the language you are using is having the impact you intend. It might help to ask yourself questions like:

"Am I promoting making mistakes but don't actually see the value in them?"

"Am I asking the children to wonder, but would really rather they just got on with the task at hand?"

"Am I trying to nudge the children to think and explore, but really think it would be quicker and easier to just tell them how to reach the answer?"

"Am I encouraging children to persevere, but really believe that some children will always struggle to stick at a task?"

Taking time to reflect on your own values will help you to unpick the classroom culture you are aiming to develop and to identify possible blocks.

Get everyone speaking learnish

Of course, it's not just you who needs to become a native speaker of learnish. You need to encourage the children to pick up on this language and use it themselves. Some of this can happen quickly and unconsciously – almost by osmosis – but learning other aspects takes more time, and a bit more concentrated effort and modelling from you. Some children pick up on the language quickly, some take a bit longer. The example of Gemma Goldenberg's assemblies illustrates this nicely.

Apart from you and the children, other adults in the classroom – learning support assistants, teachers who cover your class, and parents who volunteer, for example – will also need to become fluent in learnish. So it's worth sharing with them what you are trying to achieve, and telling them about your own learning journey. Don't be afraid to guide them and gently pick them up when they are using language that is aimed at "helping the children do it", rather than "helping them discover how to do it for themselves". In this way, you will be involving them in deepening a culture and deploying a language that develops independent, robust, challenged, and collaborative learners.

Learn by example

Here is an example of another experienced LPA teacher at work, Emma O'Regan at Sandringham School. Emma teaches a group of fifteen children who have been identified as needing extra support. This is not because they are "low ability" – as much as we object to the use of that term – or in receipt of Pupil Premium, but because they are somewhat more anxious or less-confident speakers than the other children. They are individuals who would benefit from being nurtured and having their voice heard in a smaller group.

You might like to pause here and ponder on the wisdom of grouping children on the basis of the help they need in developing specific learning muscles.

Wondering

Is there is a risk that it might be stigmatising, or make them self-conscious? How do you think this risk could be reduced or eliminated?

How could you explain this kind of differentiation in a way that avoids making it seem like there is something "wrong" with the children who are chosen? How do you think Emma set this up?

Do you think the children themselves were involved in setting up this group? Would this be a good or bad idea, do you think?

This lesson is part of a series on writing a factual report. The children have done research on their subjects, and have researched and practised different ways to design their reports, including using eye-catching banners and titles. They are at the stage of beginning to produce their final product. Emma starts the lesson by showing the children an example of a report that she had written as a student. She has deliberately chosen a page that she doesn't think is very good: rather dull and unimaginative, in fact. She discusses the example with the children, using phrases like:

> "When I reflected on this piece of writing I was quite dissatisfied with it, to be honest."

"If I'd found someone to talk to about it, my writing might have been a bit more interesting."

Emma is thinking out loud: making her thinking process visible to the children. In doing so, she is modelling the fact that reflection is part of the writing process, and that she realises she did have tools she could have used to improve the quality of her writing – in this case, sharing ideas with a friend.

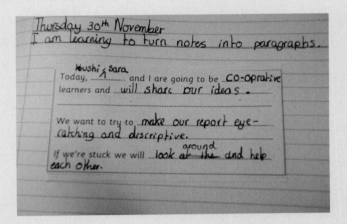

The children are then shown a framework to structure their thinking about which "learning attributes" – as the learning muscles are called at Sandringham – they might want to stretch that lesson. The framework begins, "Today, ... and I are going to be ... learners and ..." The children discuss ideas and offer answers. One child offers:

"Today, I'm going to be a reflective learner by noticing when I make a mistake, and I'll correct it."

Emma nudges her thinking on by asking, "How would you do that?"

Another child offers:

"Today, I'm going to be a cooperative learner by talking to others about what I'm going to write, and I might use their ideas."

Emma picks up on the use of the word "might", exploring the idea that you don't have to take on all the suggestions others give you, and that it's part of being a good learner to accept that yours might not be taken on.

She then explores the next part of the framework, which says, "If we're stuck, we will ..." The children offer ideas like, "stay calm", "ask a partner", "ask the teacher". Emma picks up on this final answer, asking the children, "Before asking the teacher, what could you do to help yourself?" Again, the children offer lots of ideas: "use a dictionary", "use the working wall", "ask your friend".

Just before the children go off to start working on their reports, they are given the choice of working in a pair or a group of four. They briefly discuss the advantages and disadvantages of each option. One group come up with the suggestion that pairs would be good to generate and share ideas, but that fours might be better to edit their writing. Emma's conclusion is, "If it works, then great!" The children feel trusted to make intelligent decisions about how to support their learning, to try out their own ideas about how to design their learning, and then to reflect on how it went.

The children's level of concentration during the task is palpable. And this isn't just a quiet, heads-down focus, although during parts of the lesson they are completely absorbed in their writing. At other times they are discussing ideas, drafting on whiteboards, redrafting, editing, and correcting, before getting their final ideas down on paper. Emma expertly guides children through these processes, giving just enough support and guidance to keep them on track and thinking about what they are doing.

Throughout the lesson there is an open discussion about mistakes. The children informally talk about "trying not to make mistakes" in their final piece, but they also discuss how making mistakes in the process of drafting "might happen because you're trying to write something new and unusual". They talk about their plans for the layout as their "working document". Emma says, "Well, aim for that, but make any changes along the way that you need to." Again, she is creating trust and giving permission to adjust plans as necessary. When the children come to Emma for help, she gently guides them back to their partners or groups.

Some children tell Emma they're "struggling". Emma encourages the struggle and warmly tells them to keep going. She empathises by saying understanding things like, "Sometimes we panic in the moment. Take your time. There's no rush." She feeds back to the children and nudges them towards new ideas and ways of thinking by saying things like, "What you've written is OK, but you're starting to add information about a new subject here. Are you happy with that?" Part way through the lesson, Emma comments, "There's really good cooperative learning going on here. Lots of sharing of ideas, editing, rereading, and revising. Great!" The children ask her opinion on ideas to add. She says encouraging things such as, "I don't see why not! Sounds fun!"

Experienced LPA teachers use learnish in everything they say. Everything Emma says has a positive impact on the learning culture she is aiming to create. And you can immediately see the impact this has on the children:

- They feel trusted in their decisions as learners.

- They understand what learning muscles they can stretch and how.

- They understand the value and place of mistake-making.

- They know how to get unstuck.

- They know they can use their friends for support and feedback.

- They understand when chatter is beneficial and when it's time to put your head down and think by yourself.

- They trust their teacher and each other.

- They know they are valued as learners and individuals.

All of this is created by language: by what Emma says and doesn't say. This is what we are aiming for when we talk about becoming fluent in learnish.

You might like to take stock of the language you habitually use in your classroom, and the attitudes you tend to model, in the light of our discussions and suggestions.

Wondering

Which of our key words rang a bell with you? Do you tend to think, talk, or write about the children as if you know what their "ability" is? If so, might you try to change this habit?

Do you agree that modelling fallibility makes the classroom a safer place for children to learn? Which of your own current or past learning projects, with all their struggles, could you talk more openly about with the children?

Can you check how you typically tend to respond to children when they (a) do well, (b) do badly, and (c) are struggling with something? What one small tweak could you make to your way of talking that might help them focus on their learning rather than their supposedly innate "talent" or "ability"?

Are there any ways in which you might still be giving the children "mixed messages" about what you want from them? Do your messages vary according to the subject they are studying, do you think? Or with the age of children you are teaching? Do you habitually use any words or phrases that you might now want to be on your guard about?

Bumps Along the Way

Here are some of Becky's thoughts on what you might try if things don't go quite as planned ...

What if ...	Try this ...
You want to pay attention to changing your language but it's hard to do it in the hustle and bustle of a busy school day.	This concern is totally understandable. It takes enough brain power to think about the progress of a lesson and about responding to the children without having to worry about the language you are trying to use. Teachers I've worked with have used the following methods to thread new learnish into their classrooms: • Try writing a couple of words or phrases you would like to use on the whiteboard as a reminder. Add to this list and build on it regularly so that you are expanding your learnish vocabulary. • Share with other adults – and/or the children – how you are trying to change your language. Ask them to pay attention to the words you use and to feed back to you. Try to develop your language together.

What if ...	Try this ...
	• Try out the swear box idea! Or you could turn this on its head and have a reward box – when you use positive language like "could be", you put money in the box.
The children laugh at each other's mistakes.	Be forgiving! I know this kind of behaviour can be disheartening, especially when it's the opposite of what you are aiming for. I would talk to both the child who was laughing at the mistake and the one who made it and discuss how this feels and what effect it can have on learning. I would also be quick to try to build a positive attitude to mistake-making with the class – for example, by making a "Mistake of the Week" display, as described in Chapter 4. I would also make a habit of being positive about the children learning from their mistakes. You can change attitudes around quite quickly if you raise the profile of making mistakes and keep coming back to why this is useful for learning. It might also be useful to discuss the difference between smart and sloppy mistakes, as explained earlier in the chapter.
You try to raise the value of making mistakes or of making an effort, for example, but the children don't seem to be picking up on it – the culture has just stayed the same.	There are two possible elements at play here. The first is, you are aiming for culture change and culture change takes time. Don't expect attitudes to learning to change overnight. They will change with a constant and consistent drip feed of ideas, attitudes, and values. So don't give up; keep at it. Think, are there any other ways in which you could thread this value – for example, learning from mistakes – into your teaching and the mindsets in the class? Is there another way in which you could come at it? How could you try again? Are there a few children modelling a positive attitude to making mistakes? How could you capitalise on this and share it with the class?

What if ...	Try this ...
	The second is the underlying attitudes and beliefs you hold, which are communicated in your classroom culture. Do you really believe in developing this outlook or disposition? Dig deep. Is there something holding you back? Maybe a fear of being judged by others walking into your classroom? Or a part of you that doesn't really believe in what you are trying to change? Try to find out what that barrier is and why it's there. Once you've exposed it, you might be able to analyse how it is being conveyed in your teaching. In order for learnish to be fully effective, the classroom culture and the attitudes and messages from grown-ups need to be congruent and consistent. Try to find the chinks in this message.
You are making progress with learnish and can see the children are starting to pick up on it. However, other adults in the classroom are using language that counterbalances this success.	This is a tricky one. If you really want learnish to go deep and sing from every part of the teaching and learning in your class, then everyone has to be on board. So this is going to involve having conversations with the adults in the classroom and getting them involved too. Perhaps the best way to approach this is clearly and non-confrontationally. Could you create a learnish fact file to share with adults, with a short explanation about why you are developing that vocabulary? Perhaps pick a few key areas to focus on, so as not to muddy the waters. Which aspects would have the biggest impact in your classroom? This could be part of an information pack you hand out to volunteers in your classroom – pre-empt the problem before it happens! If you have time, you could briefly explain and expand on each of the phrases you are aiming to embed. This way, instead of directly dealing with negative or unproductive

What if …	Try this …
	language, which could be confrontational, you are gently guiding adults in your classroom to be speaking from the same vocabulary list that you are.

Summary

In this chapter we have homed in on the ways in which your habits of thinking, talking, and acting impact on the development of the children's habits. As we have said, habits are contagious. The children in our classrooms spend a good chunk of their waking hours in our presence – possibly even more than with their families. So we are potent influences on their development – whether we like it or not! The way in which we behave has a lasting impact, just as much as the well-designed, interesting lessons we create. Gradually, with some self-awareness and some encouragement from friendly colleagues, we can shape our own language of learning, and our reactions to the children's learning, so that we influence their attitudes and skills as learners in a positive way. We can start with straightforward shifts in the vocabulary we use – for example, remembering to say "not yet", and to talk about "learning" rather than "work". And then we can move on to more deep-seated changes – for example, focusing our attention on improvement over time rather than on snapshots of attainment, and changing the messages we give when we respond to difficulties and mistakes. As we move in these positive directions, our classrooms become hives of learning and engagement – and results will improve too.

Chapter 6
Collaboration and Conversation

To ensure that students experience positive interdependence, teachers need to structure cooperative learning situations in which children learn the content *and* are responsible for ensuring that all group members succeed in the assigned task.

Arthur L. Costa and Bena Kallick, Teaching habits of mind, p. 63

This chapter zooms in on just one design principle, as it's quite a meaty and important one:

4.   Make ample time for collaboration and conversation.

We will also explore in more detail the learning muscles that fall under the socialising element of learning power: collaborating, accepting, imitating, empathising, and leading.

In plenty of classrooms children "do group work". In fewer do teachers deliberately structure the classroom so that children's skills as collaborators and conversationalists are systematically stretched and developed. The skills and attitudes of good collaboration are at the heart of the LPA. And, of course, building the skills and attitudes of collaboration is one of the key design principles. In fact, talking and listening well – what some people these days refer to as "oracy" – is fundamental to other elements and principles of learning power as well, such as the ability to give and receive feedback calmly and skilfully.

Learning in the real world is as much a social process as a solitary one, so children need to practise and develop all the component aspects of collaboration. You can't expect good talk or good collaboration to just happen. Sitting at a desk on your own doesn't do it, but nor does being put in a pair or a group and being told to talk. We have seen plenty of examples of unproductive group work, and it happens when teachers don't offer the children well-designed topics or questions to talk about, when the children are not clear about what they are supposed to be talking about, or when they lack the requisite skills and attitudes. Like all approaches to learning design, collaboration can be done badly – but that is no reason to dismiss it out of hand, as some traditionalists are inclined to do. The skills and sensibilities required to be a good collaborator have to be cultivated through deliberate and persistent practice, discussion, modelling, and guidance. This chapter describes a variety of ways in which teachers can build these dispositions and capabilities day by day. It is about how to design good group activities, and how to help children become skilled at working together.

> When you collaborate, you speak to each other; someone can lead and you can get all your ideas together. Other people ask questions and make your idea better.

What's So Great About Collaborative Learning?

As with any of the design principles, you will only work to embed them in your lessons if you really see the point of them. There may well be times, unless you are one of those rare teachers who are immune to these things, when you want to throw in the towel – perhaps a lesson doesn't go quite as you had planned, or some children are being particularly resistant. It may feel uncomfortable because you are taking a risk and trying something new, or because of any number of other reasons that you can't predict. So, this is the section you should come back to if you begin to feel despondent – it will

> In plenty of classrooms children "do group work". In fewer do teachers deliberately structure the classroom so that children's skills as collaborators and conversationalists are systematically stretched and developed.

remind you *why* you are making the effort to build a collaborative classroom. Table 6.1 presents some reasons for trying to deliberately build a culture of collaboration. You might have some additional ideas of your own.

Table 6.1: The Advantages of Collaborative Learning

Advantages for children	Advantages for teachers
Develops independence and interdependence.	Frees us up to give support where it's needed most.
Exercises social skills.	Creates bonds between the children, which results in fewer classroom niggles.
Improves speaking and listening skills.	Creates a happier, more relaxed classroom.
Fosters a supportive classroom and mutual respect.	Decreases stress and workload since more responsibility is given to the children.
Strengthens self-confidence in their ability to learn.	Improves behaviour because the children feel valued, trusted, and part of a class culture.
Creates class cohesion.	Increases job satisfaction because the children will start to blossom and you will see their confidence as learners growing.
Supports inclusion.	
Shifts the classroom ethos from competition to cooperation.	
Creates shared outcomes and understanding.	
Supports the idea that learning is always a process.	
Enables them to see that there are usually many solutions to one problem.	
Deepens empathy and expands flexibility.	
Sparks new friendships.	

Advantages for children	Advantages for teachers
Forms the basis for exercising other learning muscles, such as reflection and organisation. Develops growth mindsets. Reflects real-world learning.	

Let's expand a little bit on some of these benefits.

Collaboration develops independence and interdependence

If you slowly build a class culture around collaboration, you should find that the children naturally begin to rely on one another for help. Go to any Reception class during free-flow, or "planning time", and you are likely to see this cooperation already in action. If you start to explain to your class why you are getting them to collaborate, and give them the time to respond and to think for themselves about why this might be useful, you should start to see a positive response. There are plenty of ideas about how to do this coming up.

As the children are encouraged to use one another as resources, and taught how to talk to one another as partners and members of a group, you should see them getting better at solving problems together, and you can begin to step back and let them do so. In the many classes in which we have observed the LPA in action this has indeed been the case. The children are keen to learn, keen to collaborate, and keen to use one another as resources. When they get really good at this they will independently seek out friends who can help them with a specific problem. In Becky's class, they got to know each other so well as learners that they could really home in on who to ask for advice – saying, for example:

"I know, I'll ask Charlie. He's really good at spelling."

"Sammy will be able to help me solve this maths problem. She's really good at explaining things and helping people."

This understanding has been embedded through involving the children in continuous discussion about and reflection on collaboration and resourcefulness. When children know themselves as learners like this, and know they have permission to collaborate, you will be freed up to give support where it's needed most.

Collaboration develops social and oracy skills

We cannot emphasise the importance of this enough. You can't expect children to develop social skills if you don't put them in situations in which they have to be sociable. Equally, you can't expect children to improve their oracy skills if you don't find ways to structure their talk and give them opportunities to practise. This is all the more important for children who, for whatever reason, have limited opportunities to develop these skills at home.

When you first invite the children to collaborate, you could come across some resistance or anxiety, especially if they are not used to doing it. But the children who are the most resistant are generally the ones who need to develop their collaboration skills the most. By avoiding this situation, or by pretending the issue doesn't exist, we are doing these children a disservice. We need to plan to develop their social and collaboration skills in order to give them the best life chances – both now, when they need to build strong working relationships with their peers, and in the future, when they will get jobs and need to work with a whole range of different people.

Developing collaboration skills can take time and patience. Becky once taught a child on the autistic spectrum who, to begin with, would only collaborate with one friend. But with gentle and persistent encouragement and understanding, he was able to collaborate with a small circle of trusted peers by the end of the year. When writing their end-of-year reports, Becky asked the class what had helped them to learn most. This child replied, "I know that I can collaborate because if I am stuck my friends will help me." This was a huge step for him. Not only had he learned the value of collaboration, he had taken strides in his understanding that he didn't need to remain stuck – that he could find ways to move forward and that his friends were one of those resources.

If you persist – gently, supportively, and despite the resistance – you will almost certainly see the most fantastic effects on the children and their attitudes to school and to learning. New friendships will develop that you may never have expected – because you will be providing a wealth of opportunities for the children to learn with others. The children's confidence will skyrocket because they will widen their circle of friends and realise that they are liked and valued by their classmates. Have you ever had children in your class who struggle when their best mate is off sick? Say goodbye to that because they will soon have a whole class full of friends they can rely on.

Collaboration forms the basis for exercising other learning muscles

Children love to use their friends as resources. By being able to get unstuck without a teacher they feel empowered to take control of their learning. Asking their friends for help is just one of a repertoire of resources children can draw on to get unstuck without having to ask the teacher. So, by developing collaboration skills you are also beginning to develop resourcefulness. You may remember that one of Vygotsky's key insights was that children first discover and explore new mental resources in their interactions with others, and then, over time, those resources become part of how their minds work even when they are on their own.[1]

> You can learn more when you collaborate. But your partner doesn't tell you the answer, they support you so you can still figure it out yourself as your talking partner gives you ideas.

Training the basics of collaboration also lays the groundwork for effective peer marking and feedback. In order to give feedback tactfully and effectively, children need to have a basic understanding of how to work well in a pair or a group. Again, we can't just assume this will happen; we need to plan how to teach the skills needed to give and receive feedback.

---

1   See Luis C. Moll, *L. S. Vygotsky and Education* (Abingdon and New York: Routledge, 2014).

Collaboration creates cohesion

As the children become used to learning with a variety of their classmates, new bonds and friendships are created. As we have said, sometimes these friendships may surprise you! When Becky asks her class to find new learning partners, she never knows which children may pair up but is prepared to take the risk. As we explain later in this chapter, if paired activities are well-scaffolded, children mostly rise to the occasion. Sometimes, unlikely children get together and create "learning dynamite", going well beyond anything you could have expected – and aren't those the moments that we teachers love to see? LPA teachers we have spoken to have found that these partnerships create a feeling of togetherness in the class and are the basis of supportive learning.

Collaboration develops growth mindsets

By keeping groupings fluid, you are sending a message that all children can achieve and challenge themselves. Moving away from ability grouping opens up the doors to the belief and understanding that all children can excel. Sandringham School have used mixed-attainment collaborative learning for years, and have been graded "outstanding" by Ofsted. One of the highlights of their most recent Ofsted report is this:

> In lessons, pupils work diligently and hard. They are keen to learn, enjoy the opportunities presented to them and are proud of their work. Pupils show respect and genuine interest in the views and ideas of their peers. In particular, pupils work collaboratively, supporting each other as they attempt complex tasks. Incidents of behaviour that prevent others from learning are exceptionally rare.[2]

---

2   For the full report see: https://reports.ofsted.gov.uk/inspection-reports/find-inspection-report/provider/ELS/130381.

Collaboration and Conversation

✓ Build awareness and understanding of collaboration as a learning muscle.
✓ Create a display around collaboration.
✓ Plan for collaboration.
✓ Value and praise effective collaboration.
✓ Ask the children to choose their own learning partners.
✓ Create scaffolds and frames for talk.
✓ Make the shift from teacher to learning coach.
✓ Plan roles within a group.
✓ Open up discussions around group sizes.
✓ Purposefully and cumulatively develop oracy skills.
✓ Use collaboration for peer feedback and reflection.
✓ Extend, deepen, and assess collaboration.

Dipping Your Toes In

Hopefully the last section has made you hungry to get going on building up your children's collaboration and communication muscles. To begin to see how these habits can be deliberately cultivated, it is useful to get clarity on what exactly the habits are. Here are some of them. Children who are effective collaborators:

• Listen attentively and accurately to each other, and signal that they are paying attention.

• Speak clearly and look at other people when talking.

• Try to understand someone else's idea before reacting to it or evaluating it.

• Take turns to talk and know how to join a conversation without interrupting or talking over other people.

+ Remember the purpose of the conversation, keep on track, and help others to do so as well.

+ Build positively on each other's contributions.

+ Have the confidence to think aloud in the company of others.

+ Act as a good sounding board for other people as they think aloud.

+ Know how to disagree respectfully.

+ Are willing to change their minds in the light of what other people say.

+ Can be challenged or have their ideas critiqued by others without getting upset.

+ Can put themselves in other people's shoes and adopt different perspectives during a discussion.

+ Pick up on other people's good ideas and ways of operating, and learn from them.

+ Are kind and generous to others who may be struggling.

+ Help the group stay resilient and determined despite getting confused or frustrated.

+ Are aware of the group dynamics and can help a group reflect on and improve its functioning.

As you can see, collaboration is a complicated business, and it can take a lifetime to get good at all of these elements. You won't be able to complete the job of making world-class collaborators instantly, but you can certainly help all of the children in your class to make progress along the road. Some of these behaviours and abilities are obviously more sophisticated than others. Take a moment to think about your class and your school.

Wondering

Which of these components of effective collaboration are the children already good at?

Which are patchy or poor at the moment?

Can you think of particular children who might already be useful role models of some of the components of good collaboration?

Which components might the whole class be ready to start practising?

Can you think of any more behaviours that a good collaborator and conversationalist would demonstrate?

If you like, you could reflect on how well your staffroom works as a culture of collaboration and conversation. Are there any of these aspects that the staff could do with improving a bit?

So now here are some ideas to get you going. See which ones feel the most fruitful – and try them out.

Build awareness and understanding of collaboration as a learning muscle

Plan a circle time or class discussion about collaboration. Explain to the children that they will be collaborating with new partners more often. Ask them questions like:

"Why might developing collaboration be important and enjoyable?"

"What difficulties might there be?"

"What will good collaboration look, sound, and feel like?" (This will engage all the senses and really bring their understanding to life.)

"What will amazing collaboration look, sound, and feel like?"

"What could you do if a member of your group wasn't collaborating so well?"

You could use this discussion to come up with guidelines about what good collaboration looks like. Art Costa has some great suggestions in his Habits of Mind series, which we highly recommend.

Create a display around collaboration

Gather the ideas generated from your discussion about what makes a good collaborator to create a display, highlighting the points made by different children. This will give the children another chance to reflect on the ideas they came up with and will raise the profile of collaboration in the classroom. It's also a useful tool to refer to as guidance when the children are learning collaboratively. You could add examples, such as photos of the children collaborating well together or pieces of group work, to bring the display to life, as well as quotes from the children about collaborating – really try to pull out the learnish! Each time you add something new to the display, you could take a few minutes to share the example with the children and discuss how it shows good collaboration – the more you can pick apart the concept for the children, the more they will understand how to improve their skills. For example, Becky used examples of the children sharing ideas, taking turns, including others, and solving problems together; and these were demonstrated by different-sized groups, different combinations of children, and different collaborative contexts. She ensured that children who sometimes found collaboration difficult were featured on the display, so that they could see that they *could* do it. She made sure that quieter, shyer children were on the display too, so they felt valued and involved, and also included children who were taking a risk with their collaboration skills and learning with someone new. All of these carefully planned

> I didn't used to be very good at collaborating. I don't think any of us were! But now when they're talking I listen and I don't talk, and when we play games I don't argue and I play by the rules.

157

elements gave children a rich understanding of how collaboration could be useful in different contexts, built up a picture of what effective collaborative learning looks like, and provided visual proof that every child could strive to improve their collaborative skills.

Plan for collaboration

Plan a lesson which will be designed around collaboration. If planning regular collaborative learning is completely new to you, you might want to start by introducing it in lessons like PE or ICT. In some schools, it may feel like a bigger risk to start by building more collaboration into maths or English lessons. Just judge what feels like a manageable next step for you.

We would also suggest having the children hold quite short conversations in pairs at first. Then, as they gain in confidence and skill, you can slowly increase the group size, the length of conversation, and the complexity of the questions you pose for them to discuss, or the tasks for them to complete.

Also, to start with, you may want to determine the pairings ahead of time. When creating pairs you might want to take these factors into consideration:

+ Which children will be supportive of others? Are there any children who are particularly so and could you pair them up with a child who might find collaboration tricky, therefore making it more likely that you are setting them up to succeed?

+ Pre-empt pairs that might struggle to collaborate. (There is more on this in the "bumps along the way" section at the end of this chapter.)

+ Try mixed-attainment pairs. This may seem like a stretch if you are used to arranging the children in ability groups. However, the children will only begin to socialise with a range of peers if you mix them up. And you – and they – might be pleasantly surprised. Both Sandringham School and St Bernard's RC Primary School pair children up with a different learning partner at the beginning of each week. Children stay with these partners all week, using them to bounce ideas off and get themselves unstuck.

- When pairing children, it's important to bear in mind the range of skills, strengths, and interests they bring with them. For example, if pairing in ICT, does one partner have good reading skills, or good technical knowledge, that they can share?

- When you introduce collaboration to the children, it's important that it feels exciting to them. Perhaps plant the seed at the beginning of the week and begin to discuss it to build anticipation before you actually get the children to do it – there is more on this shortly.

If children are used to working in the same groups, making steps towards using more fluid groupings might feel like a challenge – for you and for them! Our advice would be to not challenge the children too much with pairings that might intimidate them to begin with, but push it just far enough so that they're not always with their best friend. We can only encourage you to be brave enough to take the plunge, and to assess and reassess as you go. The important thing is to continually review *with* the children what worked and what didn't work so well. Ask them, "How could we adjust or improve that so it might work better next time?" Teacher and blogger Matt Curtis has written an excellent post on his – often bumpy! – journey towards mixed-attainment groupings.[3] The whole piece is well worth a read as it highlights some of the potential sticking points with mixed-attainment teaching and demonstrates how taking risks in your practice can be difficult, but ultimately worth it in the end. Here is his reflection on that journey:

> Just as I was getting to the point where I was considering giving it up as a bad job and reverting to my old ways, I started to see some real chinks of light. I noticed that there were some really good relationships blossoming around the room. More confident children were getting the opportunity to verbalise their understanding of different concepts to their partners while less confident children were listening, asking questions and learning from them. The quality of interactions appeared to be much greater than I had been used to seeing in ability grouped tables. I consciously started planning more opportunities for "Maths Talk" in lessons and collaborating in this way has had a really positive effect on the way that the children participate in lessons.
>
> Matt Curtis, Transforming fixed mindsets towards maths

---

3   Matt Curtis, Transforming fixed mindsets towards maths. *Talking Maths* [blog] (6 January 2017). Available at: https://talkingmathsblog.wordpress.com/2017/01/06/transforming-fixed-mindsets-towards-maths/.

Once they become used to paired work, and more comfortable with changing partners, begin to encourage the children to choose where would be best to sit with their partner. Ask them, "Where will help you to concentrate?" "Where is the best place to complete this task?" Although the freedom might serve as a distraction to begin with, the children can often surprise you when given responsibility. For example, one child who found it hard to concentrate in Becky's class would often take himself off to a quiet table, separate from the distraction of his peers, saying, "I just find it easier to get on with my learning here."

Value and praise effective collaboration

Using whatever reward system you have in your school – house points, head teacher awards, stars of the week – begin to focus on great collaboration, highlighting this at the end of a lesson, or as you round up the day. Be as specific as you can with praise, picking apart why the collaboration was so impressive – this could look quite different for different children or different year groups. For example:

"I love the way you took a risk and chose a new partner today. It really paid off."

"You were both excellent at sharing ideas. This was definitely a two-person project."

"You often like to lead your group, but today you stepped back and let other children take the lead. Look at what a difference that made to the learning in your group!"

You get the idea!

Ask the children to choose their own learning partners

Once you have successfully tried a few collaborative lessons in which you decide the pairs, the next step could be for the children to take on that responsibility. Why? Because you will be building their independence and awareness as learners.

You will probably need some preamble to this and some ground rules. You could discuss what is going to happen with the class the day before the actual lesson. Ask the children to come up with some rules about choosing a partner for learning – for example, don't just pick your best friend! Becky tends to encourage the children from day one to be brave and seek out someone new who they've never learned with before. In doing this, she is encouraging her children to stretch their social circles, learn how to make friends, and feel encouraged to take risks.

Further down the track, you could make these choices more challenging by introducing different criteria for choosing partners. You might ask the children to choose a partner based on how they think they will go about learning. You could ask them to justify their choices in terms of the learning strengths which they think their partner will bring, and why those strengths might be relevant to the task they are going to be undertaking.

You will want to have some discussion about people's feelings – about how to accept or turn down a partnership, about how to make everyone feel included, and so on. (There is more on this in the "bumps along the way" section at the end of the chapter.)

Create scaffolds and frames for talk

Providing children with sentence starters and frames for talk will raise the quality of conversation. Share these scaffolds with the children before asking them to collaborate or to discuss a topic. Using them may seem a bit clunky at first, but as the children get used to them, the flow of their talk will become more natural and they will find their own ways of adding ideas or skilfully disagreeing with their classmates.

The set of sentence starters featured in the photo on page 161 is a scaffold used by Mariyam Seedat's class at Sandringham School. It is referred to when children are learning in small groups or pairs. You can hear children throughout the school using sentence stems from frames like this. For example, Year 3s in Katriona Rae's maths lesson used sentences like, "I can see what Charlize is saying, but I solved that problem differently." Presenting alternative methods and ideas in this way builds on suggestions without diminishing those that have gone before. Here are some possible sentence starters you could display for the children to refer to:

"I can see what ... is saying, but ..."

"To go along with ..."

"Linking to your point ..."

"On the other hand ..."

"Building on that ..."

"Adding to ..."

"I agree with ... because ..."

"I agree with ... and I'd like to add ..."

"I disagree with ... because ..."

"I noticed that ..."

"I was wondering about ..."

You can adapt these stems to suit your needs, age group, and the individuals within your class. Why not make these stems a working document – a poster maybe – and add new ideas as they come naturally from the children? The children will feel empowered when the language and structures come from them.

We encourage you to also look at the work of campaign group Voice 21 and of the English-Speaking Union, both of which have created plenty of useful resources for developing and structuring oracy in the classroom.[4] Once you've tried out a few of these ideas, spend some time taking stock and reflecting on the impact.

Wondering

What went well?

What didn't go so well?

How could you adapt your ideas and plans so they work better next time?

What about the children? What feedback have they given? Do they like collaborating? Do they find it useful?

Have you noticed a difference – good or bad! – in behaviour or attitude to learning? How could you capitalise on this or adapt your teaching to cater for it?

If you're thinking that what we have suggested so far sounds like quite a challenge, you might want to fast-forward to the "bumps along the way" section at the end of the chapter, which should help you to troubleshoot any difficulties. Remember, when you try anything new there are bound to be surprises, and maybe some frustration if it doesn't quite go to plan. Just try small tweaks to begin with so the situation can be easily salvaged if it doesn't work as well as you had hoped the first time. And don't give up! Adjust what you did in light of the experience and have another go. Some children can be quite conservative to begin with, but with gentle persistence most of them will quickly come on board.

> Remember, when you try anything new there are bound to be surprises, and maybe some frustration if it doesn't quite go to plan.

But if these ideas sound OK so far, read on!

---

4   See https://www.voice21resources.org and https://www.esu.org/our-work/esuresources.

Diving Deeper

If you're ready to take on a bit more of a challenge, here are some examples of how you can make collaboration a really integral part of your classroom culture. Bear in mind that to get to this stage can take months – and it will vary with different classes – but also be aware that the real impact will only come when collaboration becomes deeply integrated into your classroom, the children *know how* to keep improving their collaboration skills, and are *keen* to do so.

As you expand your repertoire of collaborative learning, though, remember to pay close attention to the "nitty gritty" and ask yourself – and the children:

"Is everyone included in the group? Is everyone learning? How? How do we know?"

"Is everyone involved in reaching a shared understanding of how and when collaborative learning can be useful? Does everyone have some say in when and how they collaborate?"

"Does everyone have the tools to express themselves articulately and clearly? Do they know how to make their voices heard? Are they sensitive enough to take stock, listen, and include others?"

"Is everyone improving their collaborative skills? Do they have time to reflect and learn from their mistakes?"

"Is everyone collaborating in a variety of ways? Do they understand the different roles within a group and how to shift between these roles?"

These questions may highlight the areas where group work can go wrong, and consequently why it has had such a patchy press. Being able to answer these questions could be the difference between strong, effective collaborative learning that boosts outcomes for all, and vague, undefined group work, which can be dispiriting and counterproductive. Here are some ideas about how to work towards embedding the former.

Make the shift from teacher to learning coach

As the children start to collaborate effectively with your guidance, they will begin to rely on one another for support and ideas. In this sense, your role as the teacher can shift and you can take on more the attributes of a coach; nudging, connecting, and facilitating the children's collaborative learning. You can develop your role as a learning coach in a variety of ways:

* Eavesdrop on the children while they are collaborating, nudging their learning on through your questioning. You might say things like, "I wonder how you could make sure you are being accurate in your working out?" or "Are you making sure everyone in your group is on track? How do you know they are?"

* Highlight to the children that you will be available for certain types of support. For example, some teachers create "mini-lessons" based around improvements students need to make to their writing. Children can choose which mini-lesson to take part in based on the feedback they are getting on their writing and what they need to work on. One day, they might decide to opt into a mini-lesson on descriptive detail, and another day, seek guidance on the punctuation marks which they haven't yet mastered.

* Learn alongside the children, modelling the learning habits you are looking to develop. For example, one day Becky decided to sit with a group of children and model good learning behaviour by "becoming" one of the group. The children were sharing ideas for the story maps – a sort of structured story board – they were developing, using a variety of ready-made frames. Becky modelled openness to new ideas and being resourceful by saying, "I'm not sure what to write for frame three. What have you done?" She encouraged idea-sharing by saying, "Ooh, I've just had a great idea for this picture, I'm going to include a speech bubble." The impact of this was three-fold:

1. She experienced learning from the children's point of view – a very useful thing to do from time to time.

2. The quality of the learning on that table improved – lots more ideas were shared, and lots of improvements were made – and this was done in a non-threatening, organic, and collaborative way.

3. She was asked to quieten down by learners in her group because the class had decided they should only be speaking in "whisper spy talk" (further details of which can be found in the Voiceometer strategy in Chapter 8)!

Plan roles within a group

To strengthen and develop a range of collaboration skills, you can introduce structured roles within a group, such as note taker, summariser, or task manager. Taking on a variety of roles enables children to understand their task and stay focused, hands over responsibility to them, and stretches their collaboration skills in a variety of ways. See Table 6.2 for a breakdown of possible group roles. Could you invent further roles with your class to add to this list?

Table 6.2: Roles for Collaborative Learning

Role	Description	Learning muscles stretched	Reflective questions
Note taker	Notes down key points.	Noticing Concentrating	What are the key points? How can I summarise? What information is/isn't important?
Vocab master	Gathers interesting or new vocabulary.	Noticing	Which words haven't I come across before? How can I work out their meaning?

Role	Description	Learning muscles stretched	Reflective questions
			Are there any words that jump out at me? Which words might other group members like me to note down?
Task manager	Oversees roles within a group. Ensures everyone is clear on roles and involved in task. Might pause task to fulfil role.	Planning Leading Evaluating	Are all of my group members clear on their roles? How can I support and include group members? How can I ensure everyone has a chance to contribute?
Predictor	Imagines what might happen next.	Wondering Questioning Playing with ideas	What could happen next? What makes me think that? Are there any other possibilities?
Questioner	Generates questions during task.	Questioning Contemplating	What questions could be probing? What questions would deepen the group's understanding?

Role	Description	Learning muscles stretched	Reflective questions
			What questions could I note down to research later?
Clarifier	Takes stock to ensure everyone is up to speed.	Empathising Evaluating	Are we moving too quickly/slowly? Has everything been clear up to this point? Is there anything I can ask to help clarify? Does everyone understand what we have covered so far? How do I know?
Connector	Makes links between ideas or previous learning.	Connecting	Are there any links to previous learning? Are there connections to previous reading? What does this remind me of? Where else have I seen/heard this?

Role	Description	Learning muscles stretched	Reflective questions
Challenger/ prober	Challenges ideas. Digs deeper. Doesn't take things at face value. Plays devil's advocate.	Persevering Recovering Adapting	Can my group members back up their ideas? How? Are there any other possibilities? Does this ring true? If not, why not?
Summariser	Sums up key points during and at end of learning.	Noticing Evaluating	What have we discussed? What are the salient points? How did we work together as a group? Does everyone agree?
Visualiser	Visualises images in the story. Draws pictures or diagrams of what is happening.	Noticing Imagining	What images are conjured up in this story? Does this look different from different character perspectives? How does the writer use vocabulary to paint a picture for the reader?

As you can see, alongside developing collaboration skills, each role stretches different learning muscles. For example, vocab masters need to develop keen noticing skills, while task managers will be stretching their planning skills. Note also that every role involves an element of empathy – a great group member considers the needs of the group as well as their own. In which case, children are constantly challenged to ask themselves, "I wonder what I can do or say to support and extend the other members in my group?"

At Sandringham School, teachers find lots of ways to encourage and develop various collaborative roles. In Amrita Hassan's Year 4 class, children are grouped around tables and each week one child from each table is appointed to act as the "learning mentor". They are the leader on the table and their role is to offer prompts or suggestions to the group – or to individual children – if they get stuck or are looking for someone to bounce ideas off. While Becky was observing the class, she saw learning mentors being consulted to extend vocabulary, check grammar, and develop ideas. They also read and checked each group member's writing at the end of the lesson, and offered them feedback. Special signs on each table indicated who the learning mentor was that week. Amrita explained, "All the children want to be learning mentors. Changing them weekly gives children who are more quiet a chance to take on that role." By sharing leadership roles, Amrita is gradually and purposefully developing the children's confidence in speaking and listening – and their leadership qualities – while they are learning English.

In Rakhsana Hussain's Year 1 class, learning mentors are used in a slightly different way. Children are chosen to be learning mentors at the beginning of each term. Rakhsana explained, "We choose good role models to begin with so that they can model to the other children what a good learner looks like." Learning mentors wear special necklaces so everyone knows who they are. They are in charge of noticing good learning behaviour in other children. The children regularly revisit what makes a good learner and therefore what they might pick up on. "We started this routine in planning time when the children had the space to just notice each other's learning behaviours. It's now threaded into English and maths lessons and we review who's been spotted being a good learner at the end of a lesson," Rakhsana elaborated.

Michelle Worthington's Year 3 class has a similar set-up. Each day, the children nominate fantastic learners from the previous day's learning. Children who have been spotted stretching their learning muscles go onto the "Wall of Fame", and one child is selected to be in charge of noticing amazing learning and gets to sit on a throne and wear a crown for the day. Going onto the wall has great kudos, as does being king or queen for the day! Michelle is always on hand to guide and support children's choices. Through her language she has a beautiful way of creating trust with her children – for example, by saying, "I noticed that, did you? Did you think the same thing as me? Should Liam be on the Wall of Fame today?"

These three examples illustrate how one idea – in this case, developing mentoring and leadership skills – can be adapted to suit the different dynamics and levels of readiness of particular classes and year groups. As with all the ideas in this book, you will know how best to adapt them to work in your context. In Chapter 8, we describe an example of reciprocal reading at School 21, which demonstrates in further detail how roles can be assigned within a group in this way (see pages 240–241).

Here are a number of points to bear in mind as you begin to work with these role-taking ideas:

+ There is no harm in introducing a few roles at a time so that children can familiarise themselves with each one. Feel free to target a few that you really want your children to get to grips with first. You could even discuss the different roles with the children and ask them which they would prefer to use as a class and why.

+ Be careful not to always give children "obvious" roles – for instance, giving children who are more confident writers the role of note taker.

+ Following on from the spirit of the previous point, try to stretch each child so that they learn to take on a variety of roles in a group.

+ As the children gain in confidence and understanding of the roles, they can begin to organise these themselves.

+ Don't assume that this won't work for younger children. We have seen Year 1 children effectively use roles – such as visualiser, someone who draws what they imagine in a story, and summariser, who recaps at the end – within a reading group.

Remember that you are training the children to understand and get better at these roles – so don't automatically assume that they will, or "ought to", get them right first time. It takes time, practice, and reflection to hone these skills – for adults as much as for children.

As a reflection at the end of collaborative learning, you could ask the children what went well and what didn't, what we could all improve on, and how we could work together better to include everyone in the group. Perhaps some children dominated the group or some children didn't speak. By being open about these observations in a safe environment, the children will become aware of their own attitudes and skills as collaborators, and they can begin to think about how they can improve on them in the future. Then, when they collaborate in similar groups again, you can refer to and build upon their previous reflections. You could tell the children that this term you will be developing collaborative roles within groups, opening up a discussion about how and why this might be useful. Then take some time at the end of the term to reflect upon how children have improved – and could get even better. To frame these

reflections, you could use the thinking routine, "I used to … now I …" – for example, "I used to think I was always right, but now I think that other children can help me improve my understanding" or "I used to be quite shy talking in groups, but now I'm getting much braver in speaking up."

> *I work better in a team now; I'm more fair and I let other people have a go. I don't always jump in and show off.*

Open up discussions around group sizes

In Becky's class the children are sometimes given the option to collaborate or to learn alone. Part of their whole-class time is dedicated to briefly discussing the advantages and disadvantages of collaboration in the context of the specific topic and task that they are working on. The children often give insightful, grown-up comments, such as, "I think I will collaborate today because I need someone to bounce ideas off" or "I really know how I want to approach this learning. I'd rather learn by myself." This not only develops the children's understanding of themselves as learners, it also gives them ownership over their learning. And it builds that metacognitive awareness that allows them to be flexible, and to design their own learning to suit the task and the context. At West Thornton Academy, this kind of independent thinking about how best to learn is a given – children *always* have a choice about where in the classroom and with whom they learn (following a design principle which is expanded upon further in Chapter 8).

Here's another example. When Guy visited a Year 4 English class at Bushfield Primary School in Buckinghamshire in the UK, he was surprised to see the children working in groups as big as six or seven. He asked the teacher about this, who explained that, a few weeks earlier, he had led the children in a discussion about the kinds of groups and teams they might find themselves in in their working lives when they are grown up. For example, they talked about project teams made up of people from a wide range of professional and cultural backgrounds. The children – with a little nudging – quickly agreed that it would be good if they learned how to be confident in such situations, and even better if they could learn how to help such groups function well. So the whole class agreed that for the rest of that term they would deliberately keep changing the size and the composition of their groups, in order, as they put it, to "stretch their collaborating muscles".

Guy circulated around the classroom, eavesdropping on the children's discussions. As he was listening to one table, a boy piped up, "Could we just pause for a minute … because I'm not sure how well our group is working. Could we just go around and say how we are all feeling in the group." The other children agreed, and several of them did reveal that they were feeling a bit inhibited by some of the more confident members. They quickly decided that it might be more profitable if the group split in half for the next ten minutes, and then came back together again to pool their ideas. And so, without any help from Guy or their teacher, that is what they did.

Guy was very impressed, having been in undergraduate seminars at top universities that didn't seem to house groups with that degree of social intelligence. To be honest, he has been in the odd staffroom that didn't either. But this classroom did – because the teacher had been deliberately training the children in the skills and awareness they needed. Some of the children weren't regularly exposed to this kind of discussion at home but thrived once they began to cultivate the habit in the classroom.

Purposefully and cumulatively develop oracy skills

Learning how to tactfully and effectively share ideas is the basis for effective collaboration. Breaking down and discussing with the children how to get their ideas across, how to respond to children whose opinions they agree or disagree with, and how to use their voices to build on and explain a point gives children the tools to successfully develop ideas as a group. Scaffolding this well can make the difference between successful and unsuccessful group work; the difference between all children feeling included and able to be vocal, or some feeling left out and despondent; and the difference between children feeling positive about sharing ideas, or frustrated that they can't get their message across. Picking apart the skills involved in effective oracy makes thinking visible and therefore enables children to reflect and build on them over time. This can be especially supportive for children who speak English as an additional language (EAL) as they are still learning the language structures they need in order to express themselves. It can also provide good models for talk for children who, for whatever reason, don't always have that at home. Figure 6.1 contains some thought-provoking statements that you might want to discuss with your team or think about yourself in relation to stimulating oracy. They were created by Peter Hyman, executive head teacher of School 21.

1. Speaking should have the same status as reading and writing.

2. Silent corridors and silent classrooms are the death of education.

3. We should track and test oracy skills in schools.

4. Change the staffroom conversation; change the school.

5. Learning through talk is as important as learning to talk.

6. Lack of good oral communication is the biggest barrier to inner-city pupils getting on.

7. Remove chairs and tables and oracy will flourish in the classroom.

8. Expectations about all classroom talk should be clear, modelled, and scaffolded.

9. Getting pupils to talk in assembly is the best way to get them to talk in class.

10. Speaking events should have the same profile in schools as sports days or drama shows.

Figure 6.1: Talking Points about Oracy
Source: Peter Hyman, executive head teacher, School 21

You could begin to develop oracy skills in your classroom in several ways. There isn't enough room to explore all of these areas in great detail, so we encourage you to look into James Mannion's, Oracy Cambridge's, and Voice 21's research and resources to delve deeper (details can be found in the Resources section). Here are a few suggestions to get you started:

+ Create guidelines with your class about what good "group talk" looks like. These could be similar to those you have created about good collaboration, but with a focus on listening to and sharing ideas.

+ Scaffold talk with sentence stems, as explored earlier in this chapter.

+ Demystify oracy by breaking down its elements.

+ Enable children to reflect and build on their oracy skills by making thinking visible.

The elements of oracy

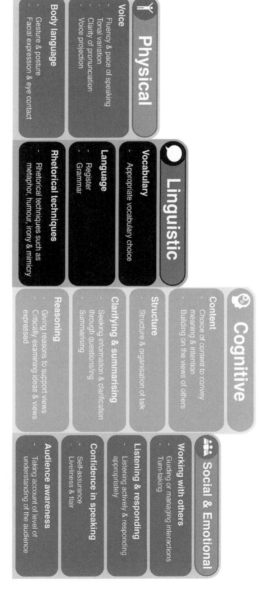

Oracy: The Four Strands

Use the oracy framework to understand the physical, linguistic, cognitive, and social and emotional skills that enable successful discussion, inspiring speech and effective communication.

Physical

Voice
- Fluency & pace of speaking
- Tonal variation
- Clarity of pronunciation
- Voice projection

Body language
- Gesture & posture
- Facial expression & eye contact

Linguistic

Vocabulary
- Appropriate vocabulary choice

Language
- Register
- Grammar

Rhetorical techniques
- Rhetorical techniques such as metaphor, humour, irony & mimicry

Cognitive

Content
- Choice of content to convey meaning & intention
- Building on the views of others

Structure
- Structure & organisation of talk

Clarifying & summarising
- Seeking information & clarification through questioning
- Summarising

Reasoning
- Giving reasons to support views
- Critically examining ideas & views expressed

Social & Emotional

Working with others
- Guiding or managing interactions
- Turn-taking

Listening & responding
- Listening actively & responding appropriately

Confidence in speaking
- Self-assurance
- Liveliness & flair

Audience awareness
- Taking account of level of understanding of the audience

Figure 6.2: Oracy: The Four Strands

Source: © Voice 21 and the University of Cambridge, used with kind permission

177

You can break down oracy into physical, linguistic, cognitive, and social and emotional skills with your children, and pinpoint which of these areas you are going to focus on one by one. When learning to perform speeches from Shakespeare in a drama lesson, the Year 5s in Sarah Saddington's class at Sandringham School began by reflecting on which areas of their physical performance they were going to work on. The children discussed how their gestures, pace, and awareness of their audience could affect their speech. With these ideas in mind, the children first visualised how the delivery of their speech might look, then wandered around the class practising, before working in small groups to perform their speeches and give one another feedback. The children made astute remarks, like, "Move around to add more emphasis and grab our attention", "Slow down, you seem hurried", and "Make more eye contact." They concluded the lesson by writing down their reflections on a prepared pro forma, detailing how they had improved and what they needed to work on next to target their physical oracy skills. Gradually and relentlessly developing oracy skills in this way builds self-confidence and results in children becoming adept and confident public speakers.

Make thinking visible

Hannah Coles, a Year 4 teacher at School 21, has found a variety of ways to make thinking visible during class conversations, and to make children aware of what she calls "derailing" – comments that change the conversation in an unconstructive way. One idea she developed is to use the Harkness model – in which the children are seated in an oval shape to facilitate idea-sharing – to visually track conversation and to highlight who has contributed and how.[5] She is particularly interested in whether they have built upon or complemented another child's contribution, or have "derailed" the discussion. Hannah commented that using this approach has raised the quality of conversation in her classroom as children could visually see and thus reflect on how their comments had added to the debate – or not. Such methods help children grow more mindful about what they are saying and how they express themselves. This photo shows an example of how you could use the Harkness model to visually track conversation.

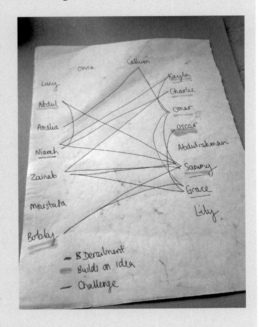

Would this work for Key Stage 1 children? Why not give it a go, adapt it, or try it with a smaller group first to find out?

---

5   For more information on the Harkness model, see: https://www.exeter.edu/exeter-difference/how-youll-learn.

Use collaboration for peer feedback and reflection

Being able to give specific, clear, and respectful feedback is an aspect of collaboration that children will need to focus on at some point. You might like to think about how you could address this and get them to practise it. When developed successfully over time, this ability not only develops children's social skills – and thus helps them to help each other improve – it also raises children's *self-awareness*, enabling them to identify their personal, and the group's collective, next steps and work towards them. In Chapter 9, we go into more detail about how you could go about scaffolding peer feedback. But if you're keen to get started, here's an idea you could try.

Speed dating

Monét Cooper teaches English at Capital City Public Charter School in Washington DC.[6] She uses a lesson protocol called speed dating to develop her students' ability to give and receive constructive feedback. The students have written drafts of an important essay assignment, and they are going to sit opposite each other, read each other's drafts, write down some feedback on a special form created for the purpose, and then tell each other the key points of their feedback. Timings in this protocol are tight – five minutes to read, five minutes to write down their suggestions, and three minutes to talk. Then they move on to the next round, working with another partner. Each round could have a different focus. For example, round one could focus on looking for spelling and grammar errors, round two could focus on looking for technical or descriptive vocabulary, and round three could focus on looking for genre-specific features and layout.

To hone their feedback, the lesson begins with the children studying a rubric that clearly defines the features that "quality work" should possess. The children look at samples of work, usually selected from a previous year's attempts to complete the same assignment – with some good and some not so good examples – and offer

---

6   You can see this lesson on the DVD that accompanies Berger, Woodfin, and Vilen's book *Learning That Lasts*. Both Monét Cooper and Anne Simpson are EL Education teachers. Anne Simpson's work is also described in *Learning That Lasts*, p. 45.

their judgements. Monét responds in a way that sharpens their understanding of what the rubric is really looking for. Then they set off on their speed-dating rounds. This method could work just as well for a maths problem, a French translation, or an art project.

Don't be fooled into thinking this kind of feedback is only relevant to older children. Anne Simpson, who teaches at Two Rivers Public Charter School, also in Washington, uses a similar protocol with her kindergarteners, except their feedback is written in the form of sticky notes, and is simplified so that children understand exactly how to feed back effectively.

Extend, deepen, and assess collaboration

As you develop these ideas and methods with your class, you will reach an ever-deeper understanding of what great collaboration looks like and how it can be useful to support learning. You can paint this picture through:

+ Planning, using, and reflecting on different kinds of collaborative learning, such as paired learning, paired feedback, using roles within a group, and using different-sized collaborative groups in different contexts.

+ Inviting the children to plan, comment, and reflect on this process. For example, give them the opportunity to choose the size of their collaborative groups and explain their choices and decisions.

+ Structuring collaborative groups, both physically – through roles – and verbally – through developing oracy skills.

+ Highlighting and valuing when children are stretching their collaborating muscles and making this part of the class ethos.

You can build on and expand your class anchor charts and displays to reflect this deepening understanding. Figure 6.3 is an example of a collaboration scale Becky developed jointly with Nicola Suddaby and Andy Moor, Key Stage 2 teacher and head teacher respectively at St Bernard's RC Primary School. It builds on a graphical tool developed by Maryl Chambers at TLO Ltd called the fishbones.[7]

Cooperates with others

1.1 Takes turns.

1.2 Listens actively.

1.3 Patient with others.

1.4 Shares own ideas.

Beginning teams

2.1 Clarifies steps to group success.

2.2 Open to ideas.

2.3 Encourages ideas.

2.4 Respects others' views.

Building teams

3.1 Thinks about the role they can play in getting things done.

3.2 Thinks about how to resolve disagreements/controversy.

3.3 Steps back for others.

3.4 Willingly tries different roles.

3.5 Checks the group's progress.

3.6 Suggests improvements.

Skills in team roles

4.1 Builds others' confidence.

4.2 Willing to change view.

4.3 Builds on and improves others' ideas.

4.4 Prioritises and plans actions.

4.5 Offers and accepts useful feedback.

---

7   See https://www.buildinglearningpower.com/2018/05/unpicking-perseverance/.

Leads others

5.1 Manages conflict.

5.2 Advocates other views.

5.3 Coordinates effort.

5.4 Evaluates outcomes.

Figure 6.3: Scale of Collaboration

Source: Becky Carlzon, Nicola Suddaby and Andy Moor, building on Maryl Chambers

---

Wondering

Why do you think it's important to provide opportunities for children to collaborate and share ideas?

What little changes are you planning to make in your classroom in order to get the children to collaborate? Can you give some specific examples?

Can you think of any deeper changes you will make to embed this design principle? Again, thinking about specific examples is useful.

What difficulties have you come across, or can you envisage, when trying to embed this design principle? How have you, or do you plan to, overcome these?

Bumps Along the Way

To conclude this chapter, let's take a quick look at some of the things that could go wrong with your initial attempts to build a collaborative learning culture in your classroom. Here are some troubleshooting tips from Becky's experience.

What if …	Try this …
The children become distracted and off task. They just aren't learning well with their partners.	How you respond to this will depend on the extent to which it is happening. Is the whole class distracted? Are many of the children off task? Just a few? If it's the latter, I would review the learning at the end, or in the middle, of the lesson and make collaboration a focus of the review. Refer back to your class tips for choosing a good learning partner. Ask the children, "Were you a good learning partner today? Did you help your partner learn? Or were you perhaps a bit distracted?" It's really important not to point fingers or cast blame here. The children need a safety net and they need to know it's OK to get things wrong – and they need to learn how to collaborate too. This is more of a reflection process for them. If a pair weren't so great at collaborating, I would remind them of it just before you get the children to collaborate again: "Remember last time we chose partners? And you didn't get on so well with your learning? Don't worry, you're going to have another chance in a minute. Who do you think could really help you with your learning today?" If the whole class is distracted, you might want to stop the lesson and bring them back to your shared anchor chart on collaboration. You could emphasise the fact that giving them a chance to collaborate means handing over trust and responsibility to them, and that you know they can take on this responsibility. It's all about second chances.

What if ...	Try this ...
You notice children pairing up who you don't think will learn well together.	Don't panic. Try not to take control and intervene immediately. To be honest, it's almost inevitable that if you give the children a chance to choose partners, some will just gravitate towards one another regardless of suitability. You need to give them a chance. One of two things will happen: (1) not much learning will occur, or (2) they will surprise you. I have witnessed both, and actually much more of the latter. I find if you trust children, they often tend to step up. It might be worth having a quick word with any dubious pairs before they go off and making sure you check in with them regularly to keep them on task. When they do surprise you and succeed together, they deserve big praise.
A child bluntly refuses a peer's offer of a learning partnership.	The best way to deal with this is to pre-empt it when you are sharing ideas about how to choose a good learning partner. I sometimes role play being a terrible partner with my learning support assistant. You can also choose a child to help you model this. This can open up a discussion about how the other person would feel if you said you didn't want to partner with them. If this still happens, it's a case of dealing with it on the spot in the same way. If there's one child left out (for example, in the case of an odd number of children in the class), I normally grab them and say, "Which kind pair will include Ruby in their group?" A whole class of hands shoots up!

What if ...	Try this ...
The class is noisier and more distracted when they are collaborating – it doesn't feel like there is as much learning going on.	This is also likely to happen at first, especially if your class has become very accustomed to working in a certain way. Stand back, take stock, and reevaluate – just as you would in any other lesson. These are the kinds of questions you could ask yourself: "Did I explain my expectations, especially with regard to collaboration, clearly enough at the beginning of the lesson?" "Did I take too many steps too early?" "Could I have structured the learning more? For example, by sending one pair off at a time to model quiet, focused learning?" "At what point did the lesson get too noisy and off task? Why might that have been? What could I do next time to prevent that?" "What did the children have to say? Did they have any ideas about improvement for next time – for both me and them?"

Summary

This chapter has hopefully given you plenty of ideas about how to build children's competence and confidence as social learners. Whatever the behaviours they have when they arrive in our classrooms, there is much we can do, quite deliberately, to help them develop the skills, attitudes, and forms of social awareness that will make them effective members of any groups in which they find themselves. We can get them interested in how collaboration works, and in the kinds of language that helps things go smoothly and productively. We can get them to make their own reminders – such as anchor charts and sentence starters – that help to guide them in positive ways when they are in the middle of their discussions. And we can build their ability to sense how to use the social situation to maximise their learning, depending on the needs, opportunities, and feelings of the moment. Teaching oracy can create children who are extraordinarily impressive in their ability to think, talk, and learn with each other, whether that be in pairs, small groups, or in front of a hall full of parents, carers, and teachers. We have seen it with our own eyes, and we have seen the jaws of other onlookers drop with amazement at what children can achieve when their teachers are committed to and skilled in the LPA.

Chapter 7
Making Learning Challenging and Adjustable

> We don't truly know what anyone is capable of until they are given interesting and difficult things to do.
>
> Mary Myatt, *Hopeful Schools*, p. 36

In this chapter we turn to two closely related design principles:

5.   Create challenge.

6.   Make difficulty adjustable.

The element of learning power we will be focusing on most is *determination*. In an LPA classroom, children's relish of challenge is tangible. They have got used to finding learning tricky and to having to struggle. They see grappling with difficulty as a normal, essential part of learning, and not as a symptom of a lack of intelligence or ability. They do not shy away from challenges; they know that learning and understanding grow when they are living at the edge of their competence, and exploring and mastering new things.

The benefits of having a roomful of determined and resilient children are obvious:

+   Children who are not scared of things that are new and difficult are more engaged in their learning. As children learn "what to do when they don't know what to do",[1] they become more optimistic and confident in their learning. Hope of success outweighs fear of failure. They are much more likely to roll their sleeves up and get stuck in than sit looking helpless and wait to be rescued from difficulty by a kindly adult.

---

1   This phrase is often attributed to the great developmental psychologist Jean Piaget when he was explaining his conception of intelligence (though no one to our knowledge has been able to track the exact quote down yet).

- The amount of low-level off-task disruption diminishes. A lot of that drifting off and messing about – the bane of many teachers' lives – kicks in when children *don't* know what to do when they don't know what to do. That makes them feel confused and inadequate, so they find ways of distracting themselves from that uncomfortable feeling. With greater resilience and resourcefulness, that feeling of inadequacy goes away, and is replaced by a robust openness to adventure and exploration.

- In school, especially come examination time, the children will need to be able to stay calm and resourceful when faced with things that they do not immediately understand – as they will in life. Building resilience and determination gives the children confidence that they can tackle tricky things, even under pressure. Children who are versed in the LPA are much less likely to go to pieces in tests and exams.

> *I like being more resilient. Now, if I don't really want to do something I will have a go anyway and see if I like it, and if I can do it.*

- With stronger determination, children are able to discover the deep sense of pride that comes when you have grappled with and succeeded at something you didn't think you could do. Having tasted this sense of satisfaction, they aim to produce work that is the best they can make it, rather than just settling for getting it done and getting an acceptable mark.

- Children grow to enjoy pushing themselves, and are keen to seek out new challenges and dig deeper in their learning. They become impatient with "easy-peasy" stuff – even if it enables them to get a good mark – because they have unleashed their own thirst for discovery and understanding. Making challenge an integral part of the classroom ethos makes deeper learning infectious.

- This attitude is empowering for all children, regardless of their presumed level of "ability", or their current level of attainment or performance. Children with determination are willing to commit themselves to the challenges of learning, and don't hold back through lack of belief. Everyone in the room is learning full throttle, so the rate of progress increases across the board.

+ Resilience and determination are aspects of children's growing self-regulation. In learning to persist with difficult things, they are also learning to manage their feelings and "delay gratification", and this, as the research shows, has wide benefits on their success in later life.[2] If children learn to be hungry for challenge, they are more likely to push themselves and persevere once they are out of school and are faced with new and uncertain situations.

Notice how the two design principles are linked together in this chapter. We are not only creating challenges for the children, but we are also making difficulty adjustable so that they can begin to play a role in moderating for themselves the level of challenge they are undertaking. In a classroom of thirty children, all with their fluctuating feelings and energies, it is impossible for the teacher to judge accurately what would make a suitable challenge for all of them, and design tasks accordingly. If a child is upset or preoccupied about something that you have no knowledge of, you might set them too hard a task and make them feel even more troubled than they were. Alternatively, a normally passive child may be inspired by the example of one of their classmates to take on a harder challenge than normal – and you could miss the opportunity to stretch them if you are not alerted to it.

> Making challenge an integral part of the classroom ethos makes deeper learning infectious.

So part of what we are up to in this chapter is building up the children's own sensitivity to their current state in learning and readiness for challenge, and giving them opportunities to choose the level to match their momentary mood and ambition. We can design versions of a task that have different degrees of difficulty and invite the children to choose the one that they think will give them a healthy stretch. Or we can design tasks that they are able to customise for themselves. We might start with a small range of difficulties – maybe just a tricky and even trickier version – and then, as the children gain in confidence, and as their intuition about the right level becomes more accurate, we can gradually offer them greater responsibility and choice. As we build up this culture, so we find that more and more of the children – more and more

---

2   See, for example, Terrie E. Moffitt et al., A gradient of childhood self-control predicts health, wealth, and public safety. *PNAS* (2011), 108(7): 2693–2698.

of the time — are really in the learning zone, grappling productively with the next challenge, and not wasting their time working at things that are either too easy or too hard for them.

So now, here are some ideas about how to build up this challenging learning culture. Remember, the LPA is about finding ideas to tweak our teaching that deliver "just a little bit more" than our current practice. If you are already well into the journey of building a culture of challenge in your classroom, keep looking out for any small ideas that could help to push you and the children another step along the path. If you already use some of these ideas, keep thinking, "How could I rack this up another notch?"

> The LPA is about finding ideas to tweak our teaching that deliver "just a little bit more" than our current practice.

Make Learning Challenging and Adjustable

- ✓ Use language and praise related to challenge.
- ✓ Use more open-ended questions.
- ✓ Use visual strategies to support risk-taking.
- ✓ Offer different degrees of difficulty.
- ✓ Get the children to design their own challenges.
- ✓ Start lessons with a grapple problem.
- ✓ Design split-screen lessons.

Dipping Your Toes In

Let's begin with some reflection time.

Wondering

How could you begin to excite the children more about the idea of challenge? Could you try asking them how they are going to challenge themselves this week?

How could you raise the profile of challenge in your classroom?

How do you already involve the children in challenging activities? How could you embed challenge even more deeply? How are you going to go about that?

What do your children have to say about challenging learning? Is that what you would like them to be saying?

Do you have some children who are gung-ho and others who are quite risk-averse? What is the balance between the two in the class? Do their friendship groups tend to cross these lines, or do children tend to stick with those who have similar learning habits to their own?

Use language and praise related to challenge

As we explored in Chapter 5, our use of language has a huge impact on children's attitudes to learning and on the ethos of a classroom. So, a good starting point to pay attention to when cultivating a relish for challenge is the language we use in the classroom.

+ Begin to use words the children might respond well to, like "grapple" or "tricky", so they come to think more positively about difficulty and learn to enjoy challenge. Share the metaphors we have been using in this book – for example, the learning river and learning muscles – so they can visualise what challenge is like.

- Praise children for challenging themselves by saying things like:

  "I like the way you challenged yourself today."
  "You really stuck with that, even though it was tricky."

- Help children to reflect back on, or during, their learning by asking questions like:

  "What was the trickiest part of your learning today?"
  "How did you, or are you going to, solve the tricky part?"
  "How could you make your learning trickier?"
  "How could you find ways to get unstuck?"

- Relate this to how the children might be feeling, so they can identify and describe how it feels when they are in the grip of a good grapple problem. And also help them learn to describe and value what it feels like to accomplish something new:

  "How did it feel when you finally got it?"
  "How does it feel when you are grappling with a tricky problem?"
  "How does it feel when learning is too easy or too tricky?"

- Talk to the children about the "sweet spot" of learning. This is when they are in the amber zone, according to the traffic light system – when they are most absorbed and learning most. This lies between the "easy-peasy" green and "dauntingly hard" red zones. Use traffic lights or refer to the learning ladder or riskometer, as described in Chapter 4, to get the children to signal where they are, so you can adjust your responses accordingly.

Talking about these feelings and experiences enables children to identify the "guts" of their learning processes, and thus normalises them. These conversations also help them to see that the learning challenge is always adjustable and that they can monitor and control their level of difficulty. Talking puts them in the driving seat of their own challenge.

Use more open-ended questions

If the questions are not causing students to struggle and think, they are probably not worth asking.

Dylan Wiliam, The right questions, the right way, 17

If you ask questions with a single right answer, you are asking the children to remember. You are not asking them to do much except look in their memory banks and see if the answer is there. But if you ask open-ended questions, you are asking them to think; and thinking is much more challenging. "What do we call the side of a right-angled triangle that is opposite the right angle?" is a right/wrong question. "Diagonal" is wrong. "Hypotenuse" is right. "Why do you think Michael Rosen wrote a book for little children about going on a *bear* hunt, and not any other kind of animal?" is an open-ended question. "When did the First World War begin?" could be mistaken for a right/wrong question, but it is actually an open-ended question. What do we mean by "begin"? Began for whom? There are some examples of open-ended questions on page 198.

Thinking involves constructing ideas, exploring possibilities, considering alternatives, discovering connections, weighing up evidence, explaining, discussing, listening, and critiquing – all things that stretch the children mentally. Open-ended questions often lead not to clear, unequivocal answers but to new, deeper questions. If we are training the children to do well on general knowledge quiz shows, then right/wrong questions are good. If we are training them to think, then open-ended questions are better. Sometimes they do need to know the right answer,

> Open-ended questions often lead not to clear, unequivocal answers but to new, deeper questions.

but a teaching style that relies too heavily on them delivering it doesn't develop the kinds of minds they are going to need in real life.

In order for the children to become comfortable with challenge, struggle, and not knowing, you could also begin to design – and co-design with the children – activities and learning with no obvious solution. For example, teachers at Sandringham School sometimes purposefully design maths problems to which there is no solution and ask the children to collaboratively grapple with them. When Becky visited the school, a Year 3 class were grappling with a "tangram" problem in groups; they had been tasked with making a square, which, with the shapes they had been given, was actually impossible. The children shared animated talk and strategies, giving them the opportunity to exercise their problem-solving skills and knowledge of shape, as well as fine-tuning their collaboration skills. You know you have reached quite a high level of learning power when the children are so engaged in the learning they are doing by grappling with an impossible problem that actually solving it becomes of only secondary importance.

James Nottingham's learning pit, which we discussed in Chapter 4, is the perfect visual tool for exploring problems with no obvious solution and for getting children used to dealing with what he calls "cognitive wobble" or "cognitive conflict". In *Challenging Learning*, James explains the thinking behind the approach:

> Cognitive conflict involves setting up a conflict of opinions within a person's mind. This conflict, or dissonance, unsettles the thinker and causes them to reflect more deeply on their assumptions.
>
> James Nottingham, *Challenging Learning*, p. 87

So, the aim of creating cognitive conflict is to build children's tolerance for being stuck in a learning impasse, and strengthen their ability to "dig deeper" into the problem, unearthing some of their own assumptions along the way, in order to find a satisfactory resolution.

James suggests that, as children gradually reach that "eureka" moment of constructing new knowledge, they could pair up with children who haven't got there yet. Their job is to help their partner out of the pit. Their partner's job is to refuse to accept what they are told at face value, and to ask questions that probe the proffered "solution" to see if it really holds water.

The learning pit can be used in every subject and with every year group. In a video on his website, James demonstrates using the learning pit with a Key Stage 2 class who are studying tourism.[3] Incidentally, in this video, James talks about the true meaning of "eureka", which in Greek means, "I found it". Not "I was *told* it" or "I *memorised* it",

---

3   See www.jamesnottingham.co.uk/learning-pit.

but "I *found* it". The children realise that achieving that moment of real, first-hand intellectual clarity in which everything finally makes sense only comes about when we have discovered it for ourselves. In the video, he asks them, "What is a tourist?" The children respond in a variety of ways at the beginning of the discussion. Each time they respond, James has a new idea that makes them think again:

Table 7.1: Statement and Response in the Learning Pit

The children say ...	James responds ...
"A tourist is someone who visits another place."	"Am I a tourist then? I'm visiting your school today ..."
"A tourist has to be having fun."	"I'm having fun."
"They take photos."	"I've been taking photos as I've been walking around."
"They spend money."	"I've spent money in your cafeteria."

At this point, the children plan to investigate tourists further using books, magazines, and the Internet and they start to collaboratively form new ideas. While they are doing this, they are in the learning pit – they are unsure of the answer, or answers, and are trying to find information to construct their understanding. The children offer ideas like, "Tourists go on tour", "It's about being on holiday", and "You're a tourist if you think you're a tourist." As they offer contributions, their classmates question these ideas by saying things like, "You could go on a tour of our school and not be a tourist" and "It was the holidays recently, we were all on holiday, but we weren't all tourists." James is always on hand to probe their thinking and to throw in a new challenge when needed.

The possibilities for using the learning pit to get the children to explore knowledge and construct ideas are endless. Here are some ideas to get you going.

"What is an odd number?"

"What was the most important reason why William of Normandy won the Battle of Hastings?"

"How and why do things grow?"

"Why do people gather together?"

"What makes a capital city?"

"There is no "I" in team?"

As you will see, some of these questions are closely linked with the P4C-style questions we explored in Chapter 5. The learning pit lends itself to these types of questions because they have no clear, right answer. However, the pit image can also be used to make the tricky thought-processes involved in solving maths problems – such as defining odd and even numbers – more visible and to explore questions that involve different perspectives – such as differing accounts of the "same" historical event.

To summarise, in the process of grappling with these kinds of questions, the children:

- Develop a growth mindset through collaboratively thinking through their ideas and eventually discovering that they can construct new knowledge.

- Build resilience, curiosity, and adventurousness through getting used to "not knowing" and wrestling with tricky ideas and problems.

- Remember what they have learned in the process of constructing their knowledge, rather than just being told.

- Become "hungry for more" as they have gone through the process of struggling and succeeding in the face of challenge.

- Learn to be supportive, collaborative learners, as the purpose of the learning pit is for all children to have the experience of climbing out unaided by an adult.

- Recognise when learning is truly cognitively satisfying, and that they shouldn't settle for less.

- Build metacognitive skills, as the final stage of the learning pit asks them to reflect on how they have constructed their knowledge and how their thinking has changed.

Use visual strategies to support risk-taking

In Chapter 4, we explored how to design a learning ladder and a riskometer. Now, you could think about how to use these throughout the day, to encourage the children to think about ways in which they could challenge themselves. For example, you could start a lesson by telling the children what the focus or topic is going to be, and then ask them, "What would risky learning look like?" Ask a few of the more confident children to plan the level of challenge they could aspire to, and ask them to move their photos to the rung on the learning ladder that represents that challenge – we'll use the learning ladder in this example for the sake of ease. When asked to explain their position, the children might say:

> "I'm going to challenge myself to use some new, exciting vocabulary from our word wall in my writing today."

> "I'm going to take a risk and try to add some three- and four-digit numbers today!"

> "I've never learned with Rashida, so I'm going to see if I can get some new ideas from her and work well in a team."

> "I'll try to look really closely at details when I'm making scientific drawings."

As you are working with a group, or circulating around the room, you could refer to the learning ladder and talk about how various children's explorations are going.

There is no harm in guiding the children to move up or down a rung on the ladder, especially when they are first getting used to using it. For example, a child might say, "I think I'm on 'good' because I am practising maths." You could nudge them by saying, "I can see what you mean, but you've also pushed yourself by trying a new method today. Perhaps you're a bit higher than that …" This open conversation about degrees of challenge helps children to build a picture about what challenge looks, sounds, and feels like for them, and so deepens their self-awareness and understanding.

Becky has often found that the end of the lesson is a good time to use the learning ladder to review the levels of thinking and exploring that the children have been engaged in. Once they are used to talking and thinking in this way, the children naturally reflect on and digest the learning that has taken place. Their reflections become increasingly astute. Becky's children have said things like:

> "To begin with I was on 'low'. I wasn't quite sure what to do and I was a bit distracted, but then Amina explained what we were doing and I started collaborating with her and I got it. I would say I was between 'good' and 'high'."

> "I was on 'high' because I tried to use lots of new descriptive words today that I hadn't used before."

> "I was on 'overstretched' for a while. It was really tricky and I couldn't work it out. But then I remembered to get a number line from the drawer and used that to count back in fives to work out the problems. I need to practise counting back in fives more."

> "I was between 'good' and 'high'. I was thinking carefully about my questions and checking and rereading my writing."

You can use the learning ladder (or the riskometer, or the learning pit) to look forward to the next day's activities. For example, you could tell the children that you have planned for them to be making some scientific observations, or learning about a religious festival, or writing a descriptive story, and ask them to think about how they could challenge themselves in this learning. Make some notes about their ideas and refer back to them the next day.

Offer different degrees of difficulty

It has become quite common for teachers to offer children a menu of tasks with varying levels of difficulty from which they can choose the one they think will challenge them in a good way. These have become known as "chilli challenges", because you can indicate the challenges' level of "hotness" by the number of chillies, just like on a typical menu in a Thai restaurant. For example, when learning to add two-digit numbers, children in Becky's Year 2 maths lesson could choose from solving problems that bridged 10s – a two-chilli challenge – or didn't –a one-chilli challenge. If they really wanted to challenge themselves they could add three or four numbers together, and then they might go into the 100s! Similarly, in English, the children were learning to use conjunctions. They collaboratively decided which conjunctions were easier to use – such as "but" and "because" – and ones which were tricky – such as "yet" – therefore coming to a shared conclusion about which ones would be harder to practise and that they should strive to include in their writing, thus creating their own chilli challenge list.

There are some key points to remember when using this technique. First, don't forget that *all* learning should be challenging. Whatever system you come up with to represent the different levels, the easiest option should still be a challenge; something the children will have to grapple with and get their teeth into. So, the baseline is challenging learning and anything above that is an

> Don't forget that *all* learning should be challenging ... the easiest option should still be a challenge; something the children will have to grapple with and get their teeth into.

extra stretch. Design the options so that some children in your class will always find the easiest option challenging! Remember Mary Myatt's quote about big-hearted classrooms:

> There is no watering down, no soft options, everyone is working hard, struggling but persevering.

The second key point is that challenge is adjustable. Show the children with your responses that it is quite acceptable to adjust the difficulty downwards if they have chosen something that turns out to be too hard. Equally, if the children aren't challenging themselves sufficiently, talk to them, perhaps using the image of the learning pit or the learning ladder, and nudge them to try something trickier. Remember to keep praising them for their determination and ingenuity, and not for how many they got right.

Third, don't let the children identify themselves according to a particular level of challenge – for example, by saying, or thinking, "I'm always a one-chilli-challenge person." Again, if the baseline is challenging learning, you should be able to avoid this. For example, when writing character descriptions of a troll, Becky's Year 1 children suggested a good three-chilli challenge could be to use similes, which resulted in one child, who sometimes struggled with writing, coming up with, "He had a boil on his nose like an exploding volcano!" Challenge is an open invitation to all children and they should be able to have a go at any level at any time.

Finally, create high-ceiling, open-ended challenges, so that there is no cap on learning – the sky is the limit! Open-ended challenge creates a buzz as you can't predict how far and in what direction the children will take their learning. The outcomes of these learning experiences can spark discussions, highlight misconceptions and provoke new and exciting learning.

The aim of creating extra challenges and making learning adjustable is to enable the children to feel brave enough to explore new ideas and come up with new learning pathways to venture down that you may not have previously foreseen. If you make the suggestions fluid and exciting, children will be tingling with "nervacitement" around learning and won't be able to resist pushing themselves just that bit further.[4]

Here's an example. Heath Vennus, a PE teacher at Sandringham School, threads child-initiated levels of challenge into every one of his lessons. When Becky observed him teach a Year 4 class, the children were deliberately practising the component skills of handball, such as hand–eye coordination, spatial awareness, and defence strategies. Each skill linked to an element of STEP, an acronym which enables children to focus on the specific skills involved in sport:

Space: How to use space in different games and contexts.

Technique: Specific techniques, like ball skills and hand–eye coordination.

---

4   Being "nervacited" means being both a bit nervous and excited at the same time. It is a very useful word that helps children to frame the experience of challenge in a positive light. Our research suggests this word was first coined by Pinkie Pie, a character in *My Little Pony*!

Equipment: Key equipment needed for each sport, such as the types of bats and balls.

People: The number of people needed in a game or needed to attack or defend.

As a warm-up to the lesson, the children were developing their hand–eye coordination. Heath started them off with sitting on the ground, throwing a ball in the air, and catching it. He made it clear to the children that the only person they were competing with were themselves: "Check your personal best. Aim to beat that." As their throws became more ambitious, so the children discovered that they also had to be more focused and precise.

Once children had practised the "easy" level of sitting down while catching the ball, Heath began to ratchet up the challenge – a notch each time – asking the children, "What's something we could change to make it harder?" All of the ideas came from the children and, each time, he referred them back to the STEP model: "Which letter are we practising now?" The children's ideas included changes in direction and movement, catching with one hand, clapping in between throws, throwing the ball higher, and changing the size of the ball. So, Heath was seamlessly incorporating two design principles: *challenge* and *independence*.[5]

He also added the design principle of *collaboration* in this lesson by planning activities in which the children worked in pairs, threes, fours, and larger groups. For example, the children practised simple throwing and catching skills in pairs; threes and fours brought in an element of defence and attack; and larger groups provided the opportunity to bring all of the skills together in goal-scoring practice. Within the larger groups, he also exercised the children's reflection muscles, as some worked as coaches feeding back ideas on how to improve – for example, by using the space better or by thinking about effective defensive strategies. This is how Heath explained his methodology:

> I try to hand as much as possible to the children. The focus is on inclusion, so they might find a way to teach someone who needs to learn a new skill, or really

---

5   We will explore independence further in the next chapter.

challenge someone who has already mastered it. After, they need to explain how they have helped that person develop that skill using STEP. We change the groups and group compositions all the time, so children experience defence, attack, and different compositions. It also breaks down the barriers of "girls vs. boys". There's none of that here. Everyone is included and supported by their teammates. Bringing in reflection and self-awareness means that the children learn how to use the space and their teammates better, rather than just hogging the ball and gathering in one spot.

Heath is purposefully planning using the LPA design principles, and the terminology of the elements of learning power, to build better learners in PE. The results are more skilled, self-aware, inclusive teammates. This is achieved with a few simple tweaks in language, by developing trust with the children, and by planning in opportunities for challenge and purposeful collaborative learning.

Get the children to design their own challenges

Once the children are used to seeking out and adjusting challenge in their learning, you can start to hand control over to them, and involve them more and more in the design of their own learning, as Heath Vennus was doing. You could begin to ask the children:

> In a learning-powered classroom there is always space for the children to design their own challenges, and their attempts to do so provide plenty of opportunities to review and discuss their learning at the end of the lesson.

"What do you think would be a good three-chilli challenge today?"

"What could you do today if you were really going to take a risk?"

Gradually make this invitation for the children to design their own challenges a core part of your classroom ethos, so they always know that they have permission to take their learning to the next level. For example, when investigating two-dimensional shapes, Becky's Year 2s were discussing shape names and properties before designing their own investigations to find out more. In the middle of the discussion, one child exclaimed, "I know! I'm going to do a five-chilli challenge! I'm going to find all the shapes with right angles in them!" She then went off with geoboards – which are mathematical manipulative boards with pegs half driven in, around which you use elastic bands to create shapes – to discover right-angled triangles, various quadrilaterals, irregular pentagons, hexagons, heptagons, and octagons. In a learning-powered classroom there is always space for the children to design their own challenges, and their attempts to do so provide plenty of opportunities to review and discuss their learning at the end of the lesson.

Start lessons with a grapple problem

> Allowing them to grapple with that question collaboratively engages them in the co-construction of knowledge and empowers them as they learn that they can discover the "answers" with their own ingenuity.
>
> Ron Berger, Libby Woodfin, and Anne Vilen, *Learning That Lasts*, p. 49

In *The Learning Power Approach*, Guy described a lesson in one of the EL Education schools.[6] It was a fifth-grade maths lesson, led by teacher Giselle Isbell, in which the children were meeting the problem of how to divide decimal numbers for the first time. The lesson began by throwing the students a grapple problem, which Giselle describes like this:

> A good grapple problem is challenging. Students might have some idea of how to enter into it. For example, they had already worked with the division of whole numbers ... but the grappling part came in because it was a decimal. They weren't sure what to do with those numbers.
>
> Quoted in Ron Berger, Libby Woodfin, and Anne Vilen, *Learning That Lasts*, Video 1

So a good grapple problem centres on learning that is just beyond the children's reach and, critically, the children have a chance to wrestle with the problem *before* they have been taught methods for tackling it. They are given time to think by themselves, and then to share their ideas and strategies with a partner. One of the

---

6   Claxton, *The Learning Power Approach*, pp. 108–110.

key purposes of a grapple problem is to level the playing field – all children have access to the problem and can solve it in any way that makes sense to them. In this way, children are using and discovering their own approaches rather than being taught one correct strategy. One child in Giselle's class explains:

> I think it is good to try something before you get taught because there are pieces of the math problem that you kind of have to piece together, and if you just learn how to do that one way, you can't piece them all together, and [through grappling] you understand the problem better.
>
> Quoted in Guy Claxton, *The Learning Power Approach*, p. 109

Her explanation is a bit tangled up, but it isn't hard to see that she is trying to articulate something rather important about the teaching and learning process. By getting children used to grappling with tricky problems, you are building their resilience, developing their problem-solving strategies, enhancing their collaboration and listening skills, cultivating a positive attitude towards "having a go", and reducing the fear of making mistakes. A fruitful discussion can take place after the grapple problem, or at the end of a lesson, about which strategies the children used and which ones might be more effective and why. However, the key message is that there's no single right way of solving a problem.

In Manzanita SEED Elementary School in Oakland, California, another EL Education school, Mark Zucker's fifth-grade class are grappling with the complexities of grammar.[7] They are learning to use conjunctions to add strength and rigour to their writing. They have been studying space and are building up to a piece of writing that compares the conditions on other planets in our solar system to those on Earth.

The children are given the following scaffolds to work with:

Cause–effect (e.g. as a result, consequently, hence, due to, in order to)

---

7   This example is detailed in Berger, Woodfin, and Vilen, *Learning That Lasts*, pp. 109–110.

_____ , so _____

_____ , because _____

_____ , thus _____

_____ , therefore _____

Because _____ , _____

Compare–Contrast (e.g. unlike, different, contrast, similar, same, both, more, -er, than)

_____ , but _____

_____ ; however, _____

_____ , whereas _____

_____ , while _____

In order to familiarise themselves with the language structures, the children first practise them in the context of subjects that are already well-known to them – for example, in talking about their friends, pets, or likes and dislikes. They also practise using them in a range of language contexts, such as poems and oral presentations. Finally, when they come to apply them to their writing about the new subject of planets, they write much more complex and well-crafted pieces than they would have done otherwise. For example:

"Venus is a beautiful light-green planet, *so* people long ago named her after the Greek god of beauty."

"*Because* Venus is closer to the Sun than Earth is, Venus is hotter than the Earth."

"Venus is so hot that any water there would be just steam, *whereas* on Earth, water can be a liquid or even solid."

By carefully planning for, structuring, and deliberately practising these structures in interesting, personal, and creative contexts, Mark enabled his fifth graders to grapple successfully with using conjunctions in a new and unfamiliar context.

Wondering

Which of these ideas are you already using? What's working? How do you know? What isn't working so well? How could you adapt your practice to change this?

Is challenge infectious in your classroom yet? How could you encourage that fever? Are all lessons challenging? Do many start with a grapple problem?

Which ideas do you think you could try? When? How?

Are the children adept at adjusting their levels of challenge independently? Has it become natural for them to do so?

Do the learning activities you design strike a good balance of being well-structured yet open-ended, so the children know that they have permission to take their learning on to new levels?

What can you do with children who seem quite resistant to the idea of challenge? How can you work away at their resistance?

Once you have begun to thread grapple problems into your maths lessons, why not branch out into other subjects? What would a good grapple problem look like in English? Or history? Or art?

Do the children understand the importance of deliberately practising the parts of learning that they are weaker on in order to improve?

Diving Deeper

Now you've had a chance to reflect on the extent to which challenge is already a part of your classroom ethos, and to explore some activities and strategies designed to strengthen that ethos, you might want to find ways to extend and embed this habit even more. The aim is to make it an integral part of every lesson – indeed, of every moment of every day. Many LPA teachers comment that as they delve into the approaches, they realise how much deeper they can go with developing their children as confident learners. How deep can *you* go with making challenge integral to your classroom culture and developing that adventurous spirit in *all* your young learners?

Design split-screen lessons

A key idea here is challenging the children to keep strengthening and stretching each of their learning muscles. Challenge doesn't just mean grappling with tricky subject matter; the deeper purpose behind these tasks is that, through engaging with them, the children will, out of necessity, have to become better at persevering, noticing, questioning, concentrating, collaborating, imagining, reflecting, and so on. Topics may be interesting or important in their own right, but they are also – if presented and tackled in the right way – potential exercise machines for developing learning power. Our job as teachers is not to keep banging on about the learning muscles; it is to create the conditions in which those muscles will have to grow. And that means psychological safety – a culture in which no one gets laughed at for engaging in trial and error – and a varied diet of engaging tasks and activities that will require the children to expand their capacity to be confident and intelligent learners. As Charlotte, a child at St Bernard's RC Primary School explains, strengthening your learning muscles:

> ... is a bit like baking a cake – you can't just add a couple of ingredients and expect to have an amazing cake! You need lots of different ingredients and sometimes they will need changing depending on the type of cake you are making. That's like learning powers – we can't just understand two or three – we need to use them all to reach our true potential.

The version of the LPA called Building Learning Power (BLP) places great stock on activities that have a dual purpose: to master particular content, and to stretch a particular learning muscle. Teachers are encouraged to think quite forensically about which learning muscle they want the children to be exercising in each lesson. "Today we are going to be learning about the Tudors, and the way in which we will be exploring the Tudors is designed to stretch your noticing muscles – or your imagining muscles, or your critiquing muscles." You may or may not actually say this out loud to the children, sometimes it might be better to leave it implicit. However, this is how BLP encourages you to think as you are planning your lessons.

Of course in real-life learning situations – as Charlotte realises – many of the learning muscles will be working together. Imagining and experimenting and questioning and planning are playing together in your learning mind like the instruments in a symphony orchestra. We want the children to get to the point where they are intuitively creating these fluid ensembles of learning powers in real-life problem-solving. But while they are getting there it can be very helpful to methodically work on the learning muscles one at a time – just as a pianist, or a dancer or an athlete, will work on developing specific components and sub-skills in practice before blending them all back together for their full performance.

> Our job as teachers is not to keep banging on about the learning muscles; it is to create the conditions in which those muscles will have to grow.

In the BLP approach, this is called Split-Screen Teaching. You might design a writing assignment that stretches children's ability to put themselves in other people's shoes, or – using the same topic – design a task that stretches their ability to offer useful, insightful, and respectful critique to each other. Or perhaps you could devise a game that challenges them to stay on task while you deliberately orchestrate a variety of tempting distractions. Split-screen lessons are cunningly designed to weave together content and process. Part of the challenge always relates to the learning muscles which the children are going to be required to use and stretch.

Here's a more detailed example. Julie Barlow teaches at Blaise Primary School on the outskirts of Bristol. One day when Guy was visiting the school, Julie was teaching a Year 6 science lesson. The subject was magnets, and Julie had laid out a "circus"[8] of small experiments round the room, each with an instruction card. The children were to form small groups and rotate around the different experiments, carrying out the instructions on the card and seeing how the magnets behaved.

So far, so familiar. But now Julie adds the BLP twist, as in this lesson they won't just be focusing on content, but on process too. She talks to the children about the washing line that hangs across the classroom. Pegged to it are seventeen laminated cards and each card corresponds to one of the learning muscles with which they are already familiar. She thinks aloud about which learning muscle she is going to get them to stretch that lesson, and decides it will be questioning. She takes down the appropriate card and sticks it in the middle of a permanent display at the front of the room that says, "Today we are stretching our ... muscles". The display serves as a reminder to the class about their learning power focus. She tells them that their job, once they have carried out an experiment and recorded the results, is to see if they can come up with a new question to explore why the magnets might have behaved in the way they did. She tells them that this is what real scientists do; they look carefully at things and then come up with a new question to test and investigate their observations. This is new ground for the class. It is not something that they have thought about or been taught before.

At the end of the lesson Julie holds a plenary session in which all the children feed back their observations and questions. She then guides them to think more carefully about what makes a good *scientific* question. Gradually, with a few nudges from Julie, they work their way towards ideas such as "hypothetico-deductive thinking", in which the question focuses in on a practical implication of a theoretical conjecture about – in this case – why magnets behave in the way they do. "If this is the reason why they behaved as they did, if we undergo this new test, they ought to behave like this ..." Just as in Giselle Isbell's maths lesson, the children are way out of their comfort zone, yet are willing and able to "flounder intelligently". They work their way, in conversation with each other,

---

8   A "circus of experiments" is common parlance among UK science teachers.

towards a deeper understanding of how science works, and what it is that scientists actually do.

Here's a second example. In Rebecca Senior's Year 6 class, in St Bernard's RC Primary School, the children have been learning about the Second World War. She wants them to practise writing diary entries while at the same time stretch their ability to empathise with others and see the world from their point of view – exercising their empathising muscles. To get the children in the mood for this learning, she shows them a photo of evacuee children leaving London on a train. Rebecca asks them what they notice, and they say that the children are a mixture of ages and that many of them look excited. She then invites them to delve a bit deeper and go from surface to deeper noticing by using the thinking routine, "I used to think … now I think …" The children begin to discuss the idea of putting on a brave face, relating this to their own experiences. They offer some deeper observations that change the atmosphere of the room:

> "At first I thought they were happy, but now I think they are just smiling to keep the little ones happy."

> "There are a lot of mixed emotions in that picture."

Rebecca takes the children on a visual journey, asking them to imagine that they are going to school during the war. She talks them through leaving school, running home to play football on the docks, not far from where they live. She then tells the children that when they get home, instead of a football on their bed, they notice a small suitcase. She displays a photo of this on the interactive whiteboard, while at the same time handing each of the children a copy of the letter that has been placed on top.

The letter is from their mother, saying she is sorry, but she must send them away. The children are visibly moved, easily empathising with the evacuees. A discussion is opened up and Rebecca invites the children to also empathise with the adults at the time and put themselves in their shoes – "What choice did they have?" she asks.

The children are shown more photos of their train journey, heading away from London and out into the open countryside. The children suggest that they could feel "apprehensive" but also "free". The discussion, exploring various points of view and relating these to their own feelings, leads up to the children putting themselves in the shoes of an evacuee child during the war, and writing imaginative diary entries describing their experiences and expressing their feelings. Imagining that they took this journey themselves not only helps the children build more vivid descriptions of their imagined experience, but also stretches their empathising muscles a little further, as they practise seeing a situation from various viewpoints.

> I was so emotional today. As soon I woke up I was in tears. I knew, I knew that day was the day, I'm leaving. Now I knew what I'm doing, what was going to happen next but one thing I didn't know... Where am I going. I was at the station waiting to be collected. I gave my mother and father as many hugs as I could. This is it. My eyes were filled with tears but I knew I had to be brave, be brave for my mother. Finally, the train arrived. This is it. This is the end...
>
> As I sat on the chair next to the window, waving to my mum I noticed, My friends, I was relieved, I'm not going on this adventure on my own

These are just two examples of the power and precision of the LPA. The elements of learning power framework gives teachers lots of options about which learning muscles they might focus on stretching in any given lesson. The emphasis is always on stretching; not merely making use of questioning or empathising, for example, but designing activities that aim to develop those capacities in new ways and in new directions. Of course, not all subjects and topics lend themselves to developing all the learning muscles, but once you get into the spirit of designing activities with the LPA in mind, you will be surprised at how creative you can be.

Wondering

What would happen if you swapped the connections in the last two examples you have just read?

Could you design a lesson in which the subject of magnets is used as an exercise machine to develop empathising muscles? Perhaps by asking the children what it feels like to be a magnet that is simultaneously being attracted to and repelled by other magnets – and getting them to draw parallels with times when they have had conflicted feelings about something. Could you come up with a better version of teaching magnets and empathy?

Alternatively, how about combining the evacuation of children during the Second World War with a stretch of the children's questioning muscles? How could you use Rebecca's material to stimulate different sorts of questions in your children's minds? Maybe they could be reporters interviewing the evacuated children's mothers? Maybe they could be the new foster parents, asking questions to get to know their new arrivals? What would be good – or bad – questions to ask? What would be fruitful, and what intrusive? How could you improve on our suggestions?

Bumps Along the Way

As usual, the course of teaching rarely runs smooth, so here are Becky's thoughts about how to troubleshoot and salvage your attempts to get the children to love being in the pit and challenging themselves.

What if ...	Try this ...
The children don't challenge themselves.	Talk with the children about their learning. Ask them, "Do you think this is tricky enough for you? How does it feel when you're not really challenging yourself?" If you are using chilli challenges, nudge them along by saying things like, "I think you might be ready for the next heat level – why not give it a go?" Again, it's important not to get frustrated, or blame the child – being able to find the right level of challenge independently is a learning curve for them too. What looks like a tiny step to an outsider might feel like a parachute jump for them!
The children choose learning that is too challenging.	Julian Swindale, inventor of the riskometer, had a group of Year 2 boys who saw it as a badge of honour to show how tough they were by always going for the hardest challenge – even though they constantly overestimated their readiness! He called them his "Cape Canaveral kids" because they were always trying to shoot as high as possible. We have to remember that it is as useful for children to learn where their limits are, and when to start from something they know, as it is for them to learn when to push themselves further. They are learning to self-regulate and this is a tricky thing for children to master. The process may take quite a few goes for some. Nudging them patiently and gently can help here too, along with some words of encouragement. I also had a learner who

What if ...	Try this ...
	really struggled with self-regulation. She loved a challenge and always pushed herself, but when learning became too tricky she got frustrated and cried. It took her all year to get better at this but it did happen – with lots of practice!
The children jump ahead too quickly.	Again, this would involve a discussion with the child or the whole class about slowing down. Ask them, "Why is it important to take your time when you're learning? What might happen if you rush ahead?" You could make a point of talking about the value of deliberate practice and of becoming really confident in one area of learning before moving. At Sandringham School, children often explore one maths problem in great detail, rather than working laboriously through reams and reams of similar problems. The children take their time to explain how to solve the problem rather than rushing through it. As a result, they deeply understand the process of learning and can explain their working out. Planning learning in this way sends the message to the children that it's better to take the time to do something well, rather than jump into something new before you are ready. Of course, sometimes it is really good to take the leap and go for something really tricky! It's all about balance.
The children give up too easily or are fragile or adverse to challenge.	Learning to relish challenge will be a journey – some children will jump on board more quickly than others. This will be largely to do with their readiness for challenge, which will be influenced by prior experience – how their parents have dealt with challenge, whether they have been "saved" quickly from struggle, what their previous learning experiences have been like, how others around them have responded to challenge, and what they have learned

What if …	Try this …
	about themselves as learners so far. Your job is to gently guide and nudge the children to become more resilient to challenge. To begin with, some children will need more support and knowing your children will be key here. Can you think of ways to scaffold the challenge? Or ways to guide them back to strategies for getting unstuck? Gently encourage the children to use one another for support, to draw on classroom resources, and to use strategies like rereading a text, taking time to think, or returning to a problem later. By consistently talking about and revisiting these strategies, as well as scaffolding learning carefully, you should begin to see good results with even the most fragile of learners.

Summary

The key point of this chapter is that learning is always about challenge. Learning is trying to do something, or understand something, that you are not yet sure you can. You are not yet sure that you have the knowledge or the know-how to get it right – so you are bound to be floundering. Our job is to make sure that the children have the skills and attitudes to flounder confidently and intelligently, rather than miserably and ineffectually. Whatever their backgrounds or personalities, we are in the business of doing whatever we can to nudge them along in the right direction – because their lifelong happiness and fulfilment depend upon it. To be an LPA teacher is to keep reminding ourselves that we have both the opportunity and the responsibility to develop children's "epistemic characters" alongside their knowledge and literacies.[9]

In this chapter we have offered you a wide range of ways in which you can get your children to be more robust and adventurous in their approach to learning. As a result they will become willing to try new things that they don't yet know they can do, and develop the skills and self-awareness to think about how they could choose, customise, and create tasks for themselves so their minds get a really good workout. They will be simultaneously deepening their understanding of the subject matter and strengthening their learning muscles. As always, our success depends upon attending to a number of different factors: how we frame activities and talk about difficulty; how we encourage the children to enjoy being in the learning zone, where things are not too easy and not too hard; and how we build up their confidence – both singly and in collaboration – to work their own way out of difficulties, rather than wait helplessly to be rescued by a kindly teacher or learning support assistant. In doing this, children's engagement with learning improves, their attainment goes up, and they are better prepared for the rigours and pleasures of a learning life.

> ... children's engagement with learning improves, their attainment goes up, and they are better prepared for the rigours and pleasures of a learning life.

9   If you want to be formal, you could say that the LPA is about the business of developing "epistemic character". Epistemic just means to do with thinking, knowing, and learning, so epistemic character is the combination of qualities that make you good at being in situations where thinking, knowing, and learning are difficult and demanding. Sometimes it is useful to be able to speak in a more formal way – though we think informal speech ("stretching their learning muscles", for example) is usually better between teachers, and definitely preferable when talking with the children and their parents.

Chapter 8
Independence and Responsibility

Students who are capable of being different, going against the grain of common thinking, and thinking of new ideas (by testing them with peers and teachers) are more likely to be successful in an age of innovation and uncertainty.

Arthur L. Costa, Describing the habits of mind, p. 35

This chapter explores how to implement two design principles to gradually hand over more ownership to the children. They are:

11.   Allow increasing amounts of independence.

12.   Give students more responsibility.

The elements of learning power that will be most in play here are those in the *reflection* category.

Why do we need to build up children's independence and willingness to take responsibility? Because they will need these attitudes in life, and because – in the traditional classroom – they tend to be neglected. Without thinking, teachers often do too much for children. We remind them, we rescue them, we explain things to them at the first opportunity, we tell them what to do, and we often tell them what is right and what to think. This is all well and good, indeed it's necessary – up to a point. But if we do it all the time – if we fall into a habit of always thinking for the children, rather than getting them to think for themselves –

> If we fall into a habit of always thinking for the children ... we may be building up the wrong kinds of habits in them.

we may be building up the wrong kinds of habits in them. They can get so used to being in a highly regulated environment that when they are faced with greater uncertainty and no one is there to rescue them, they become helpless. Employers always say that they want the people who work for them to show initiative, and complain that too many of them seem unwilling or unable to do so. Yet these individuals almost certainly weren't born that way; they were very resourceful as toddlers. Somewhere along the way they seem to have lost that spark of initiative and self-reliance, and we must make sure that our schools and our classrooms aren't the places where this happens.

In this chapter we talk about a variety of ways to gently – but relentlessly – wean children off their dependence on an adult, and to coax them into discovering and expanding just how much they can do for and by themselves – individually, and with a little help from their friends.

First, let's expand on some of the potential benefits of training your learners to take more responsibility for their learning.

- As we have said, children will need to be able to think for themselves, especially about what they need to learn and how they are going to learn it. There is one simple reason for this: they will not be followed around by an obliging teacher who tells them what to do for the rest of their lives. At some point they will each need to be resourceful and self-reliant, so teaching in a way that makes them come to depend on us is not in their long-term interests.

- The amount of cossetting they will get at college or university is much less than they get at a traditional school. So to flourish in further and higher education, they will need that independence.

- Showing initiative in the workplace – as well as having the nous to ask questions when you need to – is more likely to get you appreciated and promoted. And if you are going to be self-employed, the need for that proactive spirit is beyond question.

- Children respond to the expectations of those around them. If you give them responsibility, most of them rise to the challenge. This develops their self-esteem and self-belief: qualities that are especially important to cultivate in children who are lacking in confidence.

- You tend to get more buy-in from the children when they feel involved with their learning process. They feel greater ownership over what goes on in the classroom, and that is motivating. As the great teacher of learning Chris Watkins says, children are more engaged when they see themselves not as passengers on the good ship Education, but as crew – and, we would add, they should increasingly see themselves as "officers".[1]

+ Children often have better ideas than you do. They can come up with neat ways of learning things of which you would never have dreamed. And it is very empowering for children to see their ideas being taken seriously, and making a difference to what is happening in their classroom.

+ More independent children tend, by definition, to get on with learning by themselves – on their own or in collaboration. They will treat you as the last resort when they get stuck rather than the first. You will hear much fewer of those doleful cries of "I don't get it, Miss" or "I can't do it, Sir." Apart from the intrinsic benefit, this frees you up to spend your time in different ways: working with the children who need it most; wandering round and prodding them to think more deeply about what they are doing; eavesdropping on groups so you learn how they are thinking; and making your teaching more effective by adjusting your interventions accordingly.

+ Children who are thinking things through for themselves learn more effectively and more deeply. Instead of merely trying to remember what they have been told, they understand it, and this means they can draw on what they know more flexibly and more creatively.

As well as the benefits, there are some hurdles that you may encounter on the journey towards this greater independence. First, some children – those with what you might call "acquired weakness of learning syndrome" – may not like it to begin with. They have become so used to being rescued and protected that they feel anxious – and therefore become upset or resistant – when asked to think or do things for themselves. Some of them may try, in various ways, to get you to change your mind and go back to the comfortable old way of doing almost everything for them. You have to be ready to resist this pressure. Go slowly and gently, by all means, but don't backtrack.

Second, parents and carers who are used to treating their children with kid gloves may also distrust or dislike the fact that their children are being required to take more

---

1   Chris Watkins, *Classrooms as Learning Communities: What's in It for Schools?* (Abingdon and New York: Routledge, 2005), p. 35.

responsibility and show greater independence at school. They may demand to know why you are not "teaching them properly" – so you, and your school leaders, will need to be ready with a good rationale as to why this "toughening up" is in the children's long-term best interests. You may need to explain that, once the children have got used to thinking for themselves, the vast majority of them will rise to the challenge and enjoy "being more grown-up". They may even start to suggest more ways in which they can take responsibility.

Third, this way of teaching requires you to be willing to share rather more control with the children than you may be used to. As the children get the bit between their teeth, you may have to keep adjusting the balance between keeping things safe and orderly – and ensuring they learn what they need to know – and letting them explore new areas of responsibility. Sometimes you will judge that they are not yet ready for what they are proposing and will have to say no – but do always explain why. However, you will also need to keep thinking, "Perhaps they could ..." or "I wonder if I could let them have a go at ..." You may have to keep adjusting your expectations of how much control to keep.

> You can visualise what has happened in the past, what can happen in the future. It can help your belief in achieving something. It helps you with tasks as you can visualise what work could look like.

Some teachers have come to feel that it is a core part of their job to do all the managing, designing, and controlling of learning in the classroom. They may be concerned that the quiet order they've worked hard to establish could be jeopardised. Or they may worry that they will become deskilled if the children start playing a bigger role in making the decisions that have always been part of the teacher's professional expertise. So we will offer some suggestions about how to make this transfer of ownership so gradual that these "shocks to the system" are minimised – both for you and for the children. Bravery may be required as you take each little step, but hopefully not a daunting amount.

Developing Independence and Responsibility

✓ Offer simple choices about how to present learning.

✓ Open up discussion and choice around noise levels.

✓ Create opportunities for the children to plan and organise their learning.

✓ Open up discussion about what the children think they need to learn next.

✓ Involve the children in taking ownership of their classroom.

✓ Ask the children to determine their own success criteria.

✓ Ask for feedback on how to improve lessons.

✓ Involve the children in planning their own projects.

✓ Create opportunities for the children to teach one another.

✓ Enable the children to judge when they need support from a teacher.

✓ Timetable planning time or thinkering studios.

Dipping Your Toes In

There are probably already some ways in which you have handed responsibility and ownership over to the children. They might be in charge of looking after different parts of the classroom; watering the plants, giving out the books, or cleaning the board. In this section, we are hoping to invite you to nudge that responsibility a little further, so they are not just "teacher's little helpers" but, purposefully and gradually, have more opportunities to move into the driving seat of their learning.

First of all, it would be useful to take some time to reflect on where you are now.

Wondering

What responsibilities do the children have already in your classroom? Who decides on these responsibilities? You or the children, or both?

How do you decide who gets to do what? Do you bestow little responsibilities as rewards for good behaviour? What message would this way of selecting children send to them, or to the rest of the class, do you think?

How often do the children decide how or what they are going to learn? Sometimes? Never? Often? How do you involve them in this process?

Do the children have chances to reflect on what helps them to learn? Where they sit? Who they sit with? How they are affected by noise levels in the classroom?

Are the children involved in developing the classroom environment? How?

Do the children give feedback on your lessons? How do you respond to their feedback?

Now that you've had a chance to reflect, you might want to delve into some of the ideas below, bearing in mind what you already do or how you could thread new approaches into your classroom practice. As you try things out, try to be aware of the effect you are expecting or hoping for, and notice when and in what ways you might be feeling pleased – or disappointed – with the result.

Offer simple choices about how to present learning

One simple way in which you can hand ownership over to your children is to give them options as to how they can present their learning. Even this tiny tweak can have a profound impact on the children's engagement. By giving the children options, you are sending the message, "I value you all as learners and I trust you to choose the best option for your learning."

Options are commonplace in Becky's classroom. One example occurred when the children were exploring onomatopoeic words. Some chose to record on whiteboards, some used big pieces of sugar paper, others made annotations in their books. This happened to be a lesson during which the school governors were doing a learning walk. As they walked into the classroom, some children with behavioural difficulties jumped out of their seats, exclaiming, "Come and look at what we're doing! We love this!" This wasn't a "showy" lesson, but the fact that the children had that choice motivated them to become this absorbed in their learning.

Sandringham School also hand over ownership to the children as often as they can. For example, recall Emma O'Regan's Year 5 lesson on writing factual reports, which we described in Chapter 5, in which the children were given time to plan the formatting of their work, as well as the content. They were delighted that they could write all the way across double-page spreads in their books, as opposed to sticking to a single page. You could tell the children proudly that they are "being graphic designers" to give this even more kudos. In another lesson, children were presenting their learning in different ways in maths, demonstrating the various methods they were using to solve a problem. Below are some photos of their books. The children took great pride in their work because they had the space to present it how they thought best, bearing in mind their audience.

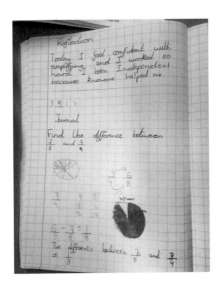
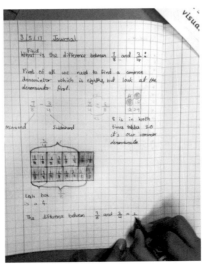

Children can also decide how they are going to demonstrate their understanding of a topic. You could offer them a menu, or – perhaps if they are a bit more experienced – let them make up their own methods. For example, in science they might perform a demonstration experiment, or decide to have one child interviewing another about the topic, or have one child demonstrate by teaching the idea to the rest of the group. In English they could show the development of a narrative through creating a graphic storyboard or by acting out vignettes, as well as through extended writing.

Open up discussion and choices around noise levels

Have you tried to open up a discussion with the children about what noise levels are best for different kinds of learning? For example, when reading, the children might need the classroom to be quiet, and when collaborating or investigating the room might be filled with excited chatter. Try sharing this observation with the children and ask them what noise levels would be best in each lesson and why. If the noise levels change undesirably, stop the class and ask them to refer back to their discussion.

Becky does this through the use of a "Voiceometer", which is positioned by her whiteboard. It has four levels:

1. Silent ninja

2. Whisper spy

3. Low flow

4. Loud crowd

At the beginning of the year, and at points throughout, the children practise what each level should sound like, therefore maintaining an understanding of the difference between each.

A teacher friend of Guy's had great success with getting her Year 5 class to think about the effect of background music on their learning. They had a discussion about the kinds of music they enjoyed listening to while doing their homework, and raised the question of whether different kinds of music might be conducive to different kinds of learning. The teacher told them that some people claimed that Mozart was the best music of all for learning, and she played them some while they were doing a Big Write – an extended piece of writing done during class time – to see what they thought. They conducted a host of different experiments during homework time – listening to Mozart, Pearl Jam, and Adele while doing their maths, for example – and reported back on how easy or difficult it was to concentrate with different kinds of music playing at different volumes.

Create opportunities for the children to plan and organise their learning

Building on the previous ideas, you could start to ask children *how* they would like to learn. As we began to explore in Chapter 6, try asking them:

> "Would it be more effective to collaborate or learn independently? Might some of you prefer one over the other?"

> "How large should the groups be to be most effective?"

> "How could we set up the groups? What are the pros and cons of it being me who decides who works with who? Do all the groups have to be the same size?"

> "Where would it be best to sit?"

> "Would it be more effective to learn at tables, on beanbags, or on the floor? Inside or outside?"

Maybe you could start to experiment with getting children to plan their own timetables. Many early education centres start coaching 4-year-olds to think about how to plan their day.

A more focused example comes from David Kehler's Year 5 class at Christian College Geelong in Australia. It was a Thursday morning when Guy visited, and the first thing David did was to give the children a list of learning jobs he wanted them to complete by the end of the next day. For the first half hour, the children worked in pairs to plan their timetables. The discussions were fascinating, and considered a wide range of factors. Which topics should the children tackle while they were freshest in the morning? Which were likely to be the most — and least — enjoyable ones, and should they do the fun things first — so they wouldn't be distracted by looking forward to them — or should they do the less agreeable tasks first and save the fun things up as rewards. Several of the groups likened it to deciding when to eat their least favourite vegetable on their plate.

After twenty minutes, David held a whole-class discussion in which all the children discussed some of the issues that were being uncovered. And then they were ready to start working through their timetables. Of course, all did not go smoothly, snags cropped up, and David sometimes needed to intervene to help sort things out. But on the whole, the children — as we have come to expect — rose to the challenge amazingly well.

However, note that this is far from the first time that these children have had this kind of experience. Their ability to handle responsibility of this magnitude had been deliberately and meticulously built up by David over the preceding months. He started out, as any beginner should, with significantly smaller-scale, bite-size options embedded in more conventional lessons, and then gradually increased the length and complexity of the planning that he was asking the children to undertake. Remember: LPA teachers always like to walk on the leading edge of what their classes might be ready to do for themselves.

> Remember: LPA teachers always like to walk on the leading edge of what their classes might be ready to do for themselves.

Open up discussion about what the children think they need to learn next

Find moments in the day to get children's input about what they would like, or need, to learn next. This can be done during plenaries, review time, snack time, or at the end of the day; and it can be formal or informal. See if you can get so used to having these conversations that it becomes a habit. You may find that this gives you useful insights into the children's interests and understanding, and it can also save you time and energy while planning new and exciting ideas.

For example, one of Becky's Year 1 children, let's call her Lily, starting drawing and playing hopscotch during one planning time session (these are explained in more detail shortly). The children were learning about the numbers 1 to 10 at the time, so Becky used Lily's idea to plan the children's next day's learning about ordering numbers up to 10. She shared photos of Lily playing and the children discussed how to order numbers on a hopscotch and how to play. They problem-solved, offering ideas about spacing out the numbers, how to draw an accurate square, and how to make sure the numbers were the right way round and in order, as well as how to challenge themselves – for example, by starting on a number other than 1 or counting backwards instead. Lily was beaming when she realised that the whole lesson had been planned around something she'd done. This was a child who sometimes struggled to join in, so the value of using her idea to make her feel included was immeasurable. Not only that, but hopscotch was much more engaging and

> You are making your learning your own responsibility. Nobody knows me better than me so I should be the one to decide what I need and how I need to do it.

meaningful to the other children than anything Becky could have planned without Lily's incidental input. As Carol Lloyd, a teacher, comments:

> When I make comments in class about the feedback and suggestions they [the children] have given me – and then act accordingly – their ownership of the class increases, as does their belief that they can make a difference.

> Quoted in Arthur L. Costa and Bena Kallick,
> *Activating and Engaging Habits of Mind*, p. 117

This sense of ownership could be achieved through using children's interests to plan lessons, as Becky did. It could also be achieved through using children's ideas to develop displays, like the Year 1 lesson example in Chapter 2, or by including children's comments and ideas in letters to parents, as will be described in Chapter 10 – or by any other means you or the children can conceive. All it takes is making a commitment to listen carefully to the children and finding ways to act on some of their ideas.

You could also try opening up a reflective discussion with the children about what they need to practise and improve upon. In doing so, children become more self-aware as learners and understand that everyone has different – or similar – areas that they don't "get" instantly, which require time and effort to master. Why not get them thinking and talking about how they might practise each of these areas? For example, when discussing spellings as an area of deliberate practice, Becky's children invented indoor and outdoor hiding games, look-cover-write-check games, sentence games, and tricks to remember particularly difficult words like "because". Tapping into the children's creativity and trusting them to design their own games created a buzz around learning spellings, and generated a plethora of ideas for the children to take home to teach their parents and brothers and sisters. It makes practice much less "boring" too!

Involve the children in taking ownership of their classroom

To what extent are your children involved in planning and developing the classroom environment? It's their learning space, so it might be a worthwhile discussion to have with them. You could ask the children:

"Where should the resources go?"

"How can we make it clear where everything goes?"

"What should we put on the walls? How can we use the walls to support our learning?"

"How could we arrange the furniture for the most effective learning?"

Of course, these discussions and this input takes time but it could well be a worthwhile investment. It might make them more proud of their classroom, and keen to take good care of it, if they have been involved in organising and designing it. Why not make developing the learning environment an extended project when you first meet your class? Ask the children, "What would help you to learn in your classroom?" Then use some of their ideas to help you design aspects of the space.

Ask the children to determine their own success criteria

What does "good quality work" look like? In some classrooms, this is never made explicit. Some teachers seem to think that talking to the children about the success criteria, and getting them to discuss examples of good and bad work – so they can see the difference – is somehow "cheating". We don't think it is. Everyone needs to have a good idea of what they are aiming for, otherwise they are just shooting in the dark, and children who – because of their home background, for example – are used to taking part in "schooly" kinds of games and activities have an unfair advantage. The EL Education schools are particularly good at helping their students to get a really clear idea of what success will look like before they start.

The next step beyond this, though, is to begin to involve the children in discovering the success criteria for themselves. Instead of just telling or showing them what "good" looks like, give them time to see if they can figure it out – at least in part.

For example, Guy once watched an RE lesson in which the children were learning about the idea of a "sermon". Hannah, their teacher, set them the activity of working in groups of three to prepare a one-minute sermon, to be delivered by one of their group to the rest of the class. The audience would then judge how "good" the different sermons were. Before they embarked on this challenge, Hannah got them to think, in their groups, about how the audience might make their judgements about a good sermon. The children came up with criteria such as, "It would be clearly expressed", "It would make us think", "It would link to our experience", and "It would be catchy and engaging." Hannah was pleased to find that the children's ideas were very similar to the ones that she had in mind. And she was also pleased to see that the "lower ability" children were at least as good at uncovering the characteristics of good work as their typically higher-achieving peers. After the class had designed and delivered their sermons, Hannah asked them how they felt about the exercise and they said things like:

"I felt more involved."

"It made it feel as if it was our project, not the teacher's."

"We knew how to improve and edit our presentation as we were making it."

"It made us feel more in control and more adult."

"Making up your own mark scheme makes you think more."

As a way of boosting engagement, ownership, self-evaluation, and reflection, this lesson certainly seems to have been a success.

Ask for feedback on how to improve lessons

At the end of some of your lessons, ask the children for feedback on how it went from their perspective and what you could do to improve. For example:

"How was that lesson for you?"

"What went well? What could we improve on?"

"Did you like learning like that? What could we do more of? What could we do less of?"

When Becky is going to teach in a new way, or try a risky lesson, she shares this with the class, putting herself on "high" on the learning ladder (as we explored in Chapter 4). This models her willingness to take risks to the children and also creates a safety net if things don't go to plan. She finds that by being open in this way the children seem more invested in the success of the lesson. It also creates an opportunity to reflect and ask how things have gone.

Remember to implement any suggestions you might want to try out at a comfortable pace. Don't try to do too much, too quickly, as the children might get rattled, and react in a way that makes them harder to control. Just work gradually and persistently at handing over little bits of responsibility, and take the time to reflect upon and notice the impact this is having. As you go along, ask yourself:

"How are the children reacting to this responsibility?"

"Are things developing as I'd hoped? If not, do I have any hunches about why not? What could I do to tweak what I'm doing and get things back on track?"

"Are we – both me and the children – ready for the next step? What might it be?"

Diving Deeper

To really develop the habit of independence in learning and give the children more ownership over what they are doing, you will need to let go of the reins more and more. Once you have tried out a few ideas that involve the children more deeply and actively in their learning, you can challenge yourself by getting them to feed ideas into your lesson planning and by getting them involved in larger-scale projects. In this section, we offer you some examples of giving responsibility to the children over a longer period of time, and of learning that might involve additional thought and planning.

We would advise delving into the examples that follow when you and the children have already been using the LPA for a while and are ready to tackle something more challenging. The strategies here are riskier in that they are more of an "unknown". For example, with some of these suggestions, it is harder to know in advance how they are going to turn out. And they are only likely to work well if the children are already quite powerful learners, used to collaborating with one another, happily making and learning from mistakes, and taking responsibility for planning. Of course, alongside this risk is the possibility of making the most impact and giving the children the chance to really shine as learners.

If you think it's worth the time, you could also involve the children in thinking creatively about how to redesign the timetable to allow these more open-ended activities to happen regularly. One way Becky does this is to ensure that the children have an afternoon a week to explore their own interests and develop learning in their own ways, as described in further detail later on in this chapter.

When teaching his Year 5 class, Julian Swindale adapted the timetable by planning cross-curricular teaching with the children, thus freeing up time to develop different kinds of learning activities. In fact, this "bought" him two afternoons a week to run workshops and planning time with his children. The children often use this time to teach skills and explain ideas to each other. Julian explained:

> We have a board on one classroom wall that breaks down the learning for that week or extended period into different skills or concepts. For example, for writing we had an image for paragraphs and an image for grammar skills, like using speech marks, and so on. When children felt they had grasped something and were confident enough to teach that key concept or skill, they would move a picture of themselves onto the image representing that learning. And in doing so they were saying, "Hey ... I feel I have got this and I'm happy to share my understanding with others."

> After a time, we would have a large group of children ready and keen to join in with the teaching on a given subject. We would then plan as a class which children were going to run workshops and on what. Sometimes the children would simply pair up – "I understand paragraphs and he understands punctuation so we are going to work together." The children plan how they were going to teach each concept, so they might take some of their "students" to the library to show them examples of how paragraphs have been used in books or may prepare posters or a presentation. The children know how to tune into their classmates, so they come up with creative and engaging ways to teach their friends.

> The process of teaching deepens their own understanding around a subject, as it does for any teacher. It has really embedded learning for the class and meant that everyone makes much deeper progress. I am careful to have a wide spectrum of skills on the wall so everyone can find themselves as teacher or learner at any given time – including myself. Most of all, I love how happy the children are to teach and be taught – it removes the idea that everyone has to know or grasp something at the same time like a race – the children have learned that progress ebbs and flows in different ways across the classroom and through time. It is communal understanding that is valued rather than being the first, only, or best. The tyranny of the race has been overthrown and replaced by a sense of communal responsibility. One day a child said, "We can take the image of paragraphs down now because we all feel we can teach it." The silence that followed was broken by a collective "Yeah!" and a qualification from one child, "I wonder if we could all get to teach 'stippling' and 'scumbling' when we do art." It was the communal "we" that was, for me, the game changer. Still is.

Julian and his class have become so comfortable with this co-construction of learning that he now plans everything with the children's input and ideas. The benefits, he says, are threefold. First, the children's ability to be independent has grown so much that they really are in the driving seat of their learning. Second, they are more engaged and make much better progress because they know exactly what they need to learn next and how to go about it, and they also know that they can rely on one another for support. And third, he claims that this method of teaching has significantly reduced the amount of form-filling he has to do to report on the children's progress. Sounds like a win-win-win!

As another example, Corngreaves Academy in Cradley Heath in the UK have a fortnightly "genius time" which is dedicated to children running workshops on their interests and learning gaps. Leading up to genius time, the children are encouraged to notice gaps in their learning, or learning they are struggling with, and are encouraged to independently research and improve on that area before running a workshop to teach others. As in Julian's class, the children can sign up to workshops based on their own interests and gaps. In both examples, the children are learning to take responsibility for their learning and to encourage and teach those around them. Noticing gaps in learning and areas that need practice is a skill that is nurtured and celebrated by the teacher.

Involve the children in planning their own projects

The possible ways in which the children could take full responsibility for a long-term project are endless. Could they plan, write, and perform their own play? Set up, stock, and run a café for parents? Design and run a workshop about the LPA for parents? With any group you have to make a judgement about what the appropriate next increment in responsibility might be. What do you think they could handle, with a little – but not too much – support? Your job is to offer only the minimal amount of guidance – usually in the form of a well-judged question – that is necessary to keep them on track and ensure that the project will be completed successfully, and to resist the temptation to do any more than that. You might ask, "Have you thought about what would happen if …?", "Where are you going to get the jam jars from?", "What will you do if you don't have enough small change?", and so on.

Take putting on a play as a fairly challenging example. The children could plan and take charge of anything and everything from: designing their own costumes; making posters, tickets, and banners; writing songs; deciding on parts; recognising which sections of the play need more practice; giving each other feedback and advice on performing; and choreographing any dances. If you have chosen the project well, the children will be abuzz with excitement, and a little anxiety, as they get down to planning and sharing ideas. Such projects give them an opportunity to truly unleash their creativity and for everyone's ideas and input to be valued. The children learn that their ideas can have an impact on the world around them and that they can move, entertain, and influence others through the power of their performance. It gives them a chance to exercise and strengthen a whole range of learning muscles, if not the entire set!

If your school teaches through topics, how much say do the children have in determining what they are going to investigate or where they are going to take their learning? West Thornton Academy leave space in their medium-term planning to add ideas from the children, and ensure that they follow up on these ideas in practice. Some of the children's ideas will probably mimic

> The children learn that their ideas can have an impact on the world around them and that they can move, entertain, and influence others through the power of their performance.

ones that teachers already had in mind, while others might be completely off-piste. As much as they can, the teachers make time to investigate both types of idea, whether as a whole class, or in small groups.

Becky strives to involve her children in the planning of topics. For example, her mixed Year 1 and 2 class were about to embark on a topic on *Alice's Adventures in Wonderland*. To conclude the topic, the children were going to have a Mad Hatter's tea party. Instead of planning what that would look like, Becky asked the children:

"How could we plan towards a Mad Hatter's tea party?"

"What could we make? What will we need to do? What will we have to learn?"

The children's imaginations were sparked and they were allowed to run wild – to begin with. Their ideas, and Becky's thoughts about incorporating them into learning, included:

* Making extravagant hats – which could have sparked a series of lessons on three-dimensional shapes, and thus stretching planning, experimenting, and collaborating muscles.

* Writing invitations to their friends and family – necessitating a lesson focusing on invitation writing and accuracy.

* Making chocolate soup for the party – requiring a lesson on measurement and on the roles which would be needed within a collaborative group.

* Designing table cloths – necessitating a design lesson which would develop attention and imagination.

* Researching new and exciting party ideas and games – which could trigger investigations into parties and celebrations in different cultures around the world, developing open-mindedness and acceptance.

The children created a planning board in the classroom, on which they posted and kept track of the ideas and suggestions as they grew throughout the term.

Of course, some of the children's ideas were totally impractical – you can make your own mind up as to whether or not you'd want to make chocolate soup in your classroom! Part of the discussion that Becky then orchestrated was about how "doable" the different ideas were, and the children had to make hard decisions about which ones to run with, and which had to be sacrificed. This was developing the children's accepting muscles, which is an important part of the learning process.

Create opportunities for the children to teach one another

There is a huge amount of value in creating opportunities for children to teach and learn from one another. By teaching a skill, the children consolidate and deepen their own learning. To teach well, they need to be empathetic, clear, and patient. Both teacher and learner will be stretching their sets of socialising and determination muscles. By teaching and leading each other, the children begin to understand that everyone has learning they find easier and learning they struggle with, and that it's smart to turn to others for help when you need to, as well as it being smart to offer help to those who need it. Sometimes, the children find a unique and effective way of explaining learning that just makes it click for the person they are trying to help. This reciprocal relationship can be naturally created with mixed-attainment pairs. Through coaching, reflection, and encouragement, the children learn to listen to, support, and extend each other's learning.

> By teaching a skill, the children consolidate and deepen their own learning. To teach well, they need to be empathetic, clear, and patient. Both teacher and learner will be stretching their sets of socialising and determination muscles.

Reciprocal reading is an effective way to develop this kind of mutual coaching. Becky observed a demonstration lesson at School 21 during their Great Oracy Exhibition – a conference showcasing great oracy practice from across the country. Four 11-year-olds worked together without support from an adult to discuss their class text. They negotiated their own roles from the following list (which were outlined in Table 6.2):

• predictor

• questioner

• clarifier

• summariser

One of them read out loud, while the other members of the group interjected with comments by putting their thumbs up if they wanted to question, clarify, or add to what had been said. Every paragraph or so the summariser recapped what had been discussed so far and drew in any members of the group who may not have contributed yet – for example, by asking the predictor what they thought might happen next. The clarifier made notes as they went along so they could track what had been said, and the questioner thought up questions to "test" the group members on their understanding. The group discussed their text for twenty minutes without adult support.

Of course, to achieve this level of independence took a great deal of focused coaching. Their teacher commented that she would often generate and plant "seeds" of ideas about how the children could improve by asking a group to model reading while the rest of the class reflected on how well they were working together. The children commented that sharing the process of reading in this way had led them to understand texts more deeply and that they now naturally make use of these different roles "inside their own heads" when they are reading independently. Although these children were only 11, they commented that they thought this approach would have helped them get to grips with reading better when they were younger. When children are coached and given a clear model to aspire to, they really can drive their own learning.

As well as homing in on the specific skill of reading, you could make time for children to teach others in the class about anything that they are interested in. Gemma Goldenberg at Sandringham School tried this with her Year 6s. Each child was given a chance to teach the others about their area of interest. Some chose to deliver more traditional lessons, like mastering a mathematical concept, but others had more "out there" ideas, like teaching the class yo-yo tricks or tips for playing computer games. Gemma commented that this opportunity gave the children a chance to shine and gain confidence in speaking to a large group.

You could also create "provocations" that invite children to dig deeper into their learning. In West Thornton Academy some of the classrooms have an investigation corner, where the children can choose to delve into difficult problems. Sometimes these are very hard problems – such as questions taken from an A level maths paper. Sometimes the corner features a curious object or picture for exploration – for example, in one Key Stage 2 classroom we saw a picture of a DNA helix. This prompted several children to investigate cell structure using the Internet. Of course, they need space and trust to research independently and this had been built up over time. As a result, they then spontaneously created a video to explain the parts of a cell, and built a model replica of DNA to bring some of their explanations to life. They shared this video with their classmates to teach them about their findings, as well as sharing it with parents. It might be worth considering how you could create the space for such investigations in your class. Sugata Mitra's self-organising learning environments (SOLEs) use this idea extensively, and he has a collection of lovely Big Questions to get the children going, such as "Why do people dance?" and "What would happen if all the insects died?"[2]

> I like to be curious and wonder about things. If there was a box and you weren't allowed to open it, I would be curious about it. Curiosity helps me to be excited about my learning.

2   See www.theschoolinthecloud.org.

Enable the children to judge when they need support from a teacher

As the children develop greater self-awareness and become more honestly reflective learners, you could begin to ask them to decide when they need support, and what might be the best source when they do. You could do this simply by asking them, "Do you think you …

"would like to complete this learning independently?"

"would like to learn with a friend for support and ideas?"

"would like to learn with an adult for support?"

In this way, children can begin to confidently judge how much support they think they will need.

West Thornton Academy take this a step further. In every classroom, the children sometimes learn with the help of an adult in a "guided group", but otherwise they have a list of independent opportunities and challenges that extend or support their learning for that week. The children choose when, where, and who they learn with, and independently design, carry out, evaluate, and complete their independent learning.

At West Thornton Academy, the children are explicitly taught how to reflect and to understand themselves better as learners. For example, the class teacher might run a workshop on speech marks (which we used to call "inverted commas" or "quotation marks") at a set time. The children are asked to think about whether they need to develop their use of speech marks and, if they want to, they can sign up to the workshop. Students at West Thornton Academy made the following comments about these workshops, or "surgeries", as they call them:

> If teachers are the only ones choosing children who need surgeries – there's no point. We might have learned things at home after a lesson and not need a surgery. Also, some children need more time to understand something properly so they can sign up for a surgery if they want it.
>
> Shiyamol, Year 5

> Choosing when and how we do things teaches us to manage our time and think about the order we do tasks. It benefits me because it's making me more independent – especially thinking about the future.
>
> Ella, Year 5

> Surgeries help me to do even better in my learning. I get to collaborate with my friends who also don't understand yet, which makes us a powerful team and we can persevere and work it out together.
>
> Jemy, Year 3

Timetable planning time or thinkering studios

Again, creating time for children to plan and develop their own projects and pursue their own interests has a two-fold impact:

1. It uses, stretches, and strengthens a whole range of learning muscles.

2. It values all the children's ideas, giving them space to bring a bit more of themselves into the classroom. This develops investment in learning and creates an inclusive classroom.

There are several ways in which you can give the children time to develop their own projects. Some schools create space in the timetable for such "planning time", "thinkering studios", or "independent learning". Children can use this time to practise a skill they need to develop, such as times tables, handwriting, or spelling. They can also develop their own longer-term projects, such as writing their own novels and non-fiction books; building and designing bridges, castles, houses, or museums; researching an area of interest; creating and developing shows; writing songs; designing and attempting tricky maths problems ... the possibilities are endless! And you can plan this time in any way you and your class see fit.

The point is, the children have the space to develop something they are interested in and they understand that the focus is on *challenge*. It's a great time for new collaborative relationships to develop and for the children to have a moment to take stock. Of course, this time needs to be planned and resourced well and the children need to be involved in a continuous dialogue about its use and purpose for it to be as effective as possible. Learning should be planned, discussed, and reviewed as it develops, and the teacher plays an essential role in nudging learning on.

Wondering

Do you give your children enough planning time, and enough opportunity to get involved in longer or more challenging projects of their own devising? Could you give them more? What difficulties might you encounter, and how could you minimise them?

Do you regularly give the children choices about the amount of help or support they need?

In general, do you think you habitually walk on the leading edge of what your children might be ready to do for themselves, or do you sometimes do too much "because it's easier"?

Do you give your children plenty of opportunity to teach and support each other? Can you think of one way in which you might be able to do this more? Do you think you might get any push-back from parents, especially those of high-achieving children? Are you ready to "hold the line" and explain to them why reciprocal teaching will help their child learn?

Bumps Along the Way

To conclude this chapter, here are some of Becky's thoughts on how to deal with possible bumps you might encounter as you try to get the children ready to be more independent and responsible learners.

What if ...	Try this ...
You let them choose how to record their learning and it is a mess! It certainly doesn't look like quality learning.	Here are some ideas I have tried to ensure a high quality of work alongside ownership and choice over its presentation: • Come up with shared success criteria before the lesson. For example, "I need to present my learning so that others can read it" or "I need to plan how to set out my work carefully before starting." • Support children's choices, even if you think they might not work. Nudge them through questioning – for example, by saying, "How will you make sure your presentation is clear to the reader?" • Open up a discussion with the children after the learning, asking them to reflect on their choices and presentation. You could ask, "Do you think you made a good choice about how you presented your learning? Why? What effect does it have on the reader?" Presenting work well independently is a learning curve too! Like taking the stabilisers off a bike, children are bound to wobble a bit at first.

What if …	Try this …
You try to give the children ownership and use their ideas but the whole lesson goes haywire!	This might be a cue to you to rein things in a little and take stock. Don't be too hard on yourself or the children – you've been brave enough to leap into the learning pit! This could be a great opportunity to model being a learner. I've often said to the children before a lesson, "I've never tried a lesson like this. It's going to be a challenge for all of you and for me. If it works, I think it might be great, but if it goes wrong, that's my fault and we'll need to try again." I put myself on "high" on the learning ladder to show I'm really challenging myself. If it goes wrong, I gather the children back, let them know the lesson hasn't gone to plan, and ask them what I – and they – need to do differently next time. This is a completely different vibe to getting cross, gathering them back, and making the interruption feel like a punishment. It builds trust with the children and models to them that you are willing to learn from your mistakes. Try to reassess what the hiccups were and how you would adjust them next time, just like you'd do with any lesson.
There's not enough freedom in the timetable to hand over ideas to the children; there is too much to get through and seemingly no room for manoeuvre.	This is a very real problem in most classrooms. It's a big enough challenge just trying to get through curriculum content without thinking about handing over ideas and ownership to the children! The first point to consider, though, is that most of the ideas in this chapter don't take up any extra time, they just involve a slightly different way of thinking. Guy has suggested that teachers walk around with a thought bubble above their heads, asking, "I wonder if they can do this for themselves yet?" I would suggest another one, "I wonder how I could involve the children in planning or developing

What if ...	Try this ...
	this learning?" By beginning to think in this way, you will start to find ways to incorporate this into your usual practice.
	Also, take a second to reflect on who are you doing this for, and why. For yourself? For Ofsted? For the children? A bit of all three? If it is mainly a bit of decoration to please someone else, then you might want to let it go. But if you really believe this is for the long-term benefit of the children, then just keep looking for opportunities, large or small, to work on building up their independence. If you look, you will find them. And even if they are only small tweaks, rather than large revolutions, please try them. You'll find it is worth it.
You plan a longer-term project with the children, which starts off OK, but then loses direction – and some of the children!	Planning a longer-term project is a big step so, first of all, congratulate yourself for being brave! Also, remind yourself why you have embarked on this project; because you want to help your children build planning, reflection, and collaborating skills, and don't want to diminish this learning by doing it for them. Right now, you're all in the learning pit and perhaps you can't quite see a way out. Why not discuss this with the children? Gather your thoughts and take stock. Have a circle time or whole-class discussion about what has gone well and how far you have come – raise the team morale. Julian Swindale often embarks on whole-class, large-scale projects. He talked to me about how he sees the teacher as being the leader of a pack: so, what does a leader do when everyone is a bit lost and demoralised? They help the team to see how far they've come and give them a reason to believe they can keep going. You could perhaps use a thinking routine here,

What if …	Try this …
	by asking, "What have we done so far?", "What's gone well so far?", "What could we improve on?", and "What do we need to do next?" By reflecting with the class in this way, you can celebrate the wins and plan next steps, whether that's a renewed focus or attitude change for some, or practical ideas to try out. If some children seem a bit lost you can nudge them and their classmates to think about how to get locked on to learning again. You could gently say, "Some children have finished this aspect and seem unsure about what to do next. How could we help them? How could they help themselves?" This is a new, more open-ended context in which they can learn how to get unstuck – and since it's a bit "messier", it's a bit more like real life too! By reflecting with the class in this way, you will collaboratively and collectively find a new focus and direction and be ready to get going again. In fact, I highly recommend having these discussions and reviews repeatedly during a whole-class project. There will still be bumps, but that's all part of the learning process – for you and for the children!

Summary

Polly, the daughter of some friends of Guy's, was approaching her fifth birthday and her parents kept telling her what a "big girl" she was going to be when she was five. She had slightly misunderstood what that meant, however, and had taken to measuring her height against a mark on a broom handle. On her birthday, her parents were woken at 6 a.m. by a very aggrieved-looking little girl, holding the broom. "Five," she thundered, "and still the same size!"

Most children seem to relish the idea of become more "grown-up". They like being involved in the adult world of thinking and decision-making, even if it is only at a junior level. They respond well to being treated as apprentices in the business of making the classroom, and all that goes on within it, the way it is. They feel pleased when their ideas are invited, taken seriously, and sometimes make a real difference. In this chapter we have given you an array of tools and examples – some of which we hope will have been new to you – for developing independence and responsibility. We have discussed a variety of choices which the children can be given as and when they are ready, choices about: how to present their work; about the working conditions that make for good learning; about what success will look like; about how to prioritise and sequence learning tasks; about who to work with; about when they need help; and about what kind of help they want. It is through the gradual escalation of such responsibility that their independence grows.

Chapter 9

Reflection, Improvement, and Craftsmanship

We now turn to our remaining two design principles, as we consider the attitudes that underpin lifelong learning.

10. Develop craftsmanship.

13. Focus on improvement, not achievement.

We would argue that these design principles in turn develop almost all of the elements of learning power. Craftsman-like learners need their curiosity. They need sharp eyes and good concentration. They need determination to see their projects through and to overcome the obstacles to excellence that they will meet. They need imagination to come up with good ideas, and thinking skills to work out their plans and arguments with clarity. They need to be able to receive feedback from others and engage collaboratively with them. And they need to be reflective and organised to make improvements and bring plans to fruition.

In the LPA the focus of both teaching and assessment is on improvement rather than achievement. Of course achievement matters, but the way to build that is through your endeavour to improve your own performance. So LPA teachers aim to build the children's desire to work towards the best product of which they are capable, knowing that to do so may well take time, effort, revision, and reflection. And that commitment will also expand their capacity to plan, think, and learn like a craftsperson. The focus on improvement puts children firmly into learning mode – trying to get better at things – for as long as possible, before they have to turn in a good performance, whether

> LPA teachers aim to build the children's desire to work towards the best product of which they are capable, knowing that to do so may well take time, effort, revision, and reflection.

that be in an examination, in a concert, or on the sports field. A relentless focus on achievement tends – if we are not careful – to put them into performance mode, not just on the occasions when they need to be at their best, but all the time. And this, of course, negatively impacts on their learning. Learning mode should be their default: the way of being they return to when there is no pressing need to be a performer, or to be protecting or defending themselves.

There is a video on YouTube, which you may well have seen, about Austin's butterfly.[1] In it, Ron Berger – he of the EL Education schools – is seen telling the story of Austin's butterfly to several groups of schoolchildren, ranging in age from 4 to around 11. Austin is a 6-year-old boy in a first-grade class at Anser Charter School in Boise, Idaho, in the United States. In his class they are learning to do accurate scientific drawings by copying photos, and Austin has chosen a tiger swallowtail butterfly.

https://www.youtube.com/watch?v=hqh1MRWZjms

His first attempt is not very good; it is as if Austin has just drawn his generic idea of a butterfly rather than looking carefully at the photo. In some schools, the teacher would make an encouraging comment and Austin would be on to the next thing, but not in Anser Charter School. His first draft is shown to a small group of his classmates, and they are coached by their teacher to offer Austin helpful suggestions about how he might improve by making a second draft. In the film, Berger shows the first draft to the children and asks them to volunteer the kinds of comments that might be helpful. As they make their suggestions, he

---

1 Ron Berger, "Critique and feedback – the story of Austin's butterfly" [video] (8 December 2012). Available at: https://www.youtube.com/watch?v=hqh1MRWZjms.

gently coaches them in how to offer feedback that is respectful, but also specific enough to be useful.

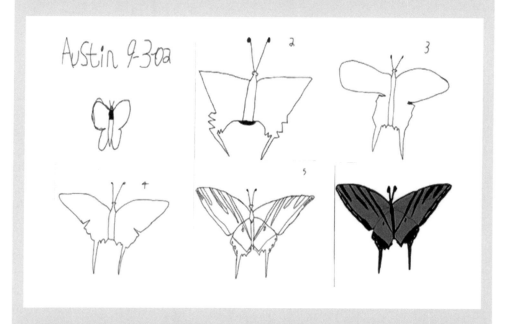

As the story unfolds, Austin produces not just two but a total of six drafts, each one an improvement on the last, until the sixth is really very good. Austin is, according to Berger's account, cheerful and committed throughout this process, and is justifiably proud of his final drawing. He has produced something that neither he nor his teacher knew he was capable of – and that is a mightily motivating experience. The groups of children listening to the story are also engrossed, and are clearly willing Austin on, wanting to find out just how good a draftsman he can be. One 4-year-old called Hadley is clearly fascinated by the idea of a "draft". She keeps using the new word out loud – "That's his third draft", "He could make a fourth draft" – as if she is getting used to the possibility that what you produce need not be judged either good or bad, but can instead be seen as a step towards getting better. At the end when Berger asks the children what they could learn from Austin's story, Hadley says, "You can make other drafts if it's not right", and you can tell by the gleam in her eye that this is an exciting and liberating discovery for her. One of the older girls, Cindy, responds to Berger's question by saying, "You don't want to just use what's in your head; you want to use your sharp eyes."

This story nicely captures the spirit of this chapter. It epitomises the LPA's approach to improvement through drafting, and the crucial role of critical reflection by the learners themselves as they take on board feedback from their peers. And it also illustrates the deliberate development of an attitude of *craftsmanship* in children; the willingness to put in the effort required, and the acceptance of critique from others, in order to come out at the end with something that is as good as you can possibly make it. Berger summed it up in the title of an earlier book, *An Ethic of Excellence: Building a Culture of Craftsmanship with Students*.[2] And this really does apply to all students – even those who are only 4 or 6 years old, or who are achieving poorly in conventional terms. Craftsmanship is underpinned by a number of our learning powers; including persevering, concentrating, imagination, accepting feedback without getting upset, and the attention to detail provided by those "sharp eyes". And a culture of craftsmanship in the classroom also means the children develop the ability to give feedback in a kindly, precise, and practical way – skills that you can see Berger coaching in his young audiences.

> Craftsmanship is underpinned by a number of our learning powers; including persevering, concentrating, imagination, accepting feedback without getting upset, and the attention to detail provided by those "sharp eyes".

You may be thinking that Berger's approach somewhat resembles the work on formative assessment, or assessment for learning (AfL), popularised by Dylan

---

2   Ron Berger, *An Ethic of Excellence: Building a Culture of Craftsmanship with Students* (Portsmouth, NH: Heinemann, 2003).

Wiliam, but there is a difference of emphasis.[3] In many schools, teachers see it as *their* job to provide the critique, carefully showing the children how to narrow the gap between their current efforts and the quality of work needed to get the required grade on a test. In the LPA, however, the emphasis is on the teacher deliberately coaching the children so that *they* can do the bulk of the diagnostic work for themselves, both individually and in collaboration. In the LPA there is also a recognition that the goal is not just to get a good mark, but to strengthen and broaden the general attitude of craftsmanship so it is applicable to a wide range of real-world situations. So AfL is a good step along the way, but the LPA is more methodical in deliberately growing and deepening children's ability to evaluate and design learning for themselves. It also takes a longer-term view of the desired outcomes of schooling, looking beyond the horizon of the next high-stakes test to the "ethic of excellence" that will last a lifetime.

> You can't just say you're finished, you keep working on things. You can keep making things better and reflection is not a learning power you are ever really done with.

In general, therefore, we recommend designing your teaching so that the children have frequent opportunities to make several attempts at a piece of work before it is ready to be "marked". We'll make some concrete suggestions about how to weave this into your lessons shortly. And we also recommend that you shift the focus of assessment from a series of disconnected, one-off tests to evaluations that track personal improvement over time. Research shows that it is much more motivating for students to be focused on how their own performance is improving, than on a series of marks or on comparisons with the rest of the class.[4]

Of course you will hear echoes of the earlier chapters, and the other design principles, in what you are reading here. Craftsmanship requires you to be in learning rather than performance mode most of the time. It needs you to look on your mistakes and

---

3   See for example, Dylan Wiliam, *Embedded Formative Assessment*, 2nd edn (Bloomington, IN: Solution Tree Press, 2017).

4   Terrence J. Crooks, The impact of classroom evaluation practices on students. *Review of Educational Research* (1988), 58(4): 438–481.

half-baked attempts not as reflections of your limited ability, but as pointers along the way to developing excellence. You certainly need to be a clear communicator and a good collaborator. Furthermore, you need to be fluent in learnish if you are going to be able to think and talk about the process of your own learning, and how to improve it. But in this chapter we home in on the role of reflection and self- and peer-critique in particular.

The Benefits of Focusing on Improvement and Reflection

For nearly 25 years it has been known that students with more elaborated conceptions of learning perform better in public examinations at age 16.

Chris Watkins, *Learning, Performance and Improvement*, p. 9

Table 9.1 summarises some of the benefits of working on building the attitudes of reflection, self-evaluation, and self-awareness that underpin craftsmanship. As you will see, we think there are significant benefits for teachers as well as for the children.

Table 9.1: The Advantages of Building an Attitude of Reflection

Advantages for the children	Advantages for teachers
Develops a built-in reflective voice. Homes in on noticing skills. Cultivates a positive attitude towards learning from mistakes. Builds resilience. Develops the attitude and skills needed to receive and act on critical feedback from employers in the future.	Impacts on progress. Reduces unnecessary marking. The children enjoy the process of reflecting on and improving their learning rather than finding it a chore – reducing resistance and behavioural issues. The children will take greater care over and pride in their learning. Builds a more generous and supportive classroom atmosphere as the children become more focused on their own self-improvement, and on helping rather than competing with others.

As you can see, the benefits of craftsmanship – and its underpinnings – are tangible. For the children, learning to think and talk about their own learning gives them greater independence and confidence. It builds their capacity for self-evaluation and self-correction, and their general awareness of "what works" and "what doesn't" as far as their own learning is concerned. That self-awareness helps to develop a calmer attitude towards difficulties and mistakes; the children panic less and think more about how they can rescue the situation for themselves. It makes them more open to advice about how to improve their work and builds their skills in giving feedback to others in a kind and helpful way. Children with these attitudes are more enjoyable to teach: they are less reactive and less dependent on the teacher for guidance and "control". And as the children develop that ethic of excellence, so they become less satisfied with just "getting it done", and more intrinsically motivated to do the best job they can, so levels of performance and achievement increase. You may also find that your workload lightens somewhat as the children get used to thinking for themselves.

Reflection, Improvement, and Craftsmanship

✓ Develop a language for reflection.

✓ Find time to focus specifically on reflection habits.

✓ Thread in reflective thinking routines.

✓ Design rubrics to structure feedback.

✓ Explicitly teach self- and peer-evaluation.

✓ Continually give and develop verbal feedback.

✓ Reflect on how to make written feedback useful and meaningful.

✓ Add an LPA boost to Two Stars and a Wish.

✓ Use protocols that develop reflection.

✓ Build a diary room.

✓ Track learning stories.

✓ Adjust assessments to focus on improvement.

✓ Plot and feed back about the growth of learning muscles.

✓ Use reflection breaks.

Dipping Your Toes In

When it comes to assessment, you probably already have a well-oiled system that works – or works to an extent – in your classroom. But it may be that you are the one who is doing most of the work – and we want the children to take over some of that responsibility. To get going, we suggest you make time to reflect on your current practice, and begin to think about how to train the children to become more meaningfully involved in the processes of assessment and improvement. So, take some time to wonder.

Wondering

How much time do you spend marking the children's work? Do you think this always leads to improvement? If so, when is it most and when is it least effective? How do you know?

Are there already times during lessons when the children have a chance to reflect on their learning? Do they do this by themselves or with others? Is it quality time? Is there a structure to scaffold reflection time? Do you or the children refer back to reflection time and use it to develop new learning?

Do you pick apart the process of learning with the children? Do your displays reflect this process?

Is your verbal or written feedback always followed by an opportunity for the children to reflect and act on what you have communicated? More importantly still, do they have a chance to adapt their learning habits in response to your feedback?

Do you have strategies and activities to develop a range of ways in which the children can self-assess, reflect, make use of feedback, and learn how to give and take critique between themselves?

Do the children have a chance to reflect on improvements in their skills as learners? Are their collaborating, noticing, questioning, and self-evaluating muscles getting stronger over time? How do the children know this?

How well did these questions about assessment and feedback in your classroom work for you? Did answering them feel comfortable? Did any questions particularly grab your attention? Perhaps some of them highlighted areas of your existing practice that you feel are strengths, and some might have stimulated thoughts about how you might like to develop or adapt what you are already doing.

The next few sections offer you some ideas that have been tried out by other teachers and found to be useful. They are all designed to strengthen the children's disposition towards reflecting on their learning and to develop the independence and skills needed to self- and peer-assess.

Develop a language for reflection

As we have seen, the language we use in the classroom – including our body language and underlying attitudes – has a major impact on the development of all the learning muscles. For example, if you would like the children to develop a positive curiosity towards their own mistakes, but you only talk about and seem to value perfect finished work, you might find that these mixed messages mean the children never quite get the idea of learning from their mistakes. In this case, start by finding small ways in which you can send the message to children that you really do value the process of learning, with all its ups and downs. And start to talk in a way that encourages the children to think about their mistakes, and to focus on continuous improvement rather than right answers. For example, you could make comments like:

"I love the way you concentrated on your writing today and took time to reread and edit as you went, just like a real author would do."

"You were so careful to check your working out today. You took your time instead of rushing through your answers without checking."

"What a great idea to ask a friend to help you spot your mistakes – it can be so tricky to notice them by yourself."

"I can see how you've responded carefully to the feedback from your friends. You can really see the improvement between your drafts."

Find time to focus specifically on reflection habits

Dedicate time to explicitly develop the children's habits of self-reflection. For example, Becky plans a weekly maths reflection session. She takes photos of the children working on their maths during the week – and, to begin their morning challenge on a Friday, the children stick these photos into their books. They then write a reflection on the learning and thinking that was going on when the photo was taken. Becky writes a thinking routine on the whiteboard to structure the process:

+ What were you learning?

+ What was the trickiest bit?

+ What is your next challenge?

She has found that even her Year 1s write some really astute comments. When learning about counting back from 100, one child wrote:

> I was doing a number line from 100 to 0. The trickiest part was when we finished a lot of ten and then went down to the next lot of ten (e.g. 90, 89 …). Next I am going to count down from 200 in fives.

This child has definitely grasped the idea of how to challenge himself! He also has a very specific understanding of which part of counting back is difficult. By sharing this reflection with the whole class, the children pinpointed that bridging tens was a difficult skill for many of them. They then planned to practise it and collectively agreed that next week's lessons should focus specifically on this skill. Sharing this reflection raised the understanding for the whole class and involved the children in planning their next steps, making the process empowering and meaningful for them. Becky regularly uses individual children's reflections in this way to create a whole-class learning dialogue about where they are and where they

> To start with I didn't like being reflective, and I didn't see the point, but now I get it that it's better to look back and find your own mistakes and figure out how to put them right. I learn better that way. Also, being reflective helps me write better stories that have all the good things in.

think they need to go next. Through conversations like this, the children develop deeper understanding of their own progress and of their learning needs.

Sandringham School plan similar reflection time into every maths lesson. The children write about their learning as they go, as if they are explaining it to a friend or parent. At the end of each lesson, they take the time to write about which mathematical methods they used and why, as well as how difficult they found their learning that day, thus distilling their thinking and practising metacognition. You can see one of these reflections in the photos of their maths books on page 225.

Thread in reflective thinking routines

In Chapter 5, we focused on a few thinking routines that you could adapt in different contexts to build deeper thinking skills. It might be worth considering which thinking routines could be incorporated to specifically embed self-reflection. A useful one for self-improvement is, "I used to think ... now I think ..." This can also be adapted to describe actions or behaviours. For example, when reflecting on collaboration, one child in Becky's class said, "I used to take over group learning, now I let other children have a go."

You could offer the children sentence prompts to use in discussion, such as:

"I wonder ..."

"I notice ..."

"If it were mine, I would do this next ..."

"Seeing this gives me the idea to change mine in this way ..."

The sentence structures can be displayed on the whiteboard or as a poster for the children to refer to when reflecting on examples of their own or their classmates' work. If you get the children to practise critiquing their work regularly as a whole class, all the children will build their understanding of what quality looks like together. Using these kinds of prompts, sentence structures, or thinking routines can purposefully develop both the quality of children's work and of their ability to reflect productively so that, over time, they take increasingly confident ownership of the reflection and improvement process.

Design rubrics to structure feedback

Rubrics provide a structure for children to understand the areas in which they can improve their learning, and how. Depending on the success criteria for the lesson, you can design structures for the children to use to reflect on their learning and next steps. For example, you could ask children to reflect on their peers' writing through the following lens:

- Ideas – What is the main idea of this piece of writing? Is it clear? How is it backed up?

- Organisation – Are the paragraphs clearly structured?

- Voice – What tone does the writing have? What words are used to create this tone?

- Style – Does the writer use a variety of sentence lengths and structures?

By ranking the success of each aspect on a scale from 1 to 5 – with clear guidance from the teacher on the difference between the levels – children can give feedback on one another's writing, justify their claims, and suggest next steps for improvement.

Explicitly teach self- and peer-evaluation

A powerful way to encourage the development of reflection and craftsmanship is to create opportunities for children to evaluate their own, and each other's, work. In fact, learning to critique other people's work is often a useful preliminary to critiquing your own. As Michelle Worthington pointed out to her Year 3 children when they were writing about Pompeii – which we saw in Chapter 2 – noticing your own mistakes is challenging but it is a really useful ability to have. To be your own teacher, you need to be able to give yourself relevant and useful ideas for improvement.

Balance, an assessment company set up by teachers for teachers, have developed the concept of learning wheels with the aim of coaching children to self- and peer-assess.[5] Learning wheels are numbered 1–9 and displayed in the classroom for the children to use to discuss their own or their peers' journey against the success criteria, objectives, or key capacities. Through internalised, peer, or whole-class discussions, the children can identify how to move forward, reflect on, or deepen their understanding. Knowing that they may not be secure in an area of learning yet, but that they're on a journey towards the 9 on the wheel, helps embed a growth mindset. As you will see later, the Balance learning wheels can also be used to reflect on the development of learning muscles within a lesson.

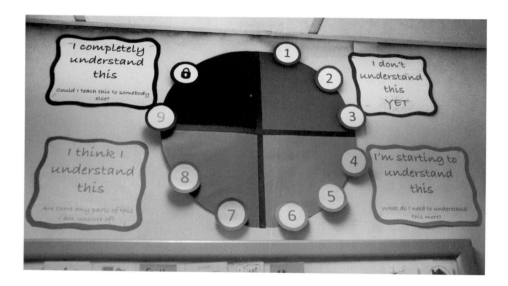

Peer-critiquing is also a very specific skill that can be cultivated directly. In order for it to be beneficial, the children need to know what effective feedback looks and sounds like, how to give and receive it, and how to respond to and learn from it. We suggest using the following guidelines as you begin to build peer-critiquing skills:

+ Use an example of a child's work to model critiquing with the class. If this is new to them, make sure you check with the child beforehand to make sure that they

---

5   See https://www.thisisbalance.co.uk/.

are happy to share their work in this way. If this is too much scrutiny for them to handle to start with, use an example from a child in a previous year, or an anonymous example from another class. Emphasise the value of learning from mistakes and what a beneficial process this will be.

- To begin with, you might tell the children what you want them to specifically pay attention to as they look at each other's work. Later on, you could share this responsibility with the children and ask them, "What do you think you'll be looking for as a good marker?" You could get the children to talk in pairs or small groups, and then, by sharing their ideas with the whole class, get them to effectively create their own success criteria. Of course, you are free to nudge their thinking so that they end up with criteria that approximate to your own! Make sure you take the time to illustrate what meeting the success criteria will look like. You could model underlining descriptive words neatly and clearly, for example, if that is an aspect the children will be looking at.

- Discuss and demonstrate the characteristics of effective, kind, and constructive feedback. Becky often role plays giving good or bad feedback with her learning support assistant. For example, bad feedback could be, "That's rubbish! Haha! I can't believe you made that mistake!" She finds the young learners in her class pay more attention when bad examples are given – it makes them laugh to see their teacher behaving badly! She asks the children to offer better ways to give constructive feedback. For example, one boy suggested, "I don't know if you noticed, but you forgot to ..." This kind of language development is key to the children feeling open to learning from their mistakes. With time, as the children become more resilient to criticism, the feedback they give and receive will not need to be so cushioned.

- As you introduce the practice of peer-critiquing, you may need to think carefully about which children to pair together, so that their experience is likely to be productive and positive. You could use the ideas from Chapter 6 to plan how to pair the children up. As the children get used to this way of working, you could start to talk to them about choosing their own partners, and the basis on which they might do so. You could discuss how to take turns to adopt the roles of learner and teacher. Children often love the idea of being the teacher.

- As they gain in confidence and experience, you can nudge the children to become more creative with their groups and roles. For example, the children in Becky's class found a way to involve everyone in the learning process when they were working in groups of three – one child's work was critiqued and given feedback, the second child focused on picking out positive strengths to build on, and the third's job was to gently point out things to improve.

- Once children have given one another feedback, they will need time to respond and improve – as Austin did with his butterfly. If you can, it is worth trying to balancing short, bite-size tasks with longer-term, more authentic tasks that require revision. For example, in writing this might mean that sometimes the children gain quick insights into the general areas that they can improve – such as spelling, handwriting, and grammar – while on other occasions, peer feedback will form part of an ongoing process of drafting, reflecting, editing, and redrafting to produce a polished final piece. It is through this continual process of revision that children will learn that their best work is often produced through cycles of rehearsal, reflection, persistence, and practice.

> *In class, as I act on other people's feedback on my work and then I also use that feedback to help others with their work. It really helps us because I learn from one bit of feedback and I have learnt to always check back on things because I know I can always make it better.*

- Regularly make time to review how the children's peer-evaluations are going. Ask them, "What's working? What isn't working? How could we make this even more useful? What would an interesting next step be?"

Continually give and develop verbal feedback

All the children – as well as the adults – in the classroom need to be in the habit of continually discussing, reflecting on, and improving their work. We need to create a culture where thinking about what you are doing, and wondering how to improve it, becomes as natural as breathing – for everyone. Thinking routines, rubrics, and visual prompts and displays will all help, but the way in which teachers talk and think aloud has a powerful impact as well. You can wonder aloud about the children's learning to invite them to reflect. For example:

"I wonder how you could make that even trickier."

"I wonder if you could do that in a different way."

"I wonder if you could explain your thinking to your partner."

You could stay to see what they do next, or you could leave these ideas sitting with them, returning later to hear how they got on. Little prompts like this nudge the children to think more deeply about their learning processes and push them to extend and explain their thinking.

The ultimate aim is for children to naturally begin to reflect without the need for adult support; for their reflective thinking routines to become second nature to them. In order to help children develop this built-in process, St Bernard's RC Primary School have created table prompts that the children can refer to during each lesson, as described in detail in Chapter 4. Figure 9.1 shows a sample table prompt the children use to develop their reflection skills. The rhino is the animal the children symbolically associate with reflection.

Reflection

Have I stopped to check that I am on the right lines?

Have I noticed how long I have left to complete the task?

Do I need to change anything?

What have I done before that could help me here?

Which learning muscles do I need to stretch more?

Why didn't that work so well? How could I alter it?

Figure 9.1: Reflection Table Prompt
Source: St Bernard's RC Primary School

Reflect on how to make written feedback useful and meaningful

Writing comments on the children's work takes a lot of teachers' time and effort. But they don't always have the desired effect. Do the children internalise your feedback and use it to continuously improve? If not, we would suggest a rethink, along the lines of some of the suggestions we've already shared. Perhaps you could have set times for the children to discuss their understanding of your comments with each other, and plan how they are going to act on them in the future. Maybe they could devise tasks for themselves, or for each other, that would require them to practise a specific improvement. Alternatively, you could try to make the uptake of feedback more effective by using visual tools such as anchor charts that clearly set out what good practice looks like.

> Think back on what you've done, reflecting on what you have learnt. It helps us improve our work and can help us in future life.

Here's another idea. When teaching in Argentina, Becky's adult learners developed a shared Google Doc to highlight common mistakes they were making in their writing. They also added elegant phrases they had used and wanted to remember. Could you develop something similar to enable your class to learn from mistakes and capture great language? It doesn't have to be online, it could be on paper. A working document like this would make a great evolving display that could be discussed and constantly developed by the whole class. Something like this would certainly encourage children to learn from mistakes, value their own ideas, build a bank of interesting phrases, and give them a greater sense of ownership over their learning.

At Corngreaves Academy, children are coached in how to give good feedback by using sticky notes. The children circulate around the classroom, looking at each other's work in progress. Each child is given four sticky notes and asked to write a suggestion on each to improve a draft produced by their classmates. Once everyone has given their feedback, the children return to their tables, each with four notes on their own draft. Their next job is to read through the feedback and decide which two notes are the most perceptive and helpful. They then begin to implement the suggested improvements. This is an effective way to open up a discussion with the children about how to give feedback that is both specific and useful.

Add an LPA boost to Two Stars and a Wish

There is a well-known routine for encouraging children to give and take feedback called Two Stars and a Wish (as well as various versions of this) doing the rounds. The idea is that one child tells another two good things about their work before offering a suggestion for improvement. It is a nice idea, but it doesn't systematically improve their ability to give and receive feedback, so it isn't really an LPA tool. But it could be. In visits to schools in Australia, Guy came across two variations that got closer to the LPA spirit.

In the first, the teacher asked her Year 4 class why they should give the two stars before they got round to the wish. The children came up with several reasons, but the main one was that often the wish can feel like a personal criticism, so to reduce hurt feelings or discouragement, the two stars help to "plump you up" so you don't get upset. The teacher then asked them how a powerful learner would respond to such feedback, and the children came to agree that they would welcome it, as it is just useful observations or suggestions to help them get better. So as a result of this conversation, the children decided that they would start out by feeding back with two stars, but then see if they could manage with just one star after a couple of weeks, as they became more robust and learned to focus on the informative nature of the feedback rather than on any emotional reaction they might have. This went so well that after another two weeks of practice the class decided that they could do without the stars altogether, and just go straight for the wish!

The second example is very simple. As well as getting the children to give each other two stars and a wish, the teacher regularly asked them to use the routine to feed back about the lesson. One child said, "I loved the examples you gave at the beginning; they really helped me to understand. And the activity was really interesting. But I would have liked it better if you had given us longer to try to work things out for ourselves, rather than jumping in quickly with the answers."

We wonder how you would react to the idea of the children giving you routine feedback on your lessons.

Wondering

Would you need the two stars before they gave you the wish?

Do you think this offers a good model of someone who is always keen to learn and improve to the children, just as you say you want them to?

Do you think this would help the children become more "conscious consumers" of their education, and, if so, would that be a good thing?

Do you see any risks in the teacher seeking feedback in this way? What are they? Can you see any way round them?

Diving Deeper

Hopefully, trying out some of these ideas and adding to or adapting the routines you already have in place will nudge you and your class along on your LPA journey. We would suggest sticking with the preceding ideas until you have embedded them completely and feel comfortable that they are part of your everyday classroom culture. To really deepen the children's sense of themselves as budding craftspeople, you might want to try some of the ideas that follow.

Use protocols that develop reflection

Here is an interesting and effective routine for the children to use to feed back to one another. Ask the children to stand in two circles, with an inner circle of children facing the outer circle. Give them a series of structured questions to prompt them to reflect on their learning. For example, you could ask:

1. What went well with your learning today? What are your "wins"?

2. What were the trickiest bits of your learning? How did you get unstuck?

3. What do you think you need to do moving forward?

4. What is still puzzling you?

5. What would you change about this lesson? What could we do differently next time?

Taking the questions one at a time, the inner-circle children talk to their outer-circle partners, whose job it is just to listen. After a minute or two they swap roles. After each question, one of the circles rotates so each child has a new talk partner.

Variations on this process could be used to share insights in maths, discuss areas for improvement in written work, critique art work, or fine-tune scientific method. As with the sticky notes example from Corngreaves Academy, the key element is that children have the opportunity to reflect with, and receive feedback from, a range of their peers. Learning from and with a range of others exposes children to a variety of viewpoints and new ways of seeing a problem.

Build a diary room

In the television show *Big Brother*, there is a diary room where contestants can go to talk to Big Brother. At St Bernard's RC Primary School, they also have a diary room where children can go to record a short video about their learning. They like to record their triumphs – for example, at having cracked a tricky problem by themselves, or having worked out a new way of explaining or understanding something. The room is set up with a tablet which the children can use at any time, and the videos of their reflections are played back on screens around the school during the day. Parents or visitors to the school who are waiting in the foyer can find themselves being regaled by excited children about their latest learning adventures.

Here are a few snippets from the diary room tapes:

"Today in PE we were learning about goal-side marking. I had to use my 'noticing' muscles. I had to intercept the ball and kick it away. I used my 'noticing' muscles to keep my eye on the ball."

"I've stretched my reflection skills today because when I wrote my letter about pets I originally chose some pretty boring words but then I made the vocabulary better."

"Today we have been learning about improving our writing in English and working together with a partner. Collaboration has helped my learning by asking questions to get everyone involved."

St Bernard's have organised the diary room as a whole-school idea, but you could easily set it up in a classroom. You could play back children's stories and reflections at the end of the day and use them as discussion points to reflect on and improve learning.

Track learning stories

New Zealand early childhood educator Professor Margaret Carr has developed an approach to tracking children's development that she calls learning stories. These are small vignettes, captured by an observer in the classroom, of a "leading edge" moment in a child's learning. A learning story might be in the form of a short written account, perhaps accompanied by photos of the child in action or of the piece of work they are engaged in. For example, here is a snippet of a learning story about a significant moment in the learning life of a 4-year-old called Nell. Nell has observed another child, Jason, making a painting tray out of cardboard, and decides she wants to do the same:

> She finds a cereal packet and says to Jason "D'you know how you can cut it? Cos I don't." ... a significant observation about Nell who up until this moment had never been seen to admit that she "didn't know" how to do something technological. She has not previously been observed attempting a technical challenge that she is unsure she can master, or asking a peer to help.
>
> Margaret Carr, *Assessment in Early Childhood Settings*, p. 66

Learning support assistants are well placed to capture these significant moments, when a child achieves a personal best in terms of their learning power. These tangible records can be displayed to encourage the children to grow in their persevering and collaborating – although you might want to write your learning stories using child-friendlier language than the example does. And they can be used as conversation starters to involve the children in reflection on their own progress. Teachers or learning support assistants can sit with a child and revisit earlier moments in their development, to give them a vivid sense of how they are progressing and growing. "Look, Nell, do you remember when you were just starting to develop your determination and your collaborating muscles, and it was quite a step for you to ask for help? But now you're much better at it, aren't you?" These techniques are now widely used in New Zealand kindergartens and primary schools, and increasingly in schools and early years settings around the world.

Adjust assessments to focus on improvement

We introduced this idea at the beginning of the chapter as it is such a big topic, so we'll only mention it briefly here. It involves designing tests and assessments that link together over time, so that the children are focusing not just on a series of isolated, one-off snapshots of their *achievement*, but on actual *progress*. By making sure that the children have time to learn from the mistakes they made on an earlier test, when the second one comes, they can see the progress they have made. "Last time, I only got 4 out of 10, but this time I got 7." This type of assessment is very motivating for children. Seeing yourself get better at something is much more encouraging than being ranked twentieth in the class, for example.

Plot and feed back about the growth of learning muscles

In Bushfield Primary School, many of the classrooms have displays on which the children can record how well their learning muscles have been functioning over a period of time. For example, one display relates to the children's ability to maintain concentration despite distractions. The children stick their photo on one of the five levels of managing distractions, which they have previously discussed as a class and all understand. This data is relayed to the head teacher, who converts them into a graph on her computer to show the performance of the class over longer periods of time. The children are delighted to look at the "worm" – the line of the graph – that shows how their concentrating muscles are steadily growing stronger. Of course, individual children could keep their own records too, and could choose which learning muscles they are going to work on for a period of time.

Using the Balance learning wheels, described earlier in this chapter, the children at St Bernard's RC Primary School regularly reflect on the development of their learning muscles. They score themselves from 1 to 9, explaining their reasoning and suggesting how they could improve next time. The children might be invited to reflect at any point in a lesson, thinking back to the last time they used the learning muscle that they are aiming to stretch, and focusing on how they could do even better during that lesson. Here are some examples of their reflections on their collaboration skills:

"I would say I've been a 7 in this class because I listened to everyone's ideas even when they were different. Maybe we could ask more questions to get other people involved."

"We were about a 3. I found collaborating hard today because we were arguing. We all had different ideas and couldn't agree. We need to take it in turns and listen to everyone's ideas before jumping in."

"I think I'm getting really good at collaborating – I'm maybe a 7 or 8! When I work with people I try to accept their ideas and also add some of my own. I could get better by giving more specific feedback and learning to collaborate with my brother!"

Use reflection breaks

When you have planned split-screen lessons that develop a particular learning muscle alongside exploring content, you could also plan in brief pauses during which the children reflect on how well they are using their learning muscles. For example, during a lesson which stretches persevering muscles, you could "press the pause button" and ask the children to reflect for a minute or so on:

"What is helping us to solve this problem?"

"What has helped us in the past?"

"What can we notice about our perseverance?"

"Who is showing really great perseverance? What are they doing? What can we learn from them?"

"What else could we use to get unstuck?"

"How can we help ourselves grow as persevering learners?"

Wondering

Which ideas from this chapter are you ready to try?

Which do you use already, but can now see a way of making more challenging?

Which ones do you think your children are not quite ready for?

How do you think you could help them become ready?

Bumps Along the Way

To round off this chapter, Becky offers some troubleshooting suggestions on developing peer feedback.

What if ...	Try this ...
There are children in the class who are so quiet, shy, or unconfident that they feel unable to give feedback – either to themselves or to a partner.	Could you or another adult give support here? If there are several pairs in which at least one partner might struggle, could they be grouped together to make it easier to provide support? You could video a pair who are really good at giving feedback and use this as a model for the

What if ...	Try this ...
	class, asking them to reflect on how effective the feedback was and why. I also get children to model in class – for example, when using talking partners I'll ask a pair to model how to take turns to speak and listen. I get them to face one another, to model paying attention to the speaker and making good eye contact, and ask them why this is important. It is a skill that will need teaching and building on throughout the year. They will all get it – but some quicker than others.
You are unsure about how to support the large number of EAL learners in the class and enable everyone to give and receive feedback effectively.	Teaching children with varied levels of English creates a brilliant opportunity to make sure expectations are clear to all as it is especially important to make sure that the content, ideas, and instructions are accessible and explained in a succinct and visual way. Here are some suggestions to bear in mind when planning to use peer feedback with EAL learners: • Think carefully about the specific elements you want the children to pick up on and feed back about before the lesson. Be specific and clear. For example, do you want them to look for effective strategies when problem-solving in maths? Or to improve their descriptive language in English? Plan this and make what they are looking for visually clear to the children beforehand by sharing and feeding back on quality examples. Use rubrics and frameworks to support and structure the feedback process.

What if ...	Try this ...
	• Can you create pictures or symbols that relate to the different aspects on which you want feedback to focus? Can the children be involved in creating these? • Utilising strong collaboration skills can be particularly effective here. Take time to pair EAL children with children who will provide a good model of language and who will be patient, sympathetic, and constructive in their feedback. • Consider using additional adults in the classroom to facilitate feedback and clarify instructions.
You teach young children who haven't yet learned to write well, or can't read their partner's writing.	When I've developed self- and peer-evaluation in Reception, I've tended to do it in the moment – so the children are less likely to forget what they have written, for example! I typically start off by building a thinking routine: "What are you really proud of? What do you think you could work on?" The children put a smiley face by the one thing they are really proud of, and I write what they think their next step might be – or they write it if they are able to. We then refer back to this next lesson. Be careful though, before you know it, there might be smiley faces all over their writing! You will need to teach them to be specific and pick just one thing. Once they have the basics of self-evaluation, you can develop peer-evaluation in the same way. Try to think

What if ...	Try this ...
	how to keep it simple and clear, then work from there.
Some children are unkind when giving feedback to their partner, saying unhelpful things like "that's rubbish!" or "I can't read it!"	Again, giving and receiving quality feedback is a skill that builds over time. The children will need to be taught how to give feedback positively. I would try pre-empting this by modelling how to give good feedback in advance, as explained earlier in this chapter. Highlight when the children are giving feedback positively. You could also use rubrics to help guide them.

Summary

Learning is all about getting better at things. It is a process that happens over time. You start out not knowing something or not being very good at it, and then you do some thinking, talking, practising, and trial and error, and you improve. Your understanding of the factors that led up to the global financial crisis of 2008 becomes deeper and more nuanced. Your free kicks curve in a more satisfying manner. Your strategies for tackling a tricky maths problem become more varied, sophisticated, and successful. To be a powerful learner, you have to want to get better at something, you need to know how to go about it, and you need to be able to track your own progress so that you know when you can be satisfied – even if only temporarily – with the progress you have made. That's what this chapter has been about: how we can teach what we have to teach in a way that builds our children's capacity and appetite for steering and appraising their own learning. We have given you a selection of ideas as to how to develop these skills and aptitudes and we hope that you will try them out.

Chapter 10

Beyond the Single Lesson

So far we have focused on strategies that you can implement in single lessons. But we are well aware that teaching involves a lot more than simply planning and delivering one-off learning episodes. You have to think about designing longer schemes of work and extended topics. You have to engage with colleagues who might either be interested in or sceptical about what is going on in your classroom. You will need to be thinking about how to help your children's parents and carers understand what you are up to, and how to win their support – especially if their child is a little disconcerted by being asked to take more responsibility for their learning. These final two points – engaging with colleagues, and engaging with parents – are what we turn the focus to later in this chapter.

You might find that the LPA way of teaching rubs up against established norms within the school, and may want to start talking to the senior leadership team about these broader aspects of whole-school culture and practice. Could broader systemic changes benefit the children? What about the length of lessons? Or the way in which the school expects reports to be written on the children's progress? Or perhaps rethinking the remit of the student council? In this final chapter we round up some of these wider issues to do with becoming an LPA teacher.

Embedding the LPA More Deeply

As you become more comfortable with the tweaks and techniques of the LPA, you may want to explore deeper and more systematic ways of developing your children's capacities as learners. There are several approaches to doing this.

First, you can think about how to involve the children directly in thinking about the long-term development of their learning muscles. You can have formative conversations with them, in small groups or individually, about their development as learners, and help them think about which learning muscles they need to work on. They may make comments like:

> "I've made a lot of progress with my collaborating skills, but now I think I need to focus more on being thoughtful and methodical about planning my own learning, and preparing for any problems that might come up."

> "I've got better at concentrating on my work, but I don't think I'm as imaginative in thinking up fresh ideas as I could be, so I need to remember to give myself 'brain time' before I dive into a painting or a piece of writing."

In many LPA classrooms each child can tell you which learning muscles they are working on at any given moment, and why.

Second, you can find ways of linking the learning muscles to your medium- and long-term planning. Take the time to think about the learning demands of an upcoming topic and ask yourself which learning muscle or muscles are going to be needed, and how you could design activities to give those muscles a good stretch. Or you might ponder whether the class as a whole has a tendency to be distractible, or disorganised, or weak in their ability to craft a detailed, logical explanation, and think about how you could harness the next few topics and themes to target the development of those capacities. Are there any thinking routines you could use as the children work their way through a topic in English or maths? If they tend to be less resilient and determined than you would like, how could you build in progressively harder levels of challenge? How could you make the activities deeper and more open-ended, so that the children really have to stretch themselves to make the grade? Could the children help you to diagnose the capacities which *they* think they need to develop? How could you involve the children

> Being in charge of my learning makes me feel proud. I am in control. It's up to me to challenge myself and if I'm not choosing work that challenges me, I won't be learning. You know your own mind so you know how to challenge yourself.

more deeply in planning and designing the kinds of activities that would stretch their learning muscles in positive ways?

First, take a moment to explore these further questions about planning to develop learning power across a series of lessons.

Wondering

What learnish might be useful in these lessons? How can you weave learnish in throughout the lessons?

How will you build reflection and craftsmanship into these lessons? What could the children reflect on? When will they reflect? At the beginning of the lesson? The middle? The end? Are there times in the week when we could specifically focus on building the skill of reflection? Would it be appropriate for the children to reflect on improvement in their learning muscles whenever they see fit, or should this be at set points?

How can you enable the children to reflect on and strengthen their learning muscles over a series of lessons? Should we concentrate on one or two this term? Which ones would be most useful to the children? What do they have to say about this?

Which lessons would be most suited to independent or collaborative learning? Or a mixture of both? Could you open up a discussion with the children about which approach would work best and why?

How can you continuously cultivate a relish of challenge within these lessons?

Are these lessons meaningful, relevant, and inspiring to the children? Will they see the point?

Once you have reflected, if you co-plan with other teachers it could be a great opportunity to share your findings about the LPA and collaboratively plan to strengthen learning capacities within your year group or key stage.

Engaging Colleagues

✓ Use window displays, doors, and notice boards.
✓ Adapt your learning environment.
✓ Reward the children for developing as learners.
✓ Link with like-minded colleagues.
✓ Mention your interest in the LPA to your year group team.
✓ Run an introductory workshop on the LPA.
✓ Talk openly to leaders about the impact you are seeing.
✓ Use the student council.
✓ Prepare an assembly to develop learning powers.

Dipping Your Toes In

Sharing the LPA can be a sticky issue. Some schools see teaching style as an inviolable expression of personality. They think that as long as you are getting good results and the children are safe and happy, it is nobody else's business to tell you how to teach. So suggesting to a colleague that there might be an alternative way of doing things can be seen as an implied criticism, or at least an unwelcome intrusion. It does no good to come across as evangelical, and you risk putting people's backs up. So, depending on the school climate, a softly, softly approach might be best, or, if your school seems open and up for it, you could start to share what you have been up to.

Whatever your situation, we've found that the best way to gain interest is to lead by example – start by making small changes in your own practice and the results will speak for themselves. Your colleagues will begin to notice changes in the way your children talk, think, behave, and learn, and many will be genuinely interested to find out more. Most teachers want the best for their children, and if they see yours being more adventurous, relishing difficult challenges, and talking in an impressively mature way about how – as well as what – they are learning, they will seek you out to find out what's behind the change. Here are just a few ideas about how – when the time is right – you can begin to broadcast what you are doing, and hopefully engage and intrigue at least some of your colleagues.

Use window displays, doors, and notice boards

The displays and notice boards in and around your classroom are first and foremost for the children and their learning. But many other people will pass by and engage with your displays – parents and carers, teachers, learning support assistants, helpers, children from other classes, senior leaders, the head teacher, and so on – which makes them a great opportunity to share what's going on in your classroom. Simple signs on the door can hook passers-by's interest. At Nayland Primary School in Suffolk in the UK you will see signs saying things like, "Watch out! Active learners in here!" or "Attention! Learnatics at work!" Not only do signs create interesting discussions with the children, but other staff, and visiting parents and carers, might wonder what is going on and ask you what they are all about.

Adapt your learning environment

Other changes to the environment in your classroom will also send signals about your philosophy and pedagogy to visitors. They might be intrigued by the fact that the layout of the furniture seems to keep changing, and you will have a chance to explain how you are aiming to stretch your learners' collaborating muscles by altering the size and composition of groups, or giving the children choices about the social arrangements for learning. If you have various drafts and works in progress on display, annotated with the children's

> Baiting your classroom walls and windows with visible signs that you are trying something different can be a non-threatening and subtle approach to sharing ideas with colleagues.

feedback and comments – instead of the usual selection of the children's best work – it makes people wonder about the purpose behind this. If you have a board celebrating the mistake of the week –as detailed in Chapter 4 – some of your visitors might think that's a good idea too, while others' first reaction might be to think you are daft. Baiting your classroom walls and windows with visible signs that you are trying something different can be a non-threatening and subtle approach to sharing ideas with colleagues, rather than trying to convert them head-on.

Reward the children for developing as learners

Do your children sometimes go to the head teacher for praise when they've shown great learning? Do they sometimes stand up in assemblies to celebrate their best work? Start celebrating the children in your class not just for the finished product, but for how they have showcased their development as strong, resilient, collaborative learners. Again, the main reason for doing this is to build your children up as powerful learners and embed the LPA values in your classroom. However, by doing this publicly, in a place where colleagues have a chance to see what is happening, some will want to know more, and this can open up a positive dialogue about what you are up to.

Link with like-minded colleagues

As you start to get the message of the LPA out there, you might find a few colleagues begin to show a particularly strong interest in your approach. Connect with these people and see if they would like to develop ideas for LPA teaching with you. This will create a support network and give you people to bounce ideas off. Inspiration breeds inspiration. If you're stuck, join Twitter – there's a great community of enthusiastic LPA practitioners out there, just waiting to share their practice. (See the Resources section at the end of the book for some suggestions.)

Mention your interest in the LPA to your year group team

If you sense your fellow teachers could be open to the LPA, suggest that you could take a few minutes in an informal meeting – over a lunchtime sandwich, say – to share what you are doing and why. Tell them about some of the quick wins you have had with the LPA and talk about the effect it has had on your class as a whole and – this is often the most powerful – on individual children who your colleagues know. We haven't come across many teachers who don't want to develop skills like concentration, empathy, and resilience in their learners. Share your current area of focus – for example, developing resilience – and see if they are interested too.

Run an introductory workshop on the LPA

If your school is on board and supportive, see if you can find a time to share your experience of the LPA with the whole staff or those from your key stage – for example, in a staff meeting or as part of a professional development day. Link with ideas that colleagues might already be familiar with, such as growth mindset. Share a little of the research behind the LPA and talk about your own personal findings in relation to the children's developing confidence. It can be powerful to share a few case studies of particular children. Short videos of the children articulating their learning and demonstrating the effect of the LPA can also have a profound impact.

Digging Deeper

As you go deeper with the LPA you might find that you begin to rub up against some structural issues which are embedded school practices – for example, the length of lessons, construction of the timetable, standard practices about marking or reporting, limited use of the student council, or attitudes towards professional development. These are not things that an individual teacher has control over; they are matters of school policy that are the consideration of the senior leadership team. We will tackle these issues from a school leader's point of view in more depth in the fourth book of this series. Here, we will just make a few suggestions about how individual teachers might go about broaching such subjects with their line managers and senior leaders, and raise the profile of the LPA within the school.

Talk openly to leaders about the impact you are seeing

Leaders are interested in how to make the biggest impact on learners. Some of this impact can be captured in the form of hard data, while other aspects may be easy to feel but harder to measure. It is not hard to tell when a child you know well is becoming more confident when asking questions, or braver about tackling new challenges, but it can be difficult to quantify. However, it would be rare to find a leader or head teacher who isn't interested in both kinds of measure. So, if you have data to show an impact on progress, share it.

For example, Becky found that her LPA teaching led many of her "lower attainers" to make accelerated progress, through coming to believe in themselves as learners, learning to relish challenge rather than feeling scared, and learning strategies to make them more resourceful in their learning. Discussion during progress meetings demonstrated the very clear impact that using the LPA was having on her learners. If you don't have data to share yet, talking about the impact on individual children – particularly on shyer children or those with behavioural difficulties – can also raise interest. In fact, if the LPA is having the effect it should, leaders will notice these changes in behaviour before you tell them.

> Becky found that her LPA teaching led many of her "lower attainers" to make accelerated progress, through coming to believe in themselves as learners, learning to relish challenge rather than feeling scared, and learning strategies to make them more resourceful in their learning.

Use the student council

Depending on the school ethos, another possible way to raise questions about whole-school practices could be through the student council. You might see if it is possible to have a discussion about the remit of the council, to see if leaders and colleagues might consider broadening it to include feedback from the children about how the school could be an even better place for them to learn. You may have to push the children to go beyond the familiar but less helpful concerns of "comfier chairs", "cleaner toilets", "better vending machines", or "less bullying" to think more deeply about what makes it easier or harder for them to learn. But soon their ideas will become more focused, and start to fall on increasingly receptive ears. You might find that this roundabout way of involving senior leaders in thinking about the more structural aspects of the school – and the ways in which they impinge on learning – works better than trying to tackle those issues head-on in a staff meeting.

Prepare an assembly to develop learning powers

Do you have the opportunity to deliver assemblies in your school? Why not plan one around resilience, learning from mistakes, or developing empathy? There are plenty of great resources to get you started. For example, you could show the children a video of an athlete, musician, or TV presenter with whom they are familiar, and talk about the great learning powers those people must possess in order to achieve what they have. Or you could read a passage from a book which opens up a discussion around empathy or learning from mistakes. You could ask them which characters in the Harry Potter series or *The Hobbit* – or whatever is currently grabbing their interest – show strengths in which learning muscles. Guy remembers an assembly a few years ago in which the children became very involved in discussing the learning strengths of the different characters in *Finding Nemo*.

You could run an assembly that really involves all the children and gets them thinking. Becky experienced an assembly like this at School 21 in London, led by Peter Hyman and fellow teachers. Attendees to the assembly were asked to consider a time when they had "used their voice" to have an impact. Everyone stood up, quietened their minds, and took some time to privately consider when they had used their voice in such a way. They then had to silently consider the sentence stem, "I want my voice to be …" After taking the time to consider this, they were asked to walk around the hall, quietly at first and without making eye contact. They then had to engage with others, first by making eye contact, then by smiling, then smiling and waving, and finally by whispering their sentence stem as they passed each other by. They played around with volume to explore the effect their voices could have, eventually building up to shouting. The children then formed groups of three and decided on roles; two told the story of how they had used their voice for impact and the third had to make a link between them. The assembly finished with the children seated in a large circle, pulling ideas together.

This assembly may be better suited to slightly older children, and would work better with a smaller group, perhaps a particular key stage or year group rather than the whole school. Remember also that the children at School 21 have spent years getting used to this kind of learning situation. You probably couldn't expect them to do this successfully right at the beginning of the LPA journey. Nevertheless, it's worth considering the impact such an assembly would have compared to the more traditional format of the children sitting in rows facing the front.

Wondering

Which format actively includes every member of the audience?

Which format actively builds the children's confidence?

Which format gets the children reflecting on their life experience?

Which format is most inclusive?

Which format purposefully builds collaboration and oracy skills?

Engaging Parents and Carers

✓ Write letters home about learning powers.
✓ Use window space and notice boards to bring the LPA to life.
✓ Use learnish in parents' meetings, letters home, and reports.
✓ Make links with home.
✓ Run a workshop for parents and carers about the LPA.

Dipping Your Toes In

Overall, we have found the majority of parents and carers to be receptive to and supportive of the LPA. Once they understand that it aims to develop their children as learners as well as their ability to do well on the tests, they tend to get on board and wholeheartedly support what you are doing. However, to reach this level, you will need to find strategies to raise their understanding of the LPA and to help them see how it benefits their child's learning. Here are some ideas that we have seen used to successfully include families in their child's learning journey and deepen their understanding of the LPA.

Write letters home about learning powers

Do you send weekly newsletters or curriculum updates home? Why not start to include information about which learning powers you are developing with the children? Perhaps you have a weekly or termly focus? You could write a couple of lines about how and why you are developing certain learning dispositions, and even invite feedback about how these learning dispositions are being developed at home. This not only informs parents and carers about how and why the children are learning to become more independent learners, but also gives them an opportunity to continue developing and stretching those learning muscles at home. Why not involve the children? Could they write a letter home explaining how they have been stretching their learning muscles? Letters from the children often get much more attention than those written by their teacher!

Use window space and notice boards to bring the LPA to life

As we have mentioned, window displays, doors, and notice boards provide great opportunities to invite discussion, provoke, and engage with other adults within your school community. Parents and carers often spend time looking at what is on display in the classroom windows when they drop off and pick up children, which makes those windows the perfect space for sharing some of the things you are doing. Put up notices about how you are developing the LPA. Display photos of children showing particularly great persevering, noticing, or analysing skills, with a short description to explain why this is important. This is even more powerful if written in child-speak.

Drip feed key ideas that underpin the LPA – such as learning from mistakes and valuing effort – into the displays. Becky displayed a large cellophane "yet" in her window for a term, challenging parents to use the word with their children as often as they could when they said they couldn't do something. Parents commented on what a positive difference it had made to family conversations around learning. Sometimes it's the most simple ideas and changes that can have the most profound impact.

If you're feeling brave, you might want to turn your classroom and the corridors that surround it into an exhibition to celebrate children's learning at the end of a project or topic. Share the idea with the children – they could plan displays and think about how to communicate with their audience. For example, they could create brochures about the exhibits or write letters home, inviting families along. As part of the planning for and reflection on the project, challenge the children to discuss

and comment on which learning muscles will be stretched at different times. On this page is a photo from St Bernard's RC Primary School, where the children concluded their songbirds project with a museum exhibition.

Use learnish in parents' meetings, letters home, and reports

When sharing the children's learning with parents and carers, both formally and informally, begin to talk about their skills as learners as well as their academic progress and achievements. Celebrate the children's successes and improvements in perseverance, attention to detail, concentration, and ability to work with others in a variety of contexts. For example, when discussing a child's writing, talk about how they have not only improved their spelling or range of styles, but also their ability to notice and learn from their mistakes. Discuss how their child has not only learned their times tables and developed their addition and subtraction skills in maths, but has also grown their ability to stick with a problem for longer and find their own ways to get unstuck. In art, talk about how their child has developed the ability to critique and to learn from feedback.

Share your intention to develop their children as adept, lifelong learners, as well as helping them do well on the tests. We have found that parents and carers generally respond positively to the idea that their children are valued in terms of their development as learners as well as their academic progress – especially when they can see for themselves that their children are learning knowledge *and* skills that will equip them to learn for themselves and survive in the big wide world.

Ideally, you can keep feeding in this message throughout the year, but you might also feed back on children's development as learners in end-of-year reports. Many schools now have a separate section in their reports for comments on "the child as a learner", as well as sections in which children can

> Share with parents your intention to develop their children as adept, lifelong learners, as well as helping them do well on the tests.

report on their learning themselves. If your school reports don't have a section like this, see if you can thread learnish in throughout the report.

West Thornton Academy have handed their report writing over to the children. They write the entire report and teachers add a short comment, responding to the children's ideas and contributing further observations of their own.

Through effective coaching in how to write these reports, children:

- Feel greater ownership of their progress and learning.

- Understand what they have learned that year more fully, as well as how it has been valuable and where they need to go next.

> • Are given an opportunity to develop their reflection and planning skills.
>
> • Better understand themselves as learners.

Your child as a learner

Eddy shows many traits of a strong, independent learner. He is curious and interested in everything, often continuing his learning at home and coming up with fantastic questions in class. He is an active listener who contributes to classroom discussions and thinks carefully about what is being said.

Eddy is equally happy to learn independently and with friends. When collaborating, he listens to the ideas of others as well as offering his own. Throughout the year, he has become better at knowing when to take a step back and let others contribute.

When learning independently, Eddy often comes up with original ideas to extend and practise his learning, such as inventing a game to learn key words. He loves to share these ideas with friends as well as noticing and adopting great ideas from others.

Figure 10.1: Report Sample from Becky's Classroom

Depending on the receptiveness of your school, you could also coach children to contribute to or run their own parent-carer consultations. Done well, this puts children in the driving seat of their learning and provides the perfect opportunity for children to stretch their reflection muscles as they plan ways to inform their parents or carers about their progress – for example, by sharing some of the big wins they have made recently. In schools where this has been effective, children are given time to curate the work they would like to share, using specific criteria. For example, they might like to find a piece of work which shows particular resilience or craftsmanship, or a piece which is a good example of when they have used their thinking skills well. The children need to be coached on how to present the information so that they don't freeze when it comes to parents' evening. The children at West Thornton Academy run their own parent-carer consultations. Since they have planned their school day to give the children complete ownership and responsibility for their learning, they have achieved remarkable outcomes. One EAL learner, independently and off his own bat, created a PowerPoint to present his learning to his teacher and parent. The presentation was in his home language and he translated it to his teacher as he went.

Digging Deeper

Once you've embedded the language of the LPA into your usual interactions with parents and carers, and hooked their interest in what you are doing, you might want to focus on actively involving them in the approach.

Make links with home

Many LPA schools have found their own smart ways to involve parents in developing learning muscles at home. In many schools, Reception and Key Stage 1 classes use puppets to demonstrate different learning dispositions. These puppets are often sent home with a diary so that the children can write about how the puppet has demonstrated use of that learning muscle in a different context. Children love the privilege of being allowed to take the class puppet home. It helps them to make links with how that learning muscle can be stretched outside the classroom and includes parents and carers by helping them understand how their children are developing as learners in school.

Remember Julian Swindale's positive learning behaviours whiteboard from Chapter 3, on which he recorded examples of effective learning throughout the day? He has found a way of sharing this with parents by collaboratively making a class e-book at the end of each week. The children – with some nudging from Julian – choose some of their best learning moments to share. They upload a photo and write a short comment ready to share on a Friday afternoon. Parents and carers gather into the classroom, and Julian guides the children through the e-book and encourages them to talk about their learning. It's a brilliant way to share and embed the classroom ethos, give the children a chance to purposefully reflect on their learning, and for parents and carers to see how to continue their children's learning at home.

Each week at St John Fisher Catholic Primary School near Liverpool, the teachers introduce a new learning muscle during assembly. But they wondered how they could involve parents and carers in this process. They sent letters home asking them to write back explaining how they used learning muscles in their jobs. These letters were then shared with the children in assembly. Some of the letters were really powerful, such as the example pictured below, explaining how one parent uses empathy in her job.

It is very important in my job to have empathy for the people that I support because although I may not have a disability myself I need to understand the problems that a person may be having so that I can help and support them in the best way possible. To have empathy means not to judge someone but to treat people like you would want to be treated if you were in that situation. It takes a lot of time, energy and compassion to see the world from another perspective and you have to pay attention so that you are able to help someone if they need it and usually this means not asking for anything in return.

There is an old saying "to walk a mile in someone else's shoes" and we may actually realise what their lives are like, but if we take the time to really get to know someone and listen to their story this can also help us to understand someone better and feel what they are feeling, see the world from their perspective and be considerate towards this. To listen you need to connect to someone and do this without the distractions of phones, televisions and computers.

Be present in the real world around you or miss the chance to help someone when they really need it.

Through this communication, everyone's learning power grows stronger and deeper. The children can see how learning powers are essential in the adult world of work, and parents and carers gain a deeper understanding of the elements of the LPA. And those essential links are made between school and home.

Run a workshop for parents and carers about the LPA

Does your school ever run maths and English workshops to share strategies for developing these skills with families? Why not run a workshop on the LPA, or dedicate a slot at a parents' evening to it? If you don't have the opportunity to do this on a larger scale, or don't feel confident about doing so yet, why not invite parents and carers into your classroom at the end of a school day? You could present some ideas, ask the children to talk about what they have been learning, share some photos of the children demonstrating using their learning powers, or bust some myths by explaining, for example, why making mistakes is such an essential part of learning. Taking the time to do this keeps everyone on board, gives the children the opportunity to share what's been going on in the classroom, and enables caregivers to continue building on the children's learning powers at home.

Wondering

Think about how your interactions with parents and carers currently go. Are they as positive and satisfying as you would like them to be? Though not all parents and carers are equally easy to get along with, can you think of a couple of small ways in which you might try to engage them in more productive and interesting conversations about their child as a learner?

Have a look at some reports you have written recently. Can you think of any ways in which you might have captured a more rounded picture of those children? Could you have said more about how they have changed over the course of a term or a year?

Could you spend time finding out more about the children's learning lives out of school? How could you weave those little conversations into the school day?

Which of your colleagues do you think you could learn most from? Are there any opportunities for you to spend time in their classrooms just watching what they do – and how the children respond?

Bumps Along the Way

As usual, here are some thoughts from Becky about how you might cope when things don't go quite according to plan.

What if ...	Try this ...
Teaching colleagues and senior leaders are quite resistant to some of the ideas in the LPA.	Depending on your school climate, some teachers might be quite resistant to new ideas or change. This attitude might have evolved from a culture of having been put down and devalued, or having had a series of new initiatives introduced – and come and gone – with little impact. So, it's understandable that some might be sceptical, especially if they don't know anything about the LPA. Sharing stories about the successes you've had with individual learners can be especially memorable and impactful. Also, I haven't yet met a teacher or leader who isn't interested in finding ways to enable their learners to become more independent or resilient. Remember to follow our advice about going softly, softly in your conversations with colleagues, certainly to begin with. It can also help to begin by discussing how the LPA targets areas of children's behaviour that many teachers have a problem with – such as giving up too quickly when they can't do something or being distractible. Exploit their natural interest in improving these behaviours.

What if ...	Try this ...
You start to develop collaboration skills within the class, which means moving away from concrete "ability" groups, causing concern for some families that their child is no longer in the top group.	Parents and carers are bound to be curious or even suspicious about change. Ultimately, they want to know that their children are getting the best out of school and being enabled to grow to their full potential. So if they have been used to their child being in the top group – and knowing that they are – they might, understandably, feel concerned that they will no longer be stretched.
	You could pre-empt this by communicating with home as you start to work on developing the children's collaborating muscles. Explain why this is an important lifelong learning skill and also why it is important to learn with a variety of people, not just the ones who happen to be in your group. You would share these insights with the children to develop their understanding, so why not get home on board too?
	It might also be worth sharing the ideas that underpin growth mindset – that habitually grouping the children can be limiting for them all – and having a discussion around attitudes towards learning. Children in the top group can often be the most averse to risk-taking and failure and be the ones who spend much of their time in performance mode, scared of making mistakes. Exposure to a range of peers with different outlooks can help to mitigate this.
	You can also talk about how you are developing a relish of challenge in your classroom and explain that all learning will be challenging – their child won't be missing out! And alongside that, they will be building an understanding of themselves as a learner and the ability to self-regulate and assess how challenging they can make their learning. But,

What if ...	Try this ...
	of course, you will be there to coach them should they need a nudge in the right direction.
	It could also be worth mentioning that it is when you try to teach a subject to someone else that you really get to grips with and understand it yourself. So by working with a variety of peers, the children are becoming able to articulate and explain their learning as well as developing key social skills.
	I find that most minds are put at ease after such conversations, but there will be a few who remain sceptical. The ultimate proof of the pudding is in the spontaneous behaviour of the children. When parents and carers start to notice positive changes in their child – such as improvements in attitude, increased willingness to give things a go, and effective use of the learning muscles at home – they tend to get on board with the LPA and are often the most enthusiastic advocates of it in the end.

Summary

There is only so much a single teacher can do to develop children's learning power. They say it takes a village to raise a child, and if the LPA is to have maximum impact on children's development, it ideally needs to be acknowledged and attended to by all members of their community: teachers, learning support assistants, parents, carers, and others. In this chapter we have assumed that you might be something of a lone wolf to begin with, and will need to work to get others on board. If that is the case, we hope that some of our ideas will be useful. However, if you are lucky, you will already be a member of a supportive and knowledgeable community of teachers who are only too willing to support you, and to learn with and from you, as you grow in confidence and experience. In this case, perhaps some of our ideas about how to strengthen your links with parents will be helpful. Or perhaps you will have some more ideas to share with other members of staff, who may be new to both your school and to the LPA, so you can invite them to join your growing pack.

Conclusion

So now we have come to the end of our book on the LPA for primary school teachers. It's likely that some of our ideas will have struck you as pretty obvious and common sense – indeed you may be doing a fair number already – while others might seem too far-fetched to try right now. But we very much hope that you have found many ideas that do make sense to you, but which are just beyond your current style and practice as a teacher, so that you have some new strategies to try out, customise, and improve upon. And even the apparently familiar things might have gained a new significance for you by being placed in the wider context of the LPA. A lot of what teachers already do can contribute to the development of children's independent learning power, but sometimes this is not as joined-up or coherent as it could be. Whatever your reaction, do let us know, via Becky's website, if you have any ideas of your own to share with us, or any comments or criticisms on the practicality of what we have suggested.[1] This book, like all teaching practice, is a work in progress, and our understanding, like all teachers', is constantly open to improvement.

> A lot of what teachers already do can contribute to the development of children's independent learning power, but sometimes this is not as joined-up or coherent as it could be.

Above all, we hope that you, like us, are convinced about the desirability of helping children grow in their capacity and appetite for real-life, lifelong learning. It is a demanding and sometimes dangerous world out there, full of perils, uncertainties, dubious invitations, and fleeting opportunities. It is fast-changing, full of conflicting advice and opinions, and often bewildering. Just having some general knowledge, some good grades, and the abilities to read, write, and calculate are not enough. To flourish in this turbulent and tricky world, a strong, agile, curious mind is an essential.

---

1   See www.learningpowerkids.com.

Without the confidence and intelligence which those learning muscles provide, children's well-being and their mental health are at risk.

The good news from cognitive science is that teaching young minds to be more supple and sophisticated is a real possibility:

> The goal of early education (and perhaps of *all* education) should not be seen as simply that of training brains whose basic potential is already determined. Rather, the goal is to provide rich environments in which to *grow* better brains.
>
> Andy Clark, *Natural-Born Cyborgs*, p. 86

We are not defined by our genes. The requisite mental habits are not fixed at birth, but develop in response to the environments in which children find themselves; just as plants grow and bend depending on the climate and the soil. As Andy Clark, one of the leading lights in the world of cognitive science, says:

> The learning device *itself* changes as a result of organism-environment interactions; learning does not just alter the knowledge base for a fixed computational engine [learning mind], it alters the computational architecture itself.
>
> Andy Clark, *Natural-Born Cyborgs*, p. 84

And, after family, school is the environment in which children find themselves the most. Helping children become properly mind-fit for the 21st century is not just desirable; it is possible too.

Not everyone in education understands this yet. Some of those who don't are in positions of power and they block the way forward. The systems within which we work are not always as supportive of this mind-expanding education as they could be, and they will be slower to change than they should be. But the *really* good news is that, despite these impediments, there is much that any teacher can do to give children the education they need. And we hope that the LPA has helped you to feel – as we do – more optimistic and enthusiastic about the dozens of little things we *can* do that add up to a really powerful send-off in life for all the children that we are honoured to teach.

Further Reading

Many useful references are given in the first book of this series, *The Learning Power Approach*. Here we focus on sources that are of particular relevance to primary and elementary school teachers. Many are cited in the text and footnotes, and we have added some further reading that we have found valuable but couldn't squeeze into the story as we have told it here.

Ampaw-Farr, Jaz (2017). "The power of everyday heroes", *TEDxNorwichED* [video] (30 March). Available at: https://www.youtube.com/watch?v=q3xoZXSW5yc.

Beaty, Andrea (2013). *Rosie Revere, Engineer* (New York: Abrams Books for Young Readers).

Berger, Ron (2003). *An Ethic of Excellence: Building a Culture of Craftsmanship with Students* (Portsmouth, NH: Heinemann).

Berger, Ron (2012). "Critique and feedback – the story of Austin's butterfly" [video] (8 December). Available at: https://www.youtube.com/watch?v=hqh1MRWZjms.

Berger, Ron, Woodfin, Libby, and Vilen, Anne (2016). *Learning That Lasts: Challenging, Engaging, and Empowering Students with Deeper Instruction* (San Francisco, CA: Jossey-Bass).

Briceño, Eduardo (2016). "How to get better at the things you care about", *TEDxManhattanBeach* [video] (November). Available at: https://www.ted.com/talks/eduardo_briceno_how_to_get_better_at_the_things_you_care_about.

Carlzon, Becky (2017). Investment + learning power = learning dynamite. *Learning Power Kids* [blog] (5 December). Available at: http://learningpowerkids.com/colearning/investment-learning-power-dynamite/.

Carr, Margaret (2001). *Assessment in Early Childhood Settings: Learning Stories* (London: Sage).

Carr, Margaret, and Lee, Wendy (2012). *Learning Stories: Constructing Learner Identities in Early Education* (London: Sage).

Clark, Andy (2003). *Natural-Born Cyborgs: Minds, Technologies, and the Future of Human Intelligence* (Oxford: Oxford University Press).

Claxton, Guy (2002). *Building Learning Power* (Bristol: TLO).

Claxton, Guy (2017). *The Learning Power Approach: Teaching Learners to Teach Themselves* [US edn] (Thousand Oaks, CA: Corwin).

Claxton, Guy (2018). *The Learning Power Approach: Teaching Learners to Teach Themselves* [UK edn] (Carmarthen: Crown House Publishing).

Claxton, Guy, Chambers, Maryl, Powell, Graham, and Lucas, Bill (2011). *The Learning Powered School: Pioneering 21st Century Education* (Bristol: TLO).

Collishaw, Stephan, Maughan, Barbara, Goodman, Robert, and Pickles, Andrew (2004). Time trends in adolescent mental health. *Journal of Child Psychology and Psychiatry*, 45(8): 1350–1362.

Common Core Writing Academy (2014). All about anchor charts. *Common Core Writing Academy* [blog] (8 October). Available at: http://commoncorewritingacademy. com/2014/10/08/all-about-anchor-charts/.

Costa, Arthur L. (2008). Describing the habits of mind. In Arthur L. Costa and Bena Kallick (eds), *Learning and Leading with Habits of Mind: 16 Essential Characteristics for Success* (Alexandria, VA: Association for Curriculum Supervision and Development), pp. 15–41.

Costa, Arthur L., and Kallick, Bena (2009). Teaching habits of mind. In Arthur L. Costa and Bena Kallick (eds), *Habits of Mind Across the Curriculum: Practical and Creative Strategies for Teachers* (Alexandria, VA: Association for Curriculum Supervision and Development), pp. 36–66.

Costa, Arthur L., and Kallick, Bena (eds) (2005). *Activating and Engaging Habits of Mind* (Cheltenham, VIC: Hawker Brownlow Education).

Costa, Arthur L., and Kallick, Bena (eds) (2008). *Learning and Leading with Habits of Mind: 16 Essential Characteristics for Success* (Alexandria, VA: Association for Curriculum Supervision and Development).

Crooks, Terrence J. (1988). The impact of classroom evaluation practices on students. *Review of Educational Research*, 58(4): 438–481.

Csikszentmihalyi, Mihaly (2002). *Flow: The Psychology of Happiness* (London: Rider).

Curtis, Matt (2017). Transforming fixed mindsets towards maths. *Talking Maths* [blog] (6 January). Available at: https:// talkingmathsblog.wordpress.com/2017/ 01/06/transforming-fixed-mindsets-towards-maths/.

Delaney, Raegan, Day, Leanne, and Chambers, Maryl (2009). *Learning Power Heroes* (Bristol: TLO).

Duckworth, Eleanor (2006). *The Having of Wonderful Ideas: And Other Essays on Teaching and Learning*, 3rd edn (New York: Teachers College Press).

Dweck, Carol S. (2000). *Self-Theories: Their Role in Motivation, Personality and Development* (Philadelphia, PA: Psychology Press).

Dweck, Carol S. (2007). *Mindset: The New Psychology of Success* (New York: Ballantine Books).

Dweck, Carol S. (2014). "The power of yet", *TEDxNorrköping* [video] (12 September). Available at: https://www.youtube.com/ watch?v=J-swZaKN2Ic.

Fullan, Michael, Quinn, Joanne, and McEachen, Joanne (2018). *Deep Learning: Engage the World Change the World* (Thousand Oaks, CA: Corwin).

Hart, Susan, Dixon, Annabelle, Drummond, Mary Jane, and McIntyre, Donald (2004). *Learning without Limits* (Maidenhead: Open University Press).

Heyes, Cecilia (2018). *Cognitive Gadgets: The Cultural Evolution of Thinking* (Cambridge, MA: Harvard University Press).

Hughes, Gwyneth (2015). Ipsative assessment: motivation through marking progress. *British Journal of Educational Studies*, 63(2): 246–248.

Katz, Lilian G., Chard, Sylvia C., and Kogan, Yvonne (2014). *Engaging Children's Minds: The Project Approach*, 3rd edn (Santa Barbara, CA: Praeger).

Kautz, Tim, Heckman, James, Diris, Ron, ter Weel, Bas, and Borghans, Lex (2017). *Fostering and Measuring Skills: Improving Cognitive and Non-Cognitive Skills to Promote Lifetime Success* (Paris: OECD).

Kidd, Celeste, Palmeri, Holly, and Aslin, Richard (2013). Rational snacking: young children's decision-making on the marshmallow test is moderated by environmental reliability. *Cognition*, 126(1): 109–114.

Langer, Ellen J. (1997). *The Power of Mindful Learning* (Cambridge, MA: Perseus Books).

Lucas, Bill, and Claxton, Guy (2010). *New Kinds of Smart: How the Science of Learnable Intelligence is Changing Education* (Maidenhead: Open University Press).

Lucas, Bill, Hanson, Janet, Bianchi, Lynne, and Chippindall, Jonathan (2017). *Learning to Be an Engineer: Implications for the Education System* (London: Royal Academy of Engineering).

Moffitt, Terrie E., Arseneault, Louise, Belsky, Daniel, Dickson, Nigel, Hancox, Robert J., Harrington, HonaLee, Houts, Renate, Poulton, Richie, Roberts, Brent W., Ross, Stephen, Sears, Malcolm R., Thomson, W. Murray, and Caspiet, Avshalom (2011). A gradient of childhood self-control predicts health, wealth, and public safety. *PNAS*, 108(7): 2693–2698.

Moll, Luis C. (2014). *L. S. Vygotsky and Education* (Abingdon and New York: Routledge).

Murdoch, Kath (2015). *The Power of Inquiry: Teaching and Learning with Curiosity, Creativity and Purpose in the Contemporary Classroom* (Northcote, VIC: Seastar Education).

Myatt, Mary (2016). *Hopeful Schools: Building Humane Communities* (Mary Myatt Learning Ltd).

Nickerson, Raymond S., Perkins, David N., and Smith, Edward E. (eds) (1985). *The Teaching of Thinking* (Hillsdale, NJ: Lawrence Erlbaum).

Nottingham, James (2016). *Challenging Learning: Theory, Effective Practice and Lesson Ideas to Create Optimal Learning in the Classroom*, 2nd edn (Abingdon and New York: Routledge).

Perkins, David (2009). *Making Learning Whole: How Seven Principles of Teaching Can Transform Education* (San Francisco, CA: Jossey-Bass).

Ritchhart, Ron (2015). *Creating Cultures of Thinking: The 8 Forces We Must Master to Truly Transform Our Schools* (San Francisco, CA: Jossey-Bass).

Ritchhart, Ron, Church, Mark, and Morrison, Karin (2011). *Making Thinking Visible: How to Promote Engagement, Understanding, and Independence for All Learners* (San Francisco, CA: Jossey-Bass).

Roberts, Hywel, and Kidd, Debra (2018). *Uncharted Territories: Adventures in Learning* (Carmarthen: Independent Thinking Press).

Sesame Street, and Monae, Janelle (2014). "Power of yet" [video] (10 September). Available at: https://www.youtube.com/watch?v=XLeUvZvuvAs.

Sherratt, Sam (2013). Parent workshops: the IB learner profile. *Making PYP Happen Here* [blog] (7 October). Available at: https://makingpyphappenhere.wordpress.com/2013/10/07/36/.

Sullivan, Anne McCrary (2000). Notes from a marine biologist's daughter: on the art and science of attention. *Harvard Educational Review*, 70(2): 211–227.

Swann, Mandy, Peacock, Alison, Hart, Susan, and Drummond, Mary Jane (2012). *Creating Learning without Limits* (Maidenhead: Open University Press).

Tough, Paul (2012). *How Children Succeed: Grit, Curiosity, and the Hidden Power of Character* (New York: Houghton Mifflin Harcourt).

Tough, Paul (2016). *Helping Children Succeed: What Works and Why* (London: Penguin Random House).

University of Birmingham (n.d.). What employers want: what attributes are most valued by employers? Available at: https://hub.birmingham.ac.uk/news/soft-skills-attributes-employers-value-most.

Walden, Tedra A., and Ogan, Tamra A. (1988). The development of social referencing. *Child Development*, 59(5): 1230–1240.

Watkins, Chris (2005). *Classrooms as Learning Communities: What's in It for Schools?* (Abingdon and New York: Routledge).

Watkins, Chris (2010). *Learning, Performance and Improvement*, Jane Reed (ed.), Research Matters series no. 34 (London: International Network for School Improvement).

Wiliam, Dylan (2014). The right questions, the right way. *Educational Leadership*, 71(6): 16–19.

Wiliam, Dylan (2017). *Embedded Formative Assessment*, 2nd edn (Bloomington, IN: Solution Tree Press).

Resources

Here is a list of links to the work of thinkers, authors, and architects of approaches that have inspired us in the development of the LPA, and in the writing of this book. You will find lots of other useful and thought-provoking ideas in their original works and on their websites.

Websites

- EL Education has plenty of free resources at https://eleducation.org.

- Ron Ritchhart's resources and publications can be found at www.ronritchhart.com.

- Arthur L. Costa and Bena Kallick's Habits of Mind and its complementary idea of "dispositional teaching", developed over many years, has resources at www.habitsofmindinstitute.org.

- The highly successful International Baccalaureate (IB) programmes are used in thousands of schools around the world. For many ideas and resources see www.ibo.org.

- The New Pedagogies for Deep Learning work is summarised in Michael Fullan, Joanne Quinn, and Joanne McEachen, *Deep Learning: Engage the World Change the World* and at www.npdl.global.

- The Learning without Limits approach is described in Susan Hart, Annabelle Dixon, Mary Jane Drummond and Donald McIntyre, *Learning without Limits* and at https://learningwithoutlimits.educ.cam.ac.uk/.

- Kath Murdoch's Power of Inquiry work, described in her book *The Power of Inquiry*, is full of practical primary classroom ideas, as is her website: see www.kathmurdoch.com.au.

- Guy and his colleagues' development of the approach known as Building Learning Power (BLP) is described in *Building Learning Power* and *The Learning Powered School*, and further information can be found at www.buildinglearningpower.com.

- More of Guy's books can be found on his website: see www.guyclaxton.net.

- Lots of good ideas get shared through the Expansive Education Network: see www.expansiveeducation.net.

- The great Chris Watkins has put many of his resources on his website: www.chriswatkins.net.
- James Mannion's research and resources can be found at https://rethinking-ed.org/blog/.
- Oracy Cambridge's research and resources can be found at www.oracycambridge.org.
- Voice 21 resources are at https://www.voice21resources.org.
- The English-Speaking Union's resources are at https://www.esu.org/our-work/esuresources.
- Conferences, ideas and pedagogy linked to teaching through mixed attainment can be found at www.mixedattainmentmaths.com.

Blogs

There are many useful and interesting blogs on primary teaching, full of practical LPA-esque ideas. These include:

- Becky Carlzon's: www.learningpowerkids.com.
- Nicola Subbay's: www.learningunlocked.creativeblogs.net
- Matt Curtis': https://talkingmathsblog.wordpress.com.

Social Media

Look at some tweets using the hashtags #learningpower, #learningpowerapproach and #LPATuesday, all of which celebrate great LPA practice, and follow Becky @beckycarlzon.

About the Authors

Guy Claxton is a cognitive scientist specialising in the expandability of human intelligence – bodily and intuitive as well as intellectual – and the roles schools play in either growing or stunting these capacities. His books for a general readership include *The Wayward Mind* and *Intelligence in the Flesh*, and for teachers, *What's the Point of School?*, *New Kinds of Smart* (with Bill Lucas), *Building Learning Power* and *The Learning Power Approach*. His practical programmes for teachers are influencing children's lives in Ireland, Spain, Poland, Dubai, South Africa, Malaysia, Indonesia, Australia, New Zealand, Argentina, and Brazil, as well as across the UK.

Becky Carlzon is an optimistic primary school teacher who specialises in the Learning Power Approach (LPA). She has adapted the LPA successfully while teaching in the UK, Argentina, and Thailand over the last twelve years. As well as teaching primary children, Becky has used the LPA to teach English to 3- to 73-year-olds, finding that no matter your age, experience, or background, you can always stretch your capacity to learn. Becky's practice is underpinned by the design principles outlined in this book, such as cultivating a relish for challenging learning and using collaboration as a launch pad for children to co-construct and critique their learning. Through staying connected with LPA schools and fellow practitioners, Becky is at the forefront of LPA practice across the globe. Her latest thoughts, reflections, and findings can be found on her website and blog: www.learningpowerkids.com.

Powering Up Students

The Learning Power Approach to High School Teaching

Guy Claxton and Graham Powell

ISBN 978-178583338-0

Building upon the foundations carefully laid by Guy's first book in the Learning Power series, *The Learning Power Approach*, this instalment embeds the ideas of his influential method in the context of the secondary or high school.

Guy and Graham provide a thorough explanation of how the Learning Power Approach's core components apply to this level of education and, by presenting a wide range of classroom examples, illustrate how they can be put into practice in different curricular areas – focusing especially on embedding the learning dispositions into students' tackling of more demanding content, while also emphasising the need to "get the grades".

Suitable for both newly qualified and experienced teachers of students aged 11–18.

Powering Up Your School

The Learning Power Approach to School Leadership

Guy Claxton, Jann Robinson, Rachel Macfarlane, Graham Powell, Gemma Goldenberg, and Robert Cleary

ISBN 978-178583456-1

Powering Up Your School illustrates in detail how school leaders can successfully embed the Learning Power Approach (LPA) in their school's culture and empower teachers to deliver its benefits to their students.

The LPA affords a clear view of the valued, sought-after outcomes of education – developing character strengths as well as striving for academic success – which underpin everything in the school: the curriculum content, the structure of the timetable, the forms of assessment, communication with parents, and the pedagogical style of every member of staff.

The school leader's job, therefore, is to provide direction and signal the standards aimed for in all these different aspects of school life – and *Powering Up Your School* sets out a detailed explanation of how this can be accomplished.

The Learning Power Approach
Teaching Learners to Teach Themselves
Guy Claxton
ISBN 978-178583245-1

In this groundbreaking book, Guy distils fifteen years' practical experience with his influential Building Learning Power method, as well as findings from a range of kindred approaches, into a set of design principles for teaching.

Complemented by engaging and informative classroom examples of the Learning Power Approach (LPA) in action – and drawing from research into the fields of mindset, metacognition, grit, and collaborative learning – *The Learning Power Approach* describes in detail the suite of beliefs, values, attitudes, and habits of mind that go in to making up learning power, and offers a thorough explanation of what its intentions and guiding principles are. Furthermore, in order to help those who are just setting out on their LPA journey, Guy presents teachers with an attractive menu of customisable strategies and activities to choose from as they begin to embed the LPA principles into their own classroom culture, and also includes at the end of each chapter a "wondering" section that serves to prompt reflection, conversation, and action among teachers.